SEA OF DREAMS

Racing Alone Around the World in a Small Boat

ADAM MAYERS

M&S

Copyright © 2004 by Adam Mayers

National Library of Canada Cataloguing in Publication

Mayers, Adam
    Sea of dreams : racing alone around the world in a small boat / Adam Mayers.

Includes bibliographical references.
ISBN 0-7710-5753-9

    1. BOC Challenge Race.   2. Hatfield, Derek.   3. Spirit of Canada (Yacht)
4. Sailing, Single-handed.   I. Title.

GV832.M38 2004   797.14'092   C2004-902658-5

We acknowledge the financial support of the Government of Canada through the Book Publishing Industry Development Program and that of the Government of Ontario through the Ontario Media Development Corporation's Ontario Book Initiative. We further acknowledge the support of the Canada Council for the Arts and the Ontario Arts Council for our publishing program.

Typeset in Bembo by M&S, Toronto
Printed and bound in Canada

McClelland & Stewart Ltd.
The Canadian Publishers
481 University Avenue
Toronto, Ontario
M5G 2E9
www.mcclelland.com

1 2 3 4 5   08 07 06 05 04

Contents

For Ben and Emily.
May you dream big dreams.

The 2002 Around Alone Fleet

CLASS I: OPEN 60S

Simone Bianchetti, thirty-five, Italy, *Tiscali*

Graham Dalton, fifty, New Zealand, *Hexagon*

Patrick de Radiguès, forty-six, Belgium, *Garnier*.

　(Withdrew from the race after completing Leg I)

Thierry Dubois, thirty-six, France, *Solidaires*

Emma Richards, twenty-eight, Great Britain, *Pindar*

Bruce Schwab, forty-three, U.S.A., *Ocean Planet*

Bernard Stamm, thirty-eight, Switzerland, *Bobst Group
　Armor Lux*

CLASS II: OPEN 40S AND 50S

John Dennis, fifty-seven, Canada, *Bayer Ascensia*

Derek Hatfield, fifty, Canada, *Spirit of Canada*

Tim Kent, fifty, U.S.A., *Everest Horizontal*

Alan S. Paris, thirty-seven, Bermuda, *BTC Velocity*

Kojiro Shiraishi, thirty-six, Japan, *Spirit of Yukoh*

Brad Van Liew, thirty-five, U.S.A., *Tommy Hilfiger
　Freedom America*

Author's Note

Canada is officially a metric country but, for the most part, her sailors still use feet when talking about boat lengths, nautical miles for distances at sea (a nautical mile is equal to 1.15 statute miles), pounds for weights, and knots to measure speed. (A wind becomes hurricane force at 64 knots, or 74 mph.) Temperatures, however, are usually expressed in Celsius. In this book, I've followed the sailors' convention.

1

Dead Calm

"For they can conquer who believe they can."

– VIRGIL

IN THE COCKPIT of his boat, Derek Hatfield stood silhouetted in the moonlight of a June night in 2002 on Lake Ontario, his reddish-brown mop of hair and thick policeman's moustache bristling in profile. He had tucked both hands into the waist of his yellow foul-weather pants to ward off the chill, and plumes of steam rose into the air as he spoke. The air temperature was around freezing. After the warmest winter on record, the upper Great Lakes basin had seen the coldest, wettest spring ever recorded. This had delayed by a month or more the seasonal warming of one of the world's largest bodies of inland water.

Hatfield's forty-foot racing sailboat, *Spirit of Canada*, was sliding down the middle of the lake, the lights of a power plant near Rochester, N.Y., visible to the south and those of the Pickering nuclear plant, east of Toronto, off the stern quarter. Hatfield was talking in measured tones about the epic journey that lay ahead of him. He stood with his legs planted wide, a man of forty-nine, of average height and compact build. Even with the bulky fleece he wore he seemed lean and spare, all sinew and muscle with not an extra ounce of weight. He leaned over and flicked on the autopilot. It whirred and clicked to life, freeing Hatfield to leave the cockpit and walk in sure-footed steps along the length of the fastest, strongest racing sailboat ever built in Canada. She had been assembled by many loving hands, including his own, to withstand the most dangerous natural forces on the planet. Yet she was so supple and swift that she would soon be breaking speed records.

Hatfield touched and tested the rigging as he went, lingering over a turnbuckle here, tugging at a line there, stopping momentarily to listen to the hiss and gurgle of water rushing along the hull. "Am I afraid?" he asked, startled by the question. "Afraid? I'm looking forward to it. I'm concerned about not being able to finish, but that's not fear. You wouldn't do this if you were afraid. You couldn't."

Many people mess around in boats, but few sail alone and fewer still sail single-handed around the world, which Hatfield was about to do. The paradox is that he dislikes being alone even though he has always liked solitary achievement. At school in Newcastle, New Brunswick, Hatfield eschewed the team play of hockey and football for the individual challenge of track and field and badminton. He savours personal victory and is unafraid of the consequences of defeat.

He came to sailing relatively late, as a married man in his mid-twenties and it took two and a half decades of ever-bigger steps to get to this starry night. He used his day jobs as a fraud-squad Mountie and later on Bay Street to support his growing sailing habit. First, Hatfield crewed aboard a neighbour's twenty-two-footer from Whitby, Ontario, about twenty-five miles east down the lake from Toronto. His experience was not much different from other novice sailors: the crew bench on Wednesday nights, learning about wind and weather, how a boat moves and why, and the arcane language of luffs and leeches and cleats and clews. He built his own seventeen-footer after reading a few books. A case of "footitis" led to a twenty-five-foot racer/cruiser. A few years later and a few more feet and along came *Gizmo*, a sleek needle-nosed racing machine in which he crossed the Atlantic Ocean and almost lost his life.

Hatfield is not sure where his love of water came from. His father, Arthur, a retired forester, never sailed, though he built small boats and lovingly helped his son construct *Spirit of Canada*. Hatfield finds it hard to discuss such emotional things, keeping a *cordon sanitaire* firmly around his feelings. He is friendly and always polite, but so self-contained and emotionally understated he appears to be passionless. He tries to be inconspicuous and unobtrusive, preferring the sidelines to the limelight, but this stance masks a hunger for adventure and a yearning for dangerous exploits. It explains why he was drawn to a cop's life and now this, an occupation that has killed far better sailors than he.

Solo sailing is an occupation the French, who are very good at it, call *solitaire*. It requires a precise mind and level head, two more of Hatfield's traits. He is not impulsive at all; he is, rather, a very deliberate man. He approaches things methodically, as a task or job to be done. Friends say he sometimes has to work at having fun, even though he can be playful, enjoying jokes and funny stories. But at his core, Hatfield is pragmatic and grounded, stimulated by difficult and involved challenges. He has tremendous patience and stamina, a willingness to work at a task for long hours without rest. He perseveres in the face of difficulty, but knows that, at sea, hardships add up quickly. Sometimes his moods are very dark and he fights feelings of hopelessness when all he wants to do is give up. This will be his hardest personal challenge during this race: maintaining equilibrium and the will to continue.

Hatfield's world for the next eight months is no bigger than a prison cell, with fewer amenities than those afforded the average killer sentenced to life. He has taken a vow of concentration which means he has no books to read, nor did he bring any music. He sees them as distractions. So there is nothing to read except weather faxes and e-mails and nothing to listen to except the whispering wind and the songs of the sea. There's no sugar, caffeine, or soft drinks on board. There is no "medicinal" alcohol either as it dulls the senses and numbs the mind. Beneath his veneer of self-confidence, there is a nagging fear of failure, of not being good enough, a concern that he lacks the juice. He worries about the effect of mood swings on his judgment because he knows he will need to stay calm and level in the face of the enormous physical and mental challenges of running the boat alone. His friends have more faith, knowing how much he likes to win, or rather, hates to lose. "If anyone has a chance of finishing, it is Derek Hatfield," says author Derek Lundy, a friend and admirer. "He'll do well. Derek has grit and determination. He's skilled, tough, and determined."

Hatfield's commitment is such that he sailed *Spirit of Canada* on Lake Ontario in January to simulate the conditions he'll encounter in the Southern Ocean, even though the lake offered only a vague approximation of what lay ahead. Hatfield discovered that every task had been harder to perform, slower to execute. On those trials he had gone home each night to a hot meal and a warm, comfortable bed. For weeks on end in the near future none of these basic amenities will be available. Instead, he'll face waves taller than his sixty-five-foot mast and winds so strong that facing them without wearing goggles might blind him. In these circumstances, any accident could prove fatal. "You can get killed doing much simpler things on land," he said with a shrug. "I'm looking forward to the challenge."

Hatfield was setting out on a journey to circumnavigate the earth in the Around Alone race, a contest that is run every four years by an elite breed of sailor. The race would last at least eight months, touch five continents, and take him through some of the worst conditions on the planet, assuming he finished. Death would be a close companion. He had been planning for the race in earnest for five years with a single-minded determination that to this point had cost him his second marriage and all his savings.

Hatfield was seeking admission into a very exclusive club. More people have blasted into space than have achieved a solo racing circumnavigation, ten times more have climbed Mount Everest. The fraternity of Canadian single-handers is even more rarefied. The last Canadian to try in a similar race was Gerry Roufs, and he perished in unimaginable conditions. The only Canadian to complete a solo racing circumnavigation, John Hughes, had done so at half Hatfield's age, and he had almost died rounding Cape Horn.

The legendary Joshua Slocum was the first Canadian to sail around the world alone. He set out in 1895 in the thirty-foot *Spray*, passing from the Atlantic to the Pacific Ocean through the Strait of Magellan, a few hundred miles north of Cape Horn. His east-to-west passage was against the prevailing wind and current, making

Derek Hatfield, alone with his thoughts, before setting out from
Port Credit, Ontario, in June 2002. *(Adam Mayers)*

it extremely difficult. In fact, he did it twice, as he was blown back
east the first time he emerged on the Pacific side of the Horn.
Slocum did not have any of the aids modern sailors take for
granted. He had no engine to manoeuvre the boat or to generate
electricity for heat and lights. There was no autopilot, so Slocum
gathered snatches of sleep as he steered, or lashed the tiller, hoping
it would keep the boat on course while he went below to warm
up. *Spray*'s hull was made of planks caulked with tar-soaked cotton
wads, not bulletproof Kevlar. Nor did he have accurate charts of
those treacherous waters, or mechanical instruments to measure
speed and distance. They did not exist yet.

In 1982, French-Canadian sailor-filmmaker Yves Gélinas made
the trip in his Alberg 30, *Jean du Sud*. Gélinas chronicled the journey
in a documentary that went on to win awards. Next was Hughes
and then Roufs. In March 2003, B.C. sailor Tony Gooch returned
home to Victoria aboard the forty-three-foot aluminum-hulled

Taonui after a non-stop around-the-world journey of 177 days. At this point Hatfield was more than halfway through his voyage.

Hatfield had no plans to come back. When he cast off his lines earlier in the day at Port Credit Yacht Club, just west of Toronto, he thought of it as signalling the first day of the rest of his life. Hatfield hoped that by doing well in the race he could build a new career as a professional sailor. The gamble was huge, the commitment total, the outcome uncertain.

The steep cost of entering the race had consumed every financial asset he could muster. But the steepest cost was one he had yet to face – the psychological cost. The Around Alone is as much a mental challenge as a physical one. Although some aspects of the sport have changed with advances in technology, what remains unchanged since Slocum's day is physical endurance and the psychological strength to stand up to the fury of the elements alone.

Some competitors train for months before setting sail, to help them cope with the fear, the solitude, and the emotional isolation. In the 1998 race, one competitor sought out a hypnotist to inculcate in him a winning attitude for his initial encounter with the Southern Ocean. In the first race of this kind, held in 1968, Englishman Donald Crowhurst committed suicide and his boat was found adrift in the middle of the Atlantic Ocean, along with thousands of words describing his descent into psychosis and death. True, much has changed since then, particularly in the field of communications. Satellite phones, e-mail, and the Internet keep sailors in twenty-four-hour touch with shore crew and with each other. That cuts both ways. A phone call is a much-anticipated event. It makes a connection across the miles, but leaves an empty longing when it ends. How far would Hatfield's psychological elastic stretch?

Just before dawn on that June day on the lake, the sky was filled with a spectacular display of stars. As the boat skipped along in a light breeze at a clip of seven knots, bubbles swirled in its wake. The water was flat and it was hard to imagine what a sixty-five-foot wave would look like. But the Southern Ocean, where almost half the race would be run, is distinguished by monstrous weather, the worst on a continuous basis of anywhere on Earth. There is no land for thousands of miles, so the waves build to enormous heights. The wind roars. There is a constant peril of icebergs. Big bergs are trailed for miles by growlers, small pieces of ice the size of cars. They can be much smaller and still punch holes in a fibreglass boat. A sort of Russian roulette takes place, because growlers are undetectable by radar. You have to be on deck, in daylight, to see them, but the cold — with the windchill around zero — means that the sailors spend as little time as possible in the cockpit, letting their autopilot steer the boat. Who knows how unlucky one might be?

If past history served as a guide, about half the boats setting sail with Hatfield would withdraw for one reason or another. As the London *Daily Mail* said in describing the race: "To compete is courageous, to finish sublime." At the end, beyond the handshake and trophy, the biggest reward would be a glow of satisfaction at some later, quiet moment. Or, perhaps, in the deep part of the night, a less pleasant reminder — a gasping for breath as the mind relived a terror that words simply cannot explain.

LEG I

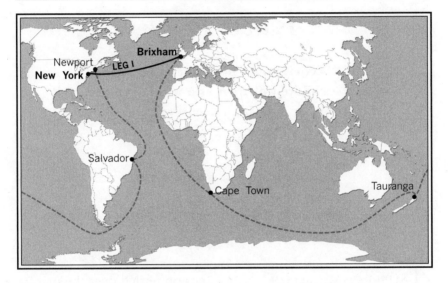

ROUTE: New York, USA, to Brixham, England

DEPARTURE: September 15, 2002

DISTANCE: 2,930 nautical miles

2

Race Day

**"Security does not exist in nature,
nor do the children of men as a whole experience it.
Life is either a daring adventure or nothing."**

– HELEN KELLER

A SUPERCHARGED FEELING of tension settled over the marina in Lower Manhattan on the morning of September 15, 2002, as the fleet of thirteen boats readied for the start of the Around Alone race. The sailors' stomachs were too tightly knotted for them to eat and their banter had a hushed, nervous tone. Shore crews went about the final preparations while the sailors spent a last few minutes with friends and family, keeping one eye on the weather. The remnants of Hurricane Gustav had boiled along the eastern seaboard for the previous two days, bringing rain and a blustery wind. Now the worst of it had moved off and the air temperature was a warm 27 degrees Celsius (80 degrees Fahrenheit). The hope was that the skies would clear in time for a noon start.

Derek Hatfield was at his boat by 7 a.m. making last-minute

adjustments, fussing here and fidgeting there, willing the clock forward so the race could begin. One of the most prepared members of the fleet, he could have set sail weeks sooner and was now itching to be on his way. He had spent the three months since that cold day on Lake Ontario sailing in stages to Halifax, then New York. In Halifax he had entered the inaugural Halifax to St. Pierre and Miquelon race, a 360-nautical mile run along the coast of Nova Scotia to the French islands off the southern coast of Newfoundland. He was first to arrive — it would have been a surprise if he hadn't been. After a few days rest, he sailed across the Atlantic to the Azores. From there it was back across the Atlantic in a two thousand-mile sprint to Newport, Rhode Island: a solo passage that was a necessary qualifier for the Around Alone race. The fleet gathered in Newport and then sailed as a group to New York for the start of the race.

Hatfield was tired of the endless preparations and just wanted to get going. And at 11 a.m. he got his wish when the boats were towed out into New York harbour, their engine transmissions locked in neutral. During the race, the sailors could use the engines only to charge their batteries, and faced a penalty if they put them in gear.

At noon, a single gunshot sounded, marking the fifteen-minute countdown to the start. In the shadow of the Statue of Liberty, the boats cruised up and down an imaginary starting line between a race committee boat and a buoy as their skippers were calculating how long it would take to reach the line given the wind speed and direction. The trick was to cross it just as the gun sounded. With a few minutes to go, in what seemed a good omen, sunshine poked through the low clouds.

At 12:15 p.m. there was a second shot and the boats were off, their long, sleek bows turned east, thousands of yards of sail filled with a fresh breeze. They would not see Newport again until the following May. Between now and then lay a lifetime of possibilities. As race organizer Sir Robin Knox-Johnston put it: "The difference between this race and climbing Everest is that when it gets tough you can't stop and climb into your tent. In this race, there is no respite. It is probably the single toughest sporting event there is."

The fleet passed under the Verrazano-Narrows Bridge and the shore crew watched as the boats gradually grew smaller. Then fog rolled in from the south and they disappeared from view. Later that night the boats cleared the Ambrose Light and set a course for England.

The Around Alone is one of just two single-handed sailing around-the-world races. It happens every four years, and the competitors cross the world's oceans in five legs, with stops of two to four weeks between each leg. The amount of time the sailors have to rest and recuperate between legs depends on how fast they complete the course, and how fast they are depends on the size of the boat. There are two classes, the sixty-foot Open 60s and the smaller Open 40s and 50s. The Open 60s could expect to sail on average 25 per cent faster than the Open 50s and 40 per cent faster than the Open 40s. "Open" refers to the fact that, beyond one or two basic rules, the boats' builders can experiment with materials and the design of the boat.

In each leg, the winning boat in each class is awarded ten points, the second-place boat nine points and third-place boat eight points, with each competitor getting points no matter where he finishes. If a boat returns to port for any reason after the leg has started it is assessed a forty-eight-hour penalty, which is added on to its time for the leg. Within each class all boats are equal despite differences in design. There is no handicapping as there is in many other sailing races.

The Vendée Globe is the other solo challenge, and many of the sailors who attempt one, attempt the other. It's a toss-up which race is tougher. The Vendée is also run every four years, but staggered with the Around Alone so that one is run every two years. The main difference between the two is that the Vendée is non-stop. It starts in Les Sables d'Olonne, France, and the winner returns to port three to four months later. Some say the endurance of 90 to 120 days at sea alone is tougher than all-out sprints with stops in between. Certainly, the psychological demands are different and so is the way the sailors race their boats. The Vendée is almost entirely the arena of professionals, or aspiring professionals, while the Around Alone has room for a Corinthian class of sailor, people who enter for the personal challenge of sailing around the world, as much as to win.

In this Around Alone race the Open 60s were skippered mainly by pros, four of them from Europe's top ranks – deep-ocean nomads who make their living by moving from course to course. Three had previously raced the Vendée Globe, but never the Around Alone, and had entered this event partly to build their resumés. These skippers were salaried employees of their sponsors. In France, the best sailors are accorded hero status and a stature equivalent to a Wayne Gretzky, Tiger Woods, or Michael Jordan in North America.

The seven boats in the Open 60s fleet were the result of multi-million dollar campaigns that enabled the sailors to buy or have built vessels that were on the leading edge of the sport in terms of design, construction, and marine electronics. That is because the Around Alone and Vendée Globe are living labs and the skippers are the equivalent of the test pilots of the early days of aviation. Their boats and equipment are a proving ground for yacht designers and the manufacturers of marine electronics and hardware. Sometimes the equipment isn't commercially available and it is supplied to solo racers for nothing so it can be tested. In this race, Emma Richards, the twenty-eight-year-old Briton sailing the Open 60 *Pindar*, was testing software manufactured by Brookes & Gatehouse that relayed information from her wind and speed instruments to her autopilots to help the boat keep a better course when sailing downwind. In an earlier race, when *Pindar* was campaigned as *Gartmore Investments*, its owner, Josh Hall, had had fibre-optic sensors installed to determine how much force was exerted on different parts of the boat during a storm. Designer Groupe Finot used the information to determine how thick to make the hull on future boats. Until then, he and other designers had had to guess at the forces exerted on the boat at sea. Brad Van Liew, sailing fifty-foot *Tommy Hilfiger*, was testing a high-end Raymarine autopilot with upgraded software to help the pilot steer a more accurate course. He was also testing a Profurl roller-furling system, an experimental 42-pound unit with a higher safety margin that replaced his 146-pound unit. Profurl had removed 100 pounds by replacing metal and rod rigging with Kevlar.

Many of these innovations trickle down to average cruising sailors. Roller-furling gear, a drum that rolls up sails like a window blind, is standard equipment on most sailboats now. Autopilots are the number-one accessory on boats after furling equipment. Both were developed to meet the needs of single-handed racing sailors and thoroughly tested in that harsh proving ground. Many manufacturers feel that if their equipment can withstand ten months at sea in a race, it has survived ten years of use by a recreational boater.

The only difference between Open 40s, Open 50s, and Open 60s is their size. A 40 or 50 is just a smaller version of a 60. Since there is no handicapping, the rules governing length, width, and

Tommy Hilfiger was so fast and her skipper so skilled that the fifty-foot
boat was often in the thick of the sixty-foot fleet. *(Billy Black)*

keel depth are pretty simple: each boat must be exactly forty, fifty,
or sixty feet long, although it can have up to a 10 per cent overhang for attachments such as the bowsprit at the front of the boat.
As the boats are experimental, their builders can use any materials
they like, making the boat as wide or narrow as they want. Most
look like slices of pizza, with a pointed bow and wide stern. Safety
rules specify how quickly the boat will right if knocked over and
require each boat to have four watertight compartments. Beyond
that, anything goes.

If pros were skippering the Open 60s, the sailors of the smaller
boats were a different group. Some like Brad Van Liew, a thirty-
five-year-old native of San Diego, aspired to the top tier of the
sport. He was a veteran of the 1998 Around Alone, when he came
third in the small-boat class. He was returning with fifty-foot *Tommy
Hilfiger Freedom America*, a well-financed challenge backed by the
clothing manufacturer, which was considering a line of Van Liew

sports clothes. Van Liew was the favourite to win this class, the one in which Derek Hatfield was entered. It has traditionally been the class for the gentleman adventurers, for dreamers, romantics, and eccentrics. These are sailors on shoestring budgets in older, smaller boats, people who go cap in hand to friends, family, and sailing pals to help pay their way. Their goal is to race, not necessarily to win. Most of them in this race just wanted to see whether they could do it, feeling that as time marched by, it was now or never.

Among them was Tim Kent, whose thick mane of white hair, matching beard, and round wire-rimmed glasses made him look like Hemingway. He is a relentlessly cheerful and friendly divorced father of two from Wisconsin. A year earlier, Kent would have described himself as an average Milwaukee soccer dad. On race day in New York, he was wandering the docks hand in hand with his daughters, Alison and Whitney, aged eight and ten. Like Hatfield, Kent did not have a major sponsor to help pay the bills and had thrown his life savings into the quest. He was also one of the least experienced members of the fleet. Kent knew Lake Michigan forwards and backwards, but he had never sailed on an ocean until he completed the Around Alone qualifying race from the Azores to Newport. His fifty-foot *Everest Horizontal* was a sturdy boat, originally built for a wealthy Californian who had the cash but not the heart for solo long-distance sailing. *Everest Horizontal* was so solid and safe, Van Liew joked it was a racing sail-boat with training wheels. One night in December 2000, over a few drinks at the Milwaukee Yacht Club, Kent and a few friends had been discussing the great "what-ifs" in life. *What if* they had all the time in the world? *What if* they had all the money in the world? What would they do? Kent declared he would sail around the world alone. It was something that had fired his imagination for more than twenty years.

Tim Kent had never
sailed beyond the
Great Lakes before
completing the Around
Alone qualifying run.
(Tim Kent photo)

Later that night one of his friends sent him a two-page e-mail. It was a plan, or a challenge, depending on how you looked at it. From that day forward, Kent slowly made his way towards the starting line. He took classes to learn the rudiments of celestial navigation, a race requirement even in the age of satellite electronics. He worked out at his gym for an hour or more each day to build stamina. He read every book he could find to soak up the lore, pick up tips, and gain insights into what he might expect from the race. He found *Everest Horizontal*, paying $250,000 (U.S.) for a boat that cost about $1 million (U.S.) to build.

By race day he was so broke, his local utility was about to cut off his electricity service for non-payment. The Milwaukee Yacht Club wanted to kick him out after twenty-two years for the same reason. When the gun fired at noon on September 15, he crossed the starting line with enough food to make it to England, and that was it. He didn't care. It would be one hell of a ride.

Kent, who was adopted at the age of six weeks, grew up in the Detroit area. He started sailing at the age of eleven, which is how he met his ex-wife and biggest fan, Cheri. He worked for a time as an auto mechanic and spent a year at University College Cork, in Cork, Ireland. Though Tim and Cheri are divorced, they remain friends and own a cruising sailboat together. It is a testament either to his salesmanship or their devotion to each other that he persuaded Cheri to act as his shore manager for the Around Alone race and lend him fifty thousand dollars. "We made a lousy married couple, but we make excellent friends," Kent says.

Cheri brought Alison and Whitney to as many stopovers as possible. She didn't understand Kent's hunger to sail solo, in fact, she thought he was quite mad. But she saluted his courage.

The Tim Kents and Derek Hatfields paid a high price to fulfill their dream. It wasn't just as simple a matter as fielding a boat. They were committed to taking a year off to run the race, losing income and quitting jobs or risking career derailment. They left families and loved ones behind, but not the mundane obligations of mortgages and car payments. It made the idea a hard sell on the home front.

It was easier for Hatfield, however. Unlike Kent, he was unencumbered by dependents, as his sons, Aron and Devon, aged twenty-eight and thirty, were self-supporting. He believed that with a strong showing he could turn pro, even though he had failed to find a major corporate sponsor for his campaign. Hatfield isn't very good at self-promotion and is the first to admit this. Nor did he have much of an ocean-racing track record to show to potential sponsors. That left a pitch as an adventuring and aspiring racing sailor, which didn't persuade anyone to sign on the dotted line. Even so, many companies and equipment suppliers helped him out. Toronto's Genco Marine, well known in the boating community, was particularly generous. Hatfield had a grassroots campaign behind him, led by a committed core of friends, but he seemed almost embarrassed to ask others to help pay his way. It was his dream, not theirs. Nonetheless, he raised about seventy-five thousand dollars, as about 1,500 people donated an average of fifty dollars each, for which their names were painted on *Spirit of Canada*'s hull. It went some way towards expenses, which amounted to some five hundred thousand dollars by race day. "I've stopped adding up the cost," he said a week before the start. "I'm a man with a van, a trailer, and a boat. And the boat's not insured. If I lose it, it's gone."

Hatfield's family lives in New Brunswick. They were puzzled by his stubborn determination, but entirely supportive. "He's putting himself in the poorhouse, that's what I don't understand," his younger brother, Hal, grumbled. "Why would you want to spend every cent you've ever saved? But it's almost like Derek has saved all that money for this purpose."

Arthur Hatfield says his oldest son has always been competitive and disciplined, his own man. Yet, even Art marvelled at his son's focus. "Derek is one of those people who has to have a challenge, whether it's racing a guy down the street or across the ocean," he says. "When I think about it, I'd sooner race with him on water than drive with him."

Hatfield spent a dozen years with the fraud squad of the Royal Canadian Mounted Police in Toronto, before embarking on a better-paid career on Bay Street, where he put his knowledge to work. He spent time at the old Toronto Stock Exchange, First Marathon Securities, and the National Bank of Canada. As he was making his final preparations for the Around Alone, he spent five months as interim director of compliance at broker Thomson Kernaghan. Bay Street provided a good pay cheque, but it was really not Hatfield's thing. The culture and values were all wrong,

at least from an ex-fraud squad cop's point of view. He had spent a
lifetime enforcing the law, while in the heart of Canada's financial
district the main sport is skirting it, bending it, or breaking it for
personal gain. The consolation for Hatfield was that the job provided the money to fund his growing affinity for deep-ocean racing.

Hatfield was twenty-five when he took up sailing, crewing
during the Wednesday-night races at clubs in Toronto and Whitby.
Then he was skipper of his own boat. By 2002, his credentials
included a single-handed voyage across the Atlantic and many
other double-handed or solo passages.

Hatfield almost died in his first solo transatlantic crossing in
1996. He was sailing in the Europe One Single-handed Transatlantic Race (OSTAR), which crosses the North Atlantic between
Plymouth, England, and Newport, Rhode Island. In the middle of
a gale his J29, *Gizmo*, was knocked on its side by a wave. The mast
dug into the water and the boat continued to roll. Hatfield was
thrown out of the cockpit and into the ocean. Luckily he was
wearing a safety harness because he ended up underneath the boat.
In the confusion he saw a seam of daylight and swam for the bright-
ness as the boat slowly righted. He climbed back in and continued
on his way. He says he was too busy to be scared.

Rigging failure prevented Hatfield from finishing higher than
seventh in a field of thirteen in the 1996 OSTAR, but determination
allowed him to complete the course. That was his first taste of
deep-ocean solo sailing and it whetted his appetite for more.

Andrew Prossin, a friend of Hatfield's, says that this noncha-
lance is pure Hatfield. Prossin helped Hatfield to ferry *Gizmo* to
England for that race. They have been sailing buddies for years. The
Halifax native is now in the adventure-travel business and guides
tours to Antarctica. It just so happened that Hatfield was expected
to round Cape Horn in March 2003 at about the same time Prossin

would be returning to Ushuaia, Argentina, from a ten-day Antarctic trip. They planned for the boats to rendezvous and for Prossin to film the historic rounding.

There was a second Canadian in the race. John Dennis was a fifty-seven-year-old real estate executive from Markham, Ontario, a northern suburb of Toronto, and for him the race was all about a promise. He had wanted to do this since he was a boy sailing with his father in Halifax harbour aboard naval training ships.

Dennis is a large, voluble man who looks every inch the old salt of popular imagination, the ship's captain on a pack of Player's cigarettes. He is blind in one eye and a diabetic. He has a marketing man's knack of instant intimacy and given half a chance launches into a sales pitch that is breezy and believable, even if the details are a bit fuzzy. Dennis sailed a lot of ocean miles in his youth but didn't own a boat. Nevertheless, he found himself drawn back to single-handed sailing time after time.

During an interview in Newport two weeks before the start, Dennis dismissed the suggestion that his age or health might be factors in his completing the race. He had arrived in Newport to join the rest of the fleet for a warm-up race to New York, where the main event would start. Dennis was just back from a twenty-nine-day, 4,000-mile round trip to the Azores, half of which he had sailed alone as the necessary qualifier to enter the race. He hadn't slept much in a week and had lost about fifteen pounds, but he looked better than most people ten years younger. He was high on the achievement and as excited as a schoolboy on the last day of class. As he inhaled with obvious pleasure on a cigarette, he said, "I don't have any suicidal tendencies. If I didn't think I was going to come back in one piece, I wouldn't go. When you look at the number of people injured in major traffic accidents in Toronto every day, my odds aren't so bad."

Dennis had approached hundreds of potential sponsors in the eighteen months before the race and had all but given up. But his perseverance paid off when three and a half months before race day, drug giant Bayer Inc. agreed to a $400,000 (U.S.) commitment.

The sponsorship was a good fit. Dennis controls his Type II diabetes through diet, and Bayer makes blood glucose monitors that people with Type II diabetes use to measure their blood sugar levels. Dennis offered Bayer a chance to build a novel marketing campaign. If things worked out, Dennis would be their poster boy, a guy who fit their demographic perfectly. His health and vitality and the adventure of the race were ideal vehicles to deliver the message that people with diabetes can still lead active, fulfilling lives. It was the third time Dennis had tried to get to the starting line and quite possibly his last chance. "This is a passion, this is a dream, and now I can do it," he said.

As the saying goes, a boat is a hole into which you pour money. Dennis didn't have a lot of time, so he spent Bayer's money quickly. He paid $130,000 (U.S.) for a boat that had been sitting in a boatyard for a year. (Dennis bought the boat from Brian Hancock, the veteran sailor and author who manned the Around Alone Web site. Hancock had bought *Great Circle* in 1995 for $150,000 (U.S.) from one of the heirs to the Upjohn drug fortune. The story goes that young Upjohn built the boat with an eye to solo sailing, but didn't have the resolve to carry through. His ex-wife then forced its sale during their divorce.) Dennis replaced most of its vital systems and ordered new sails, standing rigging, and instruments. The fifty-foot boat was repainted and renamed *Bayer Ascensia*. There were boatyard fees, wages for the skipper, crew to pay, and eight months of provisions to buy. The week before the race the money was all gone. Dennis flew to Toronto for some fundraising, hoping to persuade people to "buy" a mile of his journey for fifteen dollars and a few corporate donors to spend twenty-five thousand dollars to sponsor one leg. "Hey, I need some support and I'm not ashamed to ask for it," he said. "I have two kids in university and a mortgage."

Derek Hatfield could only look on with envy at Dennis's good fortune at finding a major sponsor. The men had bumped into each other before, and at one time Hatfield had lent Dennis equipment for one of his other sailing adventures. As Dennis was going through Bayer's cash, Hatfield opened the door to his pantry and found the cupboard bare. A week before the race, Hatfield was in Toronto. He couldn't afford the airline ticket for a return trip to Toronto, so he drove his six-year-old van the twelve hours each way. Hatfield made arrangements to cash in his retirement savings because he realized the $500,000 he'd already committed was just the beginning.

3

Sea Legs

"Nothing happens unless first a dream."

– CARL SANDBURG

~~~~~~~~~~~~~~~
~~~~~~~~~~~~~~~

*T*HE FIRST LEG of the race was a 2,930-mile sprint across the North Atlantic to Brixham, on the south coast of England. It was fast and fun. With the exception of Tim Kent, all the sailors had done it before: These waters were a known quantity as much as any ocean can be.

As the boats left New York a cold front passed over, bringing gusty winds and powerful squalls from the southwest that pushed them along. They skirted Cape Cod, the Georges Bank off the coast of Nova Scotia, and then the Grand Banks off Newfoundland. The weather was windy and the sailing good. There was a sense of release after the stress of preparation and pleasure in finding the rhythm of the sea. Gradually the winds weakened and the sailors checked forecasts to best take advantage of the weather ahead.

Among the Open 60s, Frenchman Thierry Dubois aboard *Solidaires*, an intense and moody veteran, was one of the favourites. The thirty-six-year-old Dubois was equally passionate about sailing and human rights, and although prone to dark moods and angry outbursts, he had a sense of humour that surfaced at the most unpredictable times. Dubois was making his third solo circumnavigation. He had sailed twice in the Vendée Globe. In his first attempt in 1996, he almost died when his boat capsized in a Southern Ocean storm. In the 2000 race he was disqualified partway through because he'd had to put in for repairs – which is not allowed under race rules, but completed the course anyway unofficially. He vowed the Around Alone would be his last solo circumnavigation and planned to cap his impressive career with a victory.

The man Dubois expected to beat was his friend Bernard Stamm, a boyishly handsome Swiss sailor. Stamm, thirty-eight, had worked as a lumberjack and raced motorcycles before turning to sailing as a career, steadily working his way up the race ladder. He now fielded *Bobst Group Armor Lux*, a top-notch boat sponsored by a French packaging company and a French clothing firm. Stamm had competed against Dubois in the 2000 Vendée but, like his friend, had been forced to withdraw because of mechanical problems. Stamm saw this race as a chance to vindicate that defeat and to cement his stature as a top-ranked sailor.

The thirty-four-year-old former Italian naval officer Simone Bianchetti sailing *Tiscali* was the wild card in the pre-race speculation. He had sailed around the world alone once, coming twelfth in the 2000 Vendée. It showed he had stamina and commitment. The big question was whether he could win. A poet with several published volumes to his credit, Bianchetti was at home alone on the ocean, but lost and bewildered on shore. He had a reputation for partying hard given the chance, sometimes for days at a time, but he always managed to pull himself together in time to set sail and regained his focus once out of sight of land. Some said his behaviour verged on the self-destructive. At least once during this race, while in port, friends would carry him home and put him to bed, only to find him back at the party a short time later.

Emma Richards was a rapidly rising star. Fresh-faced, unspoiled, down to earth, Richards was a media darling in Britain where the *Scottish Herald* speculated, "There is no reason why Emma cannot do for yacht racing what Anna Kournikova did for women's tennis." That marketing potential was not lost on her patron, Andrew Pindar. Pindar's printing firm sponsored her boat and was optimistic about her success. Just before the race began, he signed Richards to a three-year contract.

Richards had been a member of the Scottish National sailing squad from the ages of twelve to eighteen, racing Optimist dinghies, 420s and 470s. At Glasgow University she studied sports medicine and was captain of the University sailing team for two years. Her first big race was in 1998. She was twenty-three and was chosen as a member of Tracy Edwards's all-female crew aboard *Royal Sun Alliance* that tried to capture the Jules Verne Trophy, a trophy inspired by the Jules Verne novel *Around the World in Eighty Days*. The race rules are simple – any wind-powered yacht, any start time. The race starts from the Lizard Point on the southwest coast of England and finishes at the same spot.

They were on-course to capture the record when they were dismasted in the Southern Ocean. The next year, Richards landed a sponsorship from the Yorkshire printing firm Pindar when Andrew Pindar gambled that she had the right stuff to turn pro. She went on to victory in the fifty-foot monohull class in the 1999 double-handed race, Transat Jacques Vabre. This race is run

Emma Richards,
twenty-eight, hoped to
become the youngest
woman to race around
the world alone.
(Mark Pepper/Marinepics)

between Le Havre on the northern coast of France and Salvador in
northeastern Brazil.

The London *Sunday Times* called her "Britain's new sailing
heroine," and the *Times* was smitten by her talent, charm, self-
confidence, and drive. It didn't hurt that the package was wrapped
up in a warm smile and natural beauty. The paper compared
Richards to Britain's other sailing phenomenon, Ellen MacArthur,
declaring, "Both are small of stature but with hearts of lions. Both
women have displayed huge reserves of courage, determination,
and stamina and both have proved that they have got what it takes."
But while MacArthur had always wanted to sail alone around the
world, Richards found the loneliness at sea hard to take. She

describes herself as a team player who enjoys the company of others. The big question as she set sail from New York was her ability to take advantage of her electronic aids and turn the information into effective tactics and strategy.

Stamm's *Bobst Group* took an early lead and set the pace with average speeds in the mid-teens and spurts closer to twenty knots. Bianchetti, on *Tiscali*, had a lacklustre start, as he was suffering from the "flu" for the first forty-eight hours. By the fourth day at sea, the bug was gone and he was in third place. *Pindar* stumbled out of the gate with a series of gear problems that slowed her down.

Among the smaller boats, Brad Van Liew jumped out in front, extending his lead each day. He moved *Tommy Hilfiger* so well, he managed to keep pace with the sixty-footers for most of the leg.

Van Liew's early life was a fairy tale of wealth and privilege, servants and private school and life within the walls of a fifty-acre estate outside of San Diego that included a stable full of horses. When F. Scott Fitzgerald said, The rich are different from you and me, he might have meant Van Liew, whose patrician family roots extend back centuries in America.

Wealth breeds self-confidence, and Van Liew carries himself with the self-assured poise of people who are used to getting their way. He does not accept defeat and while he doesn't feel invincible he believes that the application of intellect, planning, and preparation can overcome most things. Van Liew's father built real estate and shopping malls in greater Los Angeles and was a millionaire many times over by the time his son entered high school. At one point the family had not one, but several airplanes. Van Liew was allowed to collect motorcycles, horses, and guns. In a 1999 interview with *Cruising World* magazine editor Herb McCormick, Van Liew admitted his upbringing had been unusual because his every adventurous whim had been encouraged by indulgent parents. He also said he couldn't have cared less about the jet-setting lifestyle he'd left behind.

He learned to sail while at a summer camp near Seattle. He loved it so much that by the age of ten he had persuaded a wealthy uncle in Newport to let him come east for the summer and sail on his forty-two-foot racing sailboat. Over the next handful of summers Van Liew learned how to race, fix, and manage boats.

By Van Liew's last year of high school, his father had shifted his focus to Houston, Texas, where an oil boom had spawned a building boom. When the boom went bust in 1986, the family fortune went with it, and his father eventually declared bankruptcy. The following summer found Van Liew in Newport taking a break from his studies at the University of Southern California. There he met the American single-hander Mike Plant, who had just won the small-boat class in the BOC Challenge, the forerunner of the Around Alone.

Plant was flat broke and the Van Liews still had a second home in Newport. They needed the help of a handyman and hired him. Plant and Van Liew hit it off, and Van Liew later helped Plant build his Open 60 *Duracell* for the 1990 Around Alone. In October 1992, the forty-two-year-old Plant disappeared at sea on his way to the start of the Vendée Globe. It would have been his fourth attempt at a single-handed circumnavigation. Van Liew tried to put together his own campaign for the 1990 race, but nobody took the twenty-two-year-old seriously. It was a humiliating experience for someone unaccustomed to defeat.

By 1992, Van Liew had graduated from the University of Southern California where he met his future wife, Meaghan. He earned his private pilot's licence and with a couple of partners formed a business that chartered and managed corporate and private airplanes. He still has a stake in that business.

When they got married, Meaghan knew the Around Alone race was part of the deal, and together the couple set their sights on the 1998 race. She would manage the business affairs, he would run the boat. He mounted a campaign sponsored by the nutrition firm Balance Bar and came in third in the small-boat class, a more than respectable showing in a race where the casualties included far more experienced sailors than he.

Van Liew was dissatisfied. He wanted to win, not just place, and join his hero, Plant, in the annals of American sailing. He mounted a new campaign, but by the fall of 2001 he still did not have all the pieces in place. He had a boat, having purchased the fifty-foot Magellan *Alpha* that had raced in the 1998 campaign, but ocean racing is a tough sell in North America and he had yet to land a major sponsor. The campaign was touch and go until he signed an agreement with clothing giant Tommy Hilfiger in April 2002, just five months before the start of the race.

In the early days of the leg, Tim Kent had problems with both his primary and his backup autopilots. Neither of them could keep the boat on a straight course, no matter how many times he reset and recalibrated them. Meanwhile, Derek Hatfield was enjoying himself, relieved to be free of the many pressures that had led up to the race. He summed up the first few days at sea as "wet and wild," with *Spirit of Canada* planing at ten to twelve knots. John Dennis was having fun too. "This old man and this old boat are holding their own," he said happily as the fleet approached the halfway mark of the leg.

By the beginning of the second week a low-pressure system settled in with high winds, rising seas, and rain. In ocean sailing these kinds of conditions do not slow the fleet down. Instead, the sailors look for ways to use the system to speed up. The worse the weather the better they like it, because it makes them go faster. The objective is not just to get through storms, but to get through them first and at the greatest speed. In conditions where a cruising sailor might lose heart, take down all his sail, and let the boat ride it out, these mariners were sailing all out. That's what it takes to win.

Simone Bianchetti, in Class I, was elated by the conditions. He called race headquarters on the fleet's sixth day at sea in great excitement to report a top speed of twenty-eight knots and of maintaining an average of twenty-three knots for four hours. Brad Van Liew's *Tommy Hilfiger* was storming along at much the same pace. *Tommy* was moving so fast, Van Liew was aiming at a twenty-four-hour speed record for a fifty-foot boat. It had been set at 333 miles four years earlier, in this race. He missed breaking the record but was as thrilled by the conditions as a kid who just got his Christmas wish.

By the tenth day at sea, Stamm and Dubois were locked in a battle for first place and nearing the English coast. Stamm was averaging 268 miles a day, at an average speed of 11.1 knots an hour. Dubois was a scant fifty miles behind. As they headed towards Land's End, and the English Channel, they set aside their friendship and poured it on.

Each man was scanning weather maps downloaded from the Internet to find the best angle of approach. Dubois was a little farther to the south than Stamm, but on a parallel course. Stamm was storming along, and could see that, behind him where Dubois was sailing, there was a small storm cell. If Dubois could hitch a ride on the squall, he could get ahead of his rival. Stamm would have the wind more squarely behind him, moving at fifteen to twenty knots of wind; Dubois would have the wind at more of an angle and be broad reaching at twenty knots.

In the end Stamm's tactics prevailed. He won the leg with a record-setting ten-day and twenty-two hour passage, even though his autopilot broke forty-eight hours from the finish, which meant he couldn't leave the cockpit. "I am very tired and looking forward to getting some rest, but now I am too excited to sleep," he said soon after arriving in Brixham, Devon. "Maybe later." A frustrated Dubois arrived eleven hours after Stamm to claim second place. *Garnier*, sailed by the Belgian Patrick de Radiguès came third, but de Radiguès withdrew at the end of the first leg to compete in the Route du Rhum that left from France in October. Emma Richards on *Pindar* recovered from her poor start to claim fourth, beating Bianchetti on *Tiscali* by three and a half hours.

As the lead Open 60s were duelling for first place, *Tommy Hilfiger* was slamming into steep seas in the middle of a storm. Stamm and Dubois had caught a lift on the front edge of the storm to carry them to a fast finish, but the smaller boats were overrun by the system. As it moved past them, the wind shifted and came straight at them. It made for rough sailing. The thirty-knot wind whipped up the seas and the motion was uncomfortable and noisy as *Tommy Hilfiger* soared off the top of waves and slammed into the troughs. The hull was made of carbon fibre, an ultra-strong, ultra-thin material, and each time the boat slammed into a wave, the hull made a "pinging" sound. The boat's bare interior even lacked floor-boards to help deaden the noise, and there was water sloshing everywhere. "I don't know how many buckets of water I have taken from the boat today, but this type of sailing has an uncanny way of finding leaks that were never there before," Van Liew said.

When *Tommy Hilfiger* arrived in Brixham, Devon, four days after Stamm, Van Liew had averaged two hundred miles a day, or 8.3 knots an hour. (This speed is based on his time at sea divided by the official 2,930-mile distance of the leg. The actual distance sailed was likely longer. Emma Richards estimated she sailed 33,500 miles over the course of the race, 17 per cent more than the official 28,700-mile course.) Even though he came within a whisker of a speed record for a boat his size, he could not overcome the laws of physics. Stamm had averaged eleven knots an hour, Van Liew, eight knots. It was a particularly sweet victory for the American. It was his first victory in a leg of the Around Alone, something that had eluded him four years earlier. "For fifteen years I have dreamed of this," he said. "I could name every person who has done it off the top of my head. I am proud to be a part of that fraternity."

Three days later, on October 3, after a seventeen-day, eight-hour-long passage, Derek Hatfield crossed the line to claim second-place honours. He had beaten Tim Kent and John Dennis, who were sailing fifty-foot boats. Kent was four hours behind him and came in third in his class. Dennis was a full twenty-four hours behind Kent and claimed fourth.

It had taken a lot out of Hatfield to place second. He had driven himself to the edge of exhaustion and the question was whether he could keep it up. Fatigue clouds judgment, and slow thinking or a sluggish reaction time can be deadly when you're alone. You can get away with it once, twice, maybe even three times, but eventually the sea wins. Five days earlier, Hatfield acknowledged that he had crossed over the line.

He had been in the same storm that Van Liew had weathered. The boat was constantly being knocked around, banging and crashing, making for a wet and miserable ride. Most of the other competitors left matters to the autopilot and stayed below but Hatfield had hand steered to get the most out of his boat. The rule of thumb is that a human helmsman can get 10 per cent more speed out of a boat than the autopilot, as people can react faster than computer software. The drawback is that over the long run, a skipper's reaction

A trim and happy John Dennis waves as he leaves the dock in Brixham for the start of Leg II.
(Billy Black)

time deteriorates and he becomes much slower than the autopilot. The trick is in knowing when to quit. "You get tired and when you get overtired, you don't make good judgments," Hatfield says. "It can get dangerous. I've come close, but you just have to recognize the signs and get some sleep."

John Dennis felt elated just to be in the race and it showed in his dispatches. While *Bayer Ascensia* beat into heavy seas, he explained the motion as akin to riding one of the old mechanical bulls, making it hard to eat, type, cook, or do any other job. Dennis was taking thirteen pills a day, and the trick was not to spill any of them.

Hatfield, Tim Kent, and Brad Van Liew all turned out in the middle of the night on October 4 to greet Dennis as he crossed the finish line after an eighteen-day passage. Brian Hancock, the Around Alone Web site correspondent, was there too.

"The first we saw was a flicker of a red navigation light followed by the dark outline of sails against an almost black horizon," he wrote. "And then he was suddenly upon us.

"John lifted his arm to acknowledge the finish gun. He could not have been dissatisfied with his fourth place finish. Just making the start line was an enormous challenge and to have successfully completed the first leg of the race was a victory in itself. It was a fit, trim and healthy John Dennis that waved to the assembled crowds. He has made the transition from businessman to sailor and looks immensely happy."

LEG II

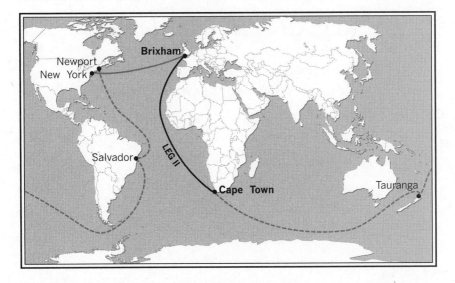

ROUTE: Brixham, England, to Cape Town,
South Africa

DEPARTURE: October 14, 2002

DISTANCE: 6,880 nautical miles

4

Bay of Biscay Blues

**"The greatest test of courage on earth
is to bear defeat without losing heart."**

– ROBERT G. INGERSOLL

THE BRITISH FONDLY call the countryside around the port of
Brixham, the English Riviera because of the unique climate.
Brixham is a well-protected port on the south coast of Devon,
about twenty miles east of Plymouth, where America's Pilgrim
Fathers set sail. Brixham sits on the bottom edge of horseshoe-
shaped Tor Bay and the heights surrounding the port protect it
from the prevailing winds. Here, the summers are long, the winters
short, and it is sunny and mild enough for palm trees to grow.

Brixham was a fitting place for the Around Alone fleet's first
stop. In the Middle Ages it was the largest port in southern
England, and in 1588 after Sir Francis Drake's fleet attacked the
Spanish Armada in the English Channel, Drake sailed one of his
prize ships into Tor Bay, the galleon *Nostra Senora del Rosario*.

During the wars against the French between 1689 and 1815, Brixham was a naval base. Napoleon Bonaparte spent a few days there as a prisoner aboard the HMS *Bellerophon*, waiting to be taken to exile on St. Helena. In the 1890s, there were about three hundred fishing trawlers based in port. A much smaller fishing fleet still calls it home today.

The sailors took advantage of the port's deep-water marina to regroup after their Atlantic crossing. Tim Kent needed to overhaul the two autopilots on *Everest Horizontal*, which had behaved so erratically on the first leg that his boat had strayed all over the course. It probably cost him second place. A team from Brookes & Gatehouse Ltd. — the company whose software Emma Richards was testing on *Pindar* — spent two days rewiring this piece of equipment. Kent also removed his Plexiglas windows, rebedding and resealing them in hopes of stopping the leaks that threatened to short out his computers and electrical instruments.

Tommy Hilfiger went through a rigorous checkup. Brad Van Liew's five-person shore team changed the engine oil and filters, replaced the primary and secondary fuel filters, and overhauled the hydraulic system that moved his keel. The winches were stripped down, rebuilt, and lubricated, as was other deck hardware. The rod rigging holding up the mast was checked and tightened. *Tommy* had also sprung leaks. These were sealed and the boat was hauled out of the water to allow the shore crew to inspect hull and keel joints. Other members of the fleet followed a similar procedure.

As it would be in all of the stops along the way, the welcome given the sailors in Brixham was warm. The local yacht club acted as host, and the marina was swarming with visitors and volunteers. There were social events and obligations to sponsors. John Dennis spent some time ashore talking to diabetic groups on behalf of Bayer. "If I motivated just a few people, [I've been] successful," he said.

The start of the second leg of the race was delayed twenty-four hours when a gale roared across western England. Then Monday, October 14, dawned clear, and the fleet was off, fighting against the prevailing current to sail the two hundred miles back down the English Channel to the point where it could safely turn south. The worry was that conditions would change, creating difficulties in rounding Brittany, on the northwest coast of France, and Île d'Ouessant, just offshore.

Brittany's coastline is dramatic and beautiful, but its currents and tides are among the most dangerous anywhere. Rocky cliffs tumble to rubble-strewn shores that have long been a graveyard for sailing ships. The water has been driven across the Atlantic Ocean for three thousand miles without any land to temper its movement, so the waves can turn short, steep, and vicious as they hit the shallow coast. Once past the bulge of Brittany, the fleet faced the Bay of Biscay, where for the length of its four hundred-mile coast the waters are extremely dangerous.

The bay indents the coast of Western Europe from Île d'Ouessant in France to Cape Ortegal in northwest Spain. The bay is noted for its sudden, severe storms and its strong currents. The rocky northeastern coasts of Biscay are irregular, with many good harbours including Brest, Saint-Nazaire, and La Rochelle. The southeastern shore is straight and sandy. The ports there include Bilbao and Santander in Spain. There are several resorts along the French coast, notably Biarritz.

A storm blowing from the west can deprive sailors of room to manoeuvre their boats if they are too close to shore. It is a situation that sailors fear – the danger of being blown onto the rocks of a lee shore.

The fleet's luck held that first day and into the starlit evening. By midnight, the leading yachts were edging into the North Atlantic.

The stars disappeared behind cloud and a light rain began falling. Then the wind picked up and the drizzle became a downpour.

By the second day at sea, the leaders were recording a wind of a steady fifty knots. While some of the boats turned south, the first and second place finishers in the first leg, Bernard Stamm and Thierry Dubois, kept heading west to put more distance between themselves and land. This leg, a marathon down the length of Europe and Africa, took the longest of any to complete. The leaders would take a minimum thirty days and the laggards as much as fifty to finish. It was a leg where the race could be won or lost, because tactics played a huge part. So for now, tactics prevailed over the need to be leading the fleet. "The first real deal," as Brad Van Liew put it.

It was the small boats' turn to face high winds at the end of the second day. The wind was all over the place, in the high twenties, then gusting into the mid-thirties with twelve-foot seas from trough to crest. Tim Kent had heard the stories about the Bay of Biscay and was as stoic as he was nervous. It was not very comfortable on board *Everest Horizontal*, not at all. It was in sharp contrast to the previous evening when Kent had fried up a steak and washed it down with a chilled Diet Coke, his preferred beverage at sea. It was the way he liked to start each leg. His boat did not have refrigeration, so he filled a cooler with ice and, for the first few days, ate his favourite fresh food.

By the evening of the second night, Kent had rolled up the headsail and was flying a storm jib, a small sail that lent the boat stability in high winds. His massive mainsail, which was almost one thousand square feet and weighed about 250 pounds, had been reefed down, reducing its size by more than two-thirds. It was an arduous task made even more difficult by his being tied to a safety harness as the boat heaved and pitched. Worse conditions lay ahead.

Everyone had their eyes glued to the weather maps. In two days, an intense, fast-moving storm would blanket them. It looked like the six Open 60s could get far enough west into the Atlantic to tough the storm out. The six smaller boats would be that much slower. They had the laws of physics working against them.

As the sailors readied for their first test, there was some comfort in the fact that they were aboard the most sophisticated sailing vessels ever built. As he had sailed down Lake Ontario in June, Derek Hatfield had emphatically declared that Open boats were "the safest and fastest boats in the world." Now he would find out.

A lot had changed in boat design and materials since race chairman Sir Robin Knox-Johnston had won the first running of any solo circumnavigation challenge in 1968. Like Industrial Revolution metallurgists who played with iron, nickel, and chromium to forge steel, the alchemists of twenty-first-century boat building played with Kevlar, carbon fibre, and fibreglass to make the fastest boats on Earth. Each one was handcrafted in a boatyard or a hometown workshop.

Bernard Stamm and Thierry Dubois built their boats, *Bobst Group* and *Solidaires*, themselves, hiring professionals only at key points. So did Hatfield. *Spirit of Canada* had been pieced together in a shed on his father's property outside Fredericton. Arthur Hatfield recalls the day Derek came for a visit and asked if he would help him build a boat. "I said you build me a shed and I'll build you a boat," Arthur says. "And I did."

Boston naval architect Bob Dresser drew up the plans, and in the fall of 1997 Arthur set to work. He had been in the forestry industry for most of his working life and had built wooden boats before, but none on this scale. Derek's sister, Tammy, and her husband, Eugene McLellan, owned a construction company and helped build the boathouse. Derek's brother, Hal, and an army of volunteers spent thousands of hours bringing the boat to life.

First they "lofted" the boat, making full-size patterns from Mylar, a strong, thin polyester film. Wooden moulds were made from the pattern. Layers of Kevlar, fibreglass, and carbon-fibre cloth were laid over the mould in alternating layers with resin to create the hull. Kevlar is the material used in bulletproof vests and won't tear or rip, which is why it has become a staple in boat building. Carbon-fibre cloth adds strength and stiffness but it can be punctured. When the two are mixed with e-glass, a fibreglass cloth used in recreational boat building, and sandwiched around a foam core, the result is a strong, light, fast boat. The final laminate is so thin that sailors complain the noise of water running under the hull is continuous and in storms can be deafening.

Hatfield couldn't afford to use expensive carbon fibre for the entire boat, instead using it to reinforce those points that would come under the greatest stress, such as the area around the mast and chainplates, where the rigging for the mast is attached to the hull. After the basic hull was formed, a layer of gelcoat was added. This material hardens to form a smooth, shiny finish on deck and on the sides of the hull. The underside of the hull was coated with epoxy resin to form a hard, waterproof seal. The deck, which had been moulded separately, was vacuum-sealed onto the hull. All this work took almost three years to accomplish.

Another chore for Hatfield was his relentless quest to reduce weight. Patianne Verburgh, Hatfield's partner and shore manager, was part of the team that helped build the boat. Her job throughout the race involved organizing provisions, arranging for the logistics of getting spares and equipment from port to port, and doing the thousand and one other jobs that keep the boat going. A tall, wiry, and intense native of Nova Scotia, Verburgh hopes one day to join the solo circumnavigating ranks. She became involved in Hatfield's campaign in late 2000 after meeting him during a race on Lake Ontario.

Verburgh recalls crawling on hands and knees over raw fibre-glass in the belly of the half-built boat looking for ways to save a few ounces here and there. She cut the end off bolts and later replaced metal shackles with nylon webbing, saving about twenty-five pounds.

The hull was trucked to Wiggers Custom Yachts in Bowmanville, Ontario, where the keel and other fittings were installed. Arthur Hatfield was very proud of the boat, but wondered if the pros at Wiggers would scoff at something built in a barn in New Brunswick. "But they didn't," Arthur says proudly. "And you know, I felt pretty good about that, because we did build it in a barn."

Open boats have long thin keels with lead bulbs on the bottom. *Spirit of Canada*'s keel is eleven feet deep with a 700-pound blade and 2,750-pound bulb. Most keels on Open boats can be moved sideways, which increases the boat's stability in high winds by keeping it flatter in the water. This lets it carry more sail in winds that would otherwise force its skipper to reduce sail at the risk of a knockdown. *Spirit of Canada*'s keel moved thirty-four degrees to either side. When fully extended, the keel's weight is the equivalent of having about three thousand pounds, or about fifteen heavy people hanging over the side of the boat.

Canting keels are a second safety feature. If the boat capsizes so its keel is up in the air and its mast is pointing to the ocean floor, the canting units can be tilted and the weight used to flip the boats upright. Prior to entering the race, all boats in the Around Alone fleet underwent a rollover test to ensure they could do this.

Spirit of Canada did its test in Toronto harbour in May 2002. A diver attached a sling to the keel and a crane pulled on the sling until the boat turned upside down with Hatfield inside. It took just a few minutes for him to right the boat. Some boats had the added feature of ballast tanks, which allow their skippers to pump water in and out of tanks, shifting weight from side to side. In *Everest Horizontal*'s case, Tim Kent could shift four thousand pounds of water this way. Older boats like *Everest* and John Dennis's *Bayer Ascensia* had fixed keels and used water ballast to move weight around.

The advent of canting keels is one reason why average speeds have increased. When the weather gets really bad you pour it on and these devices let you sail close to the edge of control, along the fine line between exhilaration and disaster.

When the French sailor Isabelle Autissier introduced the modern version of a canting keel in the 1994 Around Alone, everyone wondered whether it would work. When she beat the nearest boat into Cape Town by five days, they got their pencils out and started figuring. Since then the mechanisms have become more or less standard, proving simple and reliable for the most part. *Spirit of Canada*'s hydraulic canting system is similar to those used by other boats. A piston fits inside a cylinder filled with hydraulic fluid. When pressure is applied to the piston, it applies force to the fluid, which moves the keel.

You run into trouble when a seal breaks and the hydraulic fluid leaks out. If that happens, there's nothing to keep the keel rigid. All of a sudden you have a couple of thousand pounds of keel flopping around, with the terrifying prospect that the motion might rip a hole in the bottom of your boat. *Tommy Hilfiger* had a backup system for just this reason. Brad Van Liew installed pipes on either side of the keel that could be clamped tightly in place to keep the keel fixed along the centre line of the boat should the hydraulic

Spirit of Canada was turned upside down in Toronto harbour
in May 2002 to ensure that Derek Hatfield would be able to
right the boat while at sea. *(Adam Mayers)*

system fail. "It's one of the things I was pretty paranoid about," Van
Liew says.

These boats are all about backups. They are designed with
redundancy and reliability in mind. Multiple systems are installed so
should one fail another can take over. Backups are also expensive. A
skipper on a tight budget has to pick and choose. Hatfield couldn't
afford Van Liew's keel pipes. He had to spend his money elsewhere.

Most Open boats also use daggerboards to keep them from
being pushed sideways in a strong wind. These long thin fins on
either side of the mast are similar to centreboard keels in dinghies.
They can be raised or lowered and slide through the boat into the
water through a strong rubber sleeve.

The sailors may complain that the thin hulls make for a noisy
ride, but Open boats are strong. Tim Kent's *Everest Horizontal* was
designed by naval architect Jim Antrim and built in California by

James Betts Enterprises. Antrim came up with a bowling ball experiment to simulate a collision. The ball was swung at a sample of the hull laminate at a speed of twenty-five knots [28.7 mph]. It bounced off. Engineers then took swings at the hull with a sledge-hammer. The hammerheads bounced off. It took an axe to get through the laminate.

The disastrous 1996 Vendée Globe, which took the life of Gerry Roufs, led to a fine-tuning of safety standards. Today, the boats must meet stringent rollover requirements and have four watertight compartments. They must float even with three of the four compartments flooded. Each boat has two manual bilge pumps that can be operated from inside or outside the boat. In case the boat doesn't right itself, the skippers can leave the boat through an escape hatch in the transom at the stern. When the boat is upside down, the hatch is above the waterline. Some skippers, such as Tim Kent, went a bit further. Kent painted the bottom of his boat with fluorescent orange paint: All the better to be spotted should the vessel capsize.

The design of the mast and the rigging, which attaches the mast to the boat, involves the same quest to reduce weight and increase strength. The sixty-five-foot mast tube on *Spirit of Canada* weighs just 170 pounds. The boom is twenty-two and a half feet long, but weighs just 70 pounds. Together, these two spars hold up the large mainsail that drives the boat. This sail has the same surface area as a small bachelor apartment and weighs close to 200 pounds. Sail changes at sea are hard work.

When Brad Van Liew raced in the EDS Atlantic Challenge in 2001 as crew aboard Josh Hall's *Gartmore Investments*, the boat was wired up like a patient in intensive care to test the stresses on the rig and hull. (The race is an 8,000-mile trip from Portsmouth, England, to Baltimore, Maryland, and then from Boston to St. Malo,

France.) Groupe Finot, the boat's designers, wanted hard numbers on metal fatigue. How far could the boat be pushed before things started to fall apart?

"Fatigue is a black art," Van Liew says. "You can never really tell how much a boat will go through before things break. You have to do it to find out."

Finot is a dominant player in the design of Open class racing boats, and a Finot-designed boat had won every major solo around the world race since 1990. *Tommy Hilfiger* was a Groupe Finot design. It was built for publishing millionaire and former Special Air Service (SAS) officer Mike Garside, who campaigned the boat as *Magellan Alpha* in the 1988 Around Alone and then sold it to Van Liew.

In the EDS race, Josh Hall agreed to have sensors installed that would record how much *Gartmore*'s mast and deck flexed and how much its rod rigging twisted and stretched. The boat was also monitored to see how much gravitational or G force was applied to the skipper and the equipment as the boat catapulted off waves and slammed into troughs. These forces of acceleration and deceleration force blood from the upper part of the body, including the brain, to the legs and feet.

It was discovered that, at times, *Gartmore* pulled 3.5 Gs at the navigation station inside the cabin. In experiments with pilots, a sustained force of four to six Gs has been shown to lead to a drop in blood pressure, impaired vision, sluggish reaction times, and distorted perceptions. After about twenty seconds at six Gs, pilots start to black out.

Josh Hall says that at one spot on deck in front of *Gartmore*'s mast, the force was briefly measured at 8 Gs. This spot is where a sailor would stand to change the headsail. The force was measured in a gale as the boat surfed off a wave and landed hard in a trough.

"I've been in a situation like that many times," says Hall, an

Around Alone and Vendée Globe veteran. "The boat goes over a wave and you're left hanging in mid-air. As your body goes down, the boat is starting to come up. When the two meet, that shock force was measured at 7 to 8 Gs. That can break your legs. That's how dangerous these boats are."

By the third day into Leg II, the sailors' tactics were diverging. The winds were developing to hurricane force as the weather system spread like a two thousand-mile stain across the North Atlantic. Bernard Stamm, Thierry Dubois, and Emma Richards, the leading Open 60s, continued west, putting as much distance as possible between them and the Bay of Biscay. Stamm later joked he was being forced to sail back across the Atlantic to Newfoundland to get around the storm. By the time these boats felt the outer edge of the system, they were several hundred miles ahead of the smaller boats.

An ocean of air that reaches several hundred miles above the earth's surface surrounds the planet. The lowest layer, the troposphere, extends about twelve miles above the surface and affects us the most. The air in this layer moves in complex patterns of alternating high- and low-pressure systems, and the wind flows from high pressure to low pressure like water flowing down a hill. The flow can be gentle or, like Niagara Falls, steep, fast, and furious. The steeper the gradient, the windier it is. In high pressure regions the air slowly sinks and it usually means sunny skies and fair weather in summer. The air is often relatively cold and dry, but in summer it can also mean hot weather because of the long, sunny days. A low-pressure system is a region of mild, moist, rising air with cloud cover and rain. When a low turns into a big blow, the winds are strong, gusty, and erratic.

Weather changes because one air mass has collided with another, creating a front. On television, meteorologists are always talking about fronts – cold fronts and warm fronts. Where the two collide there are usually violent thunderstorms, high winds, or hail. Warm fronts rise over the cold fronts as warm air slides over the top of the cooler system, bringing high cloud and rain on their leading edges. As the warm air fully overtakes the colder air, the clouds become thicker and lower. Twelve hours later, or less, the weather turns foul, as the Around Alone boats discovered.

In the Northern Hemisphere, an approaching storm moves clockwise. The systems bring wind from the east, which accounts for the sailor's adage, "An east wind blows no good." As the storm passes, the winds shift to the south or southeast and increase. Finally the system moves off and the prevailing wind settles in from the west and northwest, bringing clearing skies. In the Southern Hemisphere, the pattern is reversed.

Stamm was well west of the Bay of Biscay and chose to drive straight through the storm, hoping that speed and seamanship would carry the day. He was able to overcome the sensible fear that his boat could be smashed to pieces and he might die in this vast boiling cauldron of Nature's power.

Stamm saw four tactical options: He could turn and head for port which was twenty-four hours or so away. "A wise choice, but difficult to carry out," he later mused. He could stay put, stop his boat, and ride out the storm, a technique known as heaving to. This works best with boats that have full keels, which run the length of the boat, rather than the shorter fin or dagger keels on Open boats. Racing sailboats do not to sit comfortably in these conditions and experience has shown that heaving to can be more dangerous than running before the wind. Running downwind is, after all, what the boats are designed to do best.

Option three was to sail due south and, as Stamm said, "grin and bear it" as the system swept by from west to east. That would put *Bobst Group* at right angles to the wind direction, or beam on to the seas, putting the boat at risk of being rolled over or worse if it did not handle the waves properly. Stamm chose the fourth option: To keep going southwest and aim for the heart of the beast. Sailing through the storm's centre and out the other side would mean he spent the least time but in the worst conditions. (This was the winning tactic used by the thirty-foot *Midnight Rambler* in the 1998 Sydney–Hobart race. *Midnight Rambler* chose the shortest path through the storm by sailing straight into it. Larger boats capsized trying to return to shore.)

The risk of the fourth option was that as he entered and exited the eye of the storm he would face the strongest winds and steepest seas. Inside the eye the wind might drop and the sky clear, but it would return with ferocity when he reached the far side of the system.

Stamm described what happened during the next forty-eight hours: "I met up with winds around 75 knots just before and after the centre," he said. "At the heart of the system, the wind fell to 30 knots and I even had a little fine weather for a few hours. I think that was the most dangerous moment. The boat was not being pushed along, but the seas were still just as mountainous.

"I had got the boat ready. I brought in everything from the deck, removed the halyards, which wouldn't be used. It took me about a day to do everything, battening everything down or removing it, but it was work well done, as everything came off well.

"There was just one moment when the staysail [the smallest storm sail] started to unroll from the top. I had to let the boat run free, unroll, re-roll, unroll again and roll up the staysail, until it rolled correctly. A tense moment, because if I hadn't managed to wind it up, I ran the risk of breaking the mast. Of course that sort of trouble only happens at the height of the storm."

Thierry Dubois aboard *Solidaires* and Emma Richards on *Pindar* made the same choice. Richards described her third day at sea "preparing for battle," as she put it, tying everything down that could come loose and checking her vital electronic systems, including the backup pilot and the backup compass for the backup pilot. She made extra pasta, topped up her fuel tank, and used her desalinator to make enough water for a week. She tried to sleep, figuring it would be her last chance for a while.

In a message to race officials on her fourth day at sea, Richards said that as *Pindar* fell off the crests of waves into the troughs it was all she could do to hang on. She was wearing a crash helmet to prevent a head injury as she was thrown around the cabin.

"It feels as if my arms are going to be wrenched from my sockets as I try to hang on to the navigation table," she said.

On Day Five, early in the morning, Thierry Dubois reported seventy-two knots of wind, a Category One hurricane. He hadn't been able to get far enough west to catch a favourable wind angle and was taking a pounding. The only way he'd been able to sleep was bundled up either in a sail locker or on the cabin floor. It was so small a space that he was in the fetal position. "I am hunched up in a ball to protect my head in my knees," he reported. At least he wasn't being thrown around the cabin.

"The sea is wild and I can't see to the end of this mother of a depression," he said. "It will be two days before I'm through it." He added in a later message that the conditions were "totally unbearable." The storm barred his route. He couldn't go around it, so he had to tackle it head-on. He had taken down all sail except a small storm jib. He was living in foul-weather gear and eating energy bars to keep going.

That day, New Zealander Graham Dalton sailing the Open 60 *Hexagon* checked in. Dalton was a lifelong sailor and an entrepreneur, but had the least racing experience among the big boat fleet. His boat was a thoroughbred, potentially the fastest on the course, and he was well sponsored by HSBC Bank. Dalton had chosen the southerly course that Stamm had rejected. As the storm swept through, he was battered and *Hexagon* was knocked down several times, once with so much force a stereo speaker ripped off a bulkhead wall and hit him in the back.

The six Open 40s and 50s in Class II monitored the radio chatter and e-mail traffic as the bigger boats battled on. By the third day it was clear that everyone was on a collision course with Nature in conditions most sailors avoid at all costs. However, these were not most sailors, but the sort who actively seek out the worst weather on the planet for fun, or if not fun, for competition. Bad weather makes the boats go fast and going fast makes their competitive juice flow. This is what they live for and why they do what they do. Certain people crave danger because it makes them feel more alive. These were those people.

But even racing sailors aren't totally mad. They live on the edge but most prefer not to go over. They know that safety and good seamanship mean that they will live to race another day. As Joseph Conrad said, "Any fool can carry on, but a wise man knows how to shorten sail in time."

Sailing into a hurricane was an even greater risk for them than for the Open 60 sailors. They were closer to shore and would endure the storm for longer, facing up to four days of boatbreaking conditions, compared to the two faced by the big boats.

Two more days was double the opportunity for something to go seriously wrong. They also faced the possibility of shipwreck if the winds and waves were severe enough to drive them onto the rocky shore in the Bay of Biscay. Most of them had yet to find their sea legs and some had experienced gear failure. Later on in the race they might not have the choice of continuing or sailing to the safety of a port, but now they did.

"Today is one of those knot-in-the-stomach kinda things," Brad Van Liew admitted at the end of his second day at sea. "Every time I look, the situation gets worse. There are very few options because we have had very little time to manoeuvre for the correct side of the beast. I have been cleaning house and taking care of any-thing I can think of. Basically battening down the hatches. I hope and pray that we come out of this one."

That evening and on the following day, the small boats talked among themselves. Alan Paris aboard the Open 40 *BTC Velocity* was the first to call it a day. Paris was the manager of the Ariel Sands Hotel in Bermuda, owned by actor Michael Douglas. A friendly and unassuming man, Paris has an enormous sense of humour.

John Dennis on board *Bayer Ascensia*, summed up the first two days at sea as a "baptism by fire," and like Paris did not dwell for long on his decision. He said several times his goal was to finish and that meant safety and prudence. "This is a long, hard race," he said. "Some may question my nerve, but a safe harbour looks more sen-sible right now than beating up the boat and myself." He was the next sailor to turn for shore.

Derek Hatfield seemed shocked by the quick descent into near-survival conditions during the first two days out and wondered how much worse it might be. "It was the worst storm I've ever seen," Hatfield said. "It was just horrendous. I feel like I've been run over by a bus this morning. It's just miserable."

Alan Paris put his career as a hotel manager on hold for the chance to be the first Bermudan to complete a solo race around the world.
(Ann Harley)

Hatfield used the respite between this storm and one that blew in thirty-six hours later, to clean up the boat, eat something hot, and catch a nap. He found it hard to relax knowing what was on the way and struggled with the choice. He was there to race and win and really bad weather was part of the thrill. It was a test. Each time you passed the test, it raised your experience bar. The bad weather was just earlier and more severe than expected. On the other hand, as Dirty Harry liked to say, "A man's got to know his limitations." Hatfield also headed to safety.

In the thirty-six hours since leaving Brixham *Tommy Hilfiger*'s third reefing system had broken, which meant Brad Van Liew could not fully reduce his mainsail. As a consequence, his boat would be overpowered in seventy knots of wind. He could be dismasted or worse. Van Liew, the adrenaline junkie, who described his 1988 edge-of-control Around Alone experience as "a total rush," decided it would be foolish to continue.

So as Stamm, Dubois, Richards, and Dalton sailed into the heart of the storm, one by one the Class II skippers turned for the Spanish coast, heading for Baiona, south of Cape Finesterre on the west coast of Spain. They were joined by Bruce Schwab on the Open 60 *Ocean Planet* who had left Brixham late, after repairing his boom which had broken in the first leg. They had a day or so before the worst of the weather arrived. Only John Dennis put in to the north in A Coruña on the southern edge of the Bay of Biscay.

"I'm not even going to describe the particulars," Emma Richards said of her boat on Sunday, October 20, Day Six of the leg, once she was safely through the storm. She had not been out of her foul-weather gear and safety harness in four days, except to go to the toilet. "But even then you need to pick your moment," she said.

Richards had survived on banana bread, Jaffa Cakes, and nuts. Her boat was a mess, but in one piece. She had emerged safely with just a few bangs and bruises, and as tough as it had been, she felt more confident in her abilities. The work list was long. The stove, some light fixtures and other equipment had been torn from *Pindar's* walls. Diesel fuel, tools, food, and pieces of hardware, clothes, and utensils were all sloshing around in the cabin. It was a potent mixture that smelled noxious and stung the many cuts on her hands.

"Really could do with a good massage," she grumbled in an e-mail. "My body feels like it has been in the ring for a week."

After a good start Simone Bianchetti put in to the French port of Brest on the second day of the leg to fix *Tiscali's* autopilots. They had been unreliable since he left Brixham and Bianchetti had been

Poet and former Italian
naval officer Simone
Bianchetti hoped a
good performance
would put him in the
top tier of the sport.
(James Robinson Taylor)

unable to fix them via teleconference calls with experts. As conditions deteriorated, the frustrated sailor knew it would be impossible to sail to Cape Town without their help.

On Day Six, as the Class II skippers toasted their safe arrival in Baiona, Bianchetti ran into more bad luck. He had left Brest after a short stopover and was sailing southwest in a moderate twenty knots of wind when, without warning, his mast snapped in three places and the rig fell in splinters onto his deck. Bianchetti was able to make a jury rig and hobble back to A Coruña, where John Dennis had put in. Bianchetti would be stuck there for almost three weeks.

Hatfield, Van Liew, Kent, and the other Class II sailors holed up in Spain for five days while the storm pounded the coast. The weather was so bad that all the ports along the Portuguese coast were closed. Lisbon was the sole exception. The storm was later described as a "weather bomb," a phenomenon that caused the many deaths in the 1999 Sydney–Hobart race and was the subject of Sebastian Junger's book *The Perfect Storm*. Three low-pressure systems had converged, hitting each other and forming one massive, slow-moving low that churned and boiled across the northern Atlantic. It took three days for the storm to subside and another two days of gradually moderating winds before the fleet could leave port.

In Baiona, the red carpet was rolled out at the Monte Real Club de Yates (Royal Baiona Yacht Club) which had sponsored Spain's America's Cup Challenge. The sailors were wined and dined, fêted with parties, and given the run of the place. Long dinners began at 11 p.m. and ran into the small hours. During the day the sailors went sightseeing and got to know each other, a process that would normally not have taken place so early on.

On the fourth day ashore Derek Hatfield drove up to A Coruña to see John Dennis and witness the sealing of his engine transmission. The same thing had been done to all the boats in Baiona, as race rules specify that engines cannot be used except to charge batteries while the boats are racing. Each member of the fleet would incur a forty-eight-hour penalty for the stop, but since all of them had put in to port, it was a level playing field. On October 23, the boats were towed out to sea in the order in which they arrived and one by one they headed out.

A few days later, Hatfield was ghosting past Lisbon under a blue sky and in a light breeze. He was sure the decision to seek shelter had been the right one. "That storm would have busted the boat up for sure," he said.

Single-handed sailing is emotionally draining, with as many bleak lows as exhilarating highs. A high might come from surfing at great speed down a wave or making the best distance that day in the fleet. A low might be caused by a day with light winds, listening to the banging and clattering of the rig as the boat wallows with the swells, in the knowledge that there is nothing you can do to change it. It can be caused because the skipper is in last place or second place or for no reason at all. The blues can be triggered by a long-awaited call from home that ends up feeling bittersweet, as unsettling thoughts intrude: Why am I doing this? Is it worth it? I must be a fool. They need me. Why am I here?

Single-handing requires a rare mental toughness because there is no one on board to tell the sailor to get going, work harder. There is no taskmaster to push you forward relentlessly. Sometimes routine tasks become paralyzing and the thought of sailing another one thousand or three thousand miles debilitating. Two-time Around Alone sailor David Adams, who won Class II in 1994, spent a lot of time on mental preparation in the months leading up to the race. One of his tricks at these times was to adjust his focus from the large goal of winning or finishing the leg to a smaller, more immediate goal. If he was floating on a calm sea, there was nothing he could do to make the boat move. But he could repair sails, cook, enjoy a good meal, and catch up on his rest.

John Dennis did not have time for the mental preparations that Adams deemed so important. He had been working full tilt since May when Bayer agreed to sponsor him. He had acquired, stripped down, and refit the boat and had sailed to the Azores and back to qualify. There were the thousand and one details of organization to keep him busy. Now, while his fellow sailors were resting and relaxing in Baiona and waiting out the storm, in A Coruña John Dennis crashed emotionally. He was more or less on his own for five days, doing his laundry, repairing and tidying up *Bayer Ascensia*, but otherwise with plenty of time on his hands. The reception wasn't as friendly as in Baiona and for the first time in months he wasn't a man in motion. All the things that had been pushed aside while he readied for the race closed in. Dennis had time to consider the emotional and financial cost of his undertaking. While the other Class II sailors let off steam by sharing their frustrations, all the worries in John Dennis's world rattled around in his head.

He was worried about his forty-eight-year-old wife, Penny, who was so distressed by his entry in the race, she had taken a medical leave from her administrative job at a hospital in Markham, north of Toronto, soon after Dennis set sail. She worried about Dennis's safety and the more practical matters of mortgage payments, car loans, and university fees. Their twenty-three-year-old daughter, Stephanie, was in her last year at the University of Toronto but moved home to help out. Penny went to bed at night unable to sleep and with her stomach tied in knots. "I knew John had sponsorship and I thought, Okay, I can handle this," Penny said. "But I don't think either of us totally understood what it was going to be like."

Dennis turned fifty-eight on the fleet's third day back at sea after the Bay of Biscay storm. It was the fourteenth day since leaving Brixham. The boyish glee he'd felt on leaving Newport was long gone and he felt old, tired, depressed, and guilty about the toll the trip was taking on his family, something he had not fully considered before he set sail. He had expected to miss them, but had not expected the pangs of loneliness to outweigh the pleasure of the journey. Phone calls and e-mails became painful stews of anticipation and regret. Dennis mused that he should have lived his dream twenty-five years earlier when he was healthier and less encumbered.

More than a week after his birthday, this brooding introspection was still apparent to observers. Dennis dwelled on the selfishness of his quest, but equally firmly said he was committed to continuing. He talked about how low he'd felt around his birthday, so low that other members of the fleet had feared for his safety. "I lost it for a few days," he said. "I know what it costs to run a house, I know what the mortgage is, I know what the car payment is. I know what the fees are and the utilities. It ain't cheap." Then he added, "I'm fine now and I'm going to stay fine. You don't come this far to give it up."

Two days into the fifth week of the leg, Dennis was not far off the coast of Mauritania on the west coast of Africa, not yet halfway to Cape Town. His melancholy continued. The going was slow, he had read three books, but found it hard to concentrate. He gamely professed to enjoy the ride, but kept returning to the costs of fulfilling the dream. At one point, he paused mid-conversation with a journalist to note that there was nothing to see out the huge glass windows on *Bayer Ascensia* but swells and water in every direction. "It's just empty," Dennis said.

"If you asked me if I would do it again, I would definitely tell you no. Not that I won't be happy and proud when I finish. But it's whether it's worth the agony and the worry. I don't think it is. Quite honestly, until you get out here, it's just hard to imagine how lonely it can be."

As Derek Hatfield sailed south towards the equator he too faced pressures, but unlike John Dennis, he didn't have a family to worry about.

"This is a very self-centred thing," Hatfield said. "When John's finished, what is he going to be able to say? What is it going to do for him? Absolutely nothing. It's not going to make him rich or famous. A year after the race, people will have forgotten the whole thing. Sometimes I question why I'm here, but it's my own money and I have nobody to answer to."

So why do solo sailors bother? Why cross five oceans alone in a small boat? Why do so many of these sailors up the ante from crewed trips to solo circumnavigation? One characteristic they share is the enjoyment of danger. It makes these sailors feel much more alive, heightening their senses. It is why they go back time after time. John Hughes, the first Canadian to have sailed around the world alone in a race, barely survived. He was sailing a Cayenne 42, a modified cruising boat, which was dismasted as he left Australia. Rather than give up, he built a jury rig and kept going. He almost died rounding Cape Horn, but twenty years later, in middle age, with a great job and wonderful family, he daydreams about doing it again. "If the phone rang tonight and someone said would you be interested in doing this in a winning boat I would say absolutely," Hughes says. "It's a huge rush, huge."

These men and women are adventurers and the race takes them through the most remote and least-known parts of the planet. To succeed they must be able to react positively to fear and even embrace it. Fear makes the guts turn to liquid. It makes the heart pound. But when the threat is over and the fear is gone, the chemical release is a sense of euphoria that others achieve through mind-altering drugs.

Derek Lundy says that in parts of the race, the sailors sometimes pass into an "unknown zone." It is the place where their lives twitch on a thread as they battle alarming winds, waves, and atrocious weather. Survival in these conditions is a matter of luck and timing and the strength or failure of some small metal part. If they are weak, tired, or slow, the sea will win. If an aluminum rivet or stainless-steel pin fails while they are asleep or not paying attention, they may die. It's that simple. But the skippers accept the risk, just to race and to sail – and to do it alone.

Sir Robin Knox-Johnston says that if sailing around the world and surviving were easy, who would want to do it? There would be no satisfaction.

5

In the Doldrums

**"Without heroes, we are all plain people
and don't know how far we can go."**

– BERNARD MALAMUD

~~~~~~~~~~~~~~~~~~~~~~
~~~~~~~~~~~~~~~~~~~~~~

BY EARLY NOVEMBER, the Class II fleet had put the trials of the
Bay of Biscay behind them and had latched on to the northern
trade winds, a warm, steady wind from the east that carried them
on a southwesterly course. They passed east of the Madeira Islands
and west of the Canary Islands, then headed in a gentle arc towards
Brazil. It was fast going after a slow start and before long the smaller
boats were entering the Doldrums.

Among the many sailing myths is the image of languid sailors
snoozing on deck as their boats roll on a glassy sea. The reality is
much different. The belt of calm seas known as the Doldrums is
one of the most mentally and physically exhausting points in the
race. The sailors work the boats in punishing heat to move just a
few yards. Every sailor knows the frustration of light wind and no

wind. Those conditions for days at a time are excruciating. "What's it like?" said Kent. "It makes you want to scream."

The Doldrums is the name given to a band of weather about three hundred miles deep and six hundred miles long that straddles the Atlantic Ocean between five degrees north and five degrees south of the equator. Here, sailors frequently encounter towering thunderheads, high winds, and torrential rains, followed by squalls with lots of rain and no wind, or lots of wind and no rain. The volatility in the region comes from the collision of the great air masses that circle the Northern and Southern Hemispheres. It is tremendously hot and the air is moist. The conditions are perfect for storms, some of which can become hurricanes.

There is little chance to rest or relax as one moment the ocean is flat calm, the next it is whipped up as a squall line roars by. At one time Tim Kent saw fifteen squalls forming around him on the horizon and rushed to lower sail. He muscled down several hundred pounds of mainsail to the third reef point. It was 38 degrees Celsius (100 degrees Fahrenheit) on deck in the sun and 10 degrees (20 degrees on the Fahrenheit scale) hotter in the cabin. The storms rolled harmlessly by. Fed up, he hoisted the mainsail again, set a light air spinnaker and a squall came roaring through and almost knocked his boat down.

This game can go on day after day. The skipper watches the horizon or his radar screen in the cabin, trying to anticipate what will strike and when. At night, thermals can give the boat a lift as the sun sets and the temperature changes at sea level, creating wind. But there's no rest when the thermals die, and the possibility of squalls is constant. Lightning constantly illuminates the horizon and thunder echoes across the water. As Kent says, it is hard to tell which of the storms "are packin' and which ones are posin'."

The skippers sleep for four to five hours a day in fifteen-minute

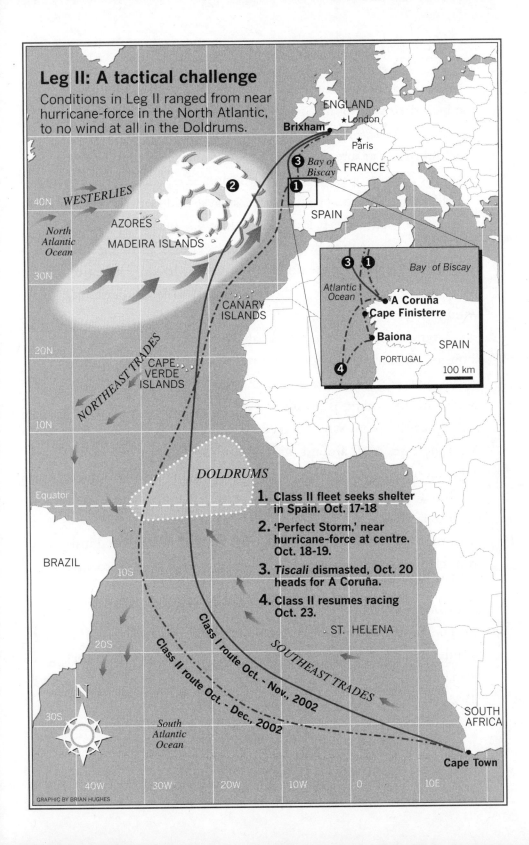

Leg II: A tactical challenge

Conditions in Leg II ranged from near hurricane-force in the North Atlantic, to no wind at all in the Doldrums.

ENGLAND
★London
Brixham
Paris
Bay of Biscay
FRANCE
SPAIN

❷

WESTERLIES

40N

North Atlantic Ocean

AZORES
MADEIRA ISLANDS

30N

Inset map:
❸ **❶** Bay of Biscay
Atlantic Ocean
A Coruña
Cape Finisterre
Baiona
SPAIN
PORTUGAL
❹
100 km

CANARY ISLANDS

20N

NORTHEAST TRADES

CAPE VERDE ISLANDS

10N

DOLDRUMS

Equator

1. Class II fleet seeks shelter in Spain. Oct. 17-18

2. 'Perfect Storm,' near hurricane-force at centre. Oct. 18-19.

3. *Tiscali* dismasted, Oct. 20 heads for A Coruña.

4. Class II resumes racing Oct. 23.

BRAZIL

10S

ST. HELENA

Class I route Oct. - Nov., 2002

Class II route Oct. - Dec., 2002

SOUTHEAST TRADES

20S

N

30S

South Atlantic Ocean

SOUTH AFRICA

Cape Town

40W   30W   20W   10W   0   10E to one-hour snatches. They watch, they fuss, they play with the sails and inch their way south. Some catch up on maintenance because it is one of the few times in the race when the boats aren't heeled over and they can spread out their tools. Sometimes though, they curse, they swear, or even cry in frustration.

"It's been going on like this for two days," said Hatfield in early November. "Flat calm. It looks like a July day on Lake Ontario."

Hatfield worked the boat through the zephyrs, grinding out a few extra miles, playing the tiny puffs of wind with determination. As he approached the edge of the Doldrums and the southern trade winds, the period between calms grew shorter.

A typical day here is clouds at daybreak, with squalls and showers. By mid-morning the sun burns away the clouds and the squalls disappear. A breeze builds and by mid-afternoon it blows nicely and the sailing is great. As evening approaches, the winds pick up to the point where a reef or sail change is required. The wind increases until around midnight when the heat dies down, but sometimes holds through the night, bringing rain and squalls.

To let off steam, many skippers listen to music or read. Some carry DVD players and watch movies. In each of his three solo passages through the Doldrums, Josh Hall has had a range of music from classics to rock to keep him company and had good cockpit speakers so he could blast the tunes on deck and sing along with his favourite bands.

Tim Kent loved music but couldn't afford good speakers. He found it helped him to unwind if he read a book. "When the boat wasn't moving I didn't sleep too much because I was antsy," he says. "But I found I could rest by reading. That would refresh me."

Van Liew brought plenty of books but couldn't relax long enough to read one. He did have DVDs. He would watch films in ten-minute sessions, so it could take him three days to watch an entire movie. Hatfield's view was that if there were only a few knots of breeze it was his job to move the boat. This steadfast concentration on getting ahead – on winning – meant that he did not bring a single diversion aboard. Not a book, a magazine, or CD. Now, with the benefit of hindsight, he says he would be less dogmatic. "I would have some kind of CD player. It would break the monotony on those days when you need to pump yourself up a bit."

Another myth of single-handed sailing is the notion of the boat disappearing into the sunset alone, not to be heard from for months. But nowadays, skippers are never truly alone. They talk to the race committee by phone, send and receive e-mails from friends, families, and fans. They fire up their wireless Internet connections and cruise the race Web site for the latest news or download weather files. They take phone calls from journalists, join phone-in radio shows, and read their press clippings on-line. The problem now is keeping the world out. Brad Van Liew refused to check his e-mail in the middle of the night even if he was awake. He considered those hours downtime.

The phone can ring in the middle of a storm or while the sailors are changing a sail in the most isolated place on Earth. As the jingle goes, they never lose the long-distance feeling. "It isn't like earlier races when you went off and didn't talk to people for weeks at a time," Hatfield said in one telephone interview as his boat bobbed listlessly in the Doldrums. "The phones make it easier. You're not with [your family and friends], but you're speaking to them."

The boats have multiple communications backups, another facet of the redundant systems rule of single-handed sailing. It says, more or less, that if something can break it will, so you had better have more than one. All boats carry a VHF radio for use within twenty miles from shore and to talk to competitors at sea. They also have a single side-band radio (SSB), two or three satellite telephones – one for talking and one or two for sending and receiving e-mails and connecting to the Internet.

The downside for the unsponsored sailors is the horrendous cost of these wireless communications. Satellite phone conversations run at $4 (U.S.) a minute, so the bills can quickly mount to thousands of dollars a month. The winner of the 2000 Vendée Globe reportedly rang up a $330,000 phone bill during the race. Iridium Satellite LLC and Stratos Global sponsored Brad Van Liew's phone calls, so he was home free. When he got the chance, he would spend several hours on the Internet or looking at weather faxes to plot the best route to the finish. Stratos Global also sponsored Emma Richards's phone calls. She spent an average thirty minutes a day making calls. Derek Hatfield might be able to afford just a minute or two a day. He was paying $1,400 (U.S.) a month to download weather files once or twice a week, something Van Liew could do three or four times daily.

Hatfield was frustrated by this financial handcuff, which he saw as a tactical disadvantage. Those who could afford it could access every piece of information available on the Around Alone Web site, including a daily summary of the race, a map showing the race positions, and e-mail from the other skippers to the site. From these reports filed by their competitors they could glean information about their tactics and about the weather that lay ahead.

"I never thought the money would be such a big issue," Hatfield said at one point. "It's a travesty, because after you've spent half a million dollars, $40,000 or $50,000 is nothing. But when you don't have it and you have no way of getting it, it's huge."

Even with advances in communications, the sailors are in a realm that is about as far removed from twenty-first-century life as possible. They eat, they sleep, and they tend their boats. Life is reduced to an elemental, primitive rhythm.

Their living space is no bigger than a walk-in closet. The space includes a kitchen, bedroom, and office. Many of the cabins have a distinctive dome of thick Plexiglas that affords a 360-degree view of conditions when they are so bad that the sailors can't go outside. *Spirit of Canada*'s cabin was twelve feet long by ten feet wide. At the front was a navigation station with its array of computers, phones, screens, and readouts that make it look more like the cockpit of a plane than a boat. The seat in front of the navigation station doubled as a box covering the engine. Hatfield slept there sometimes. On *BTC Velocity*, Alan Paris had a captain's chair in front of his instruments, with over-the-shoulder seat belts so he could strap himself in like a fighter pilot. John Dennis had a similar chair but without the seat belts.

The interiors of the cabins are stripped bare and have none of the conveniences of a modern cruising sailboat. The walls and floors are unfinished fibreglass. There are no refrigerators or hot and cold running water. Food and other essentials in mesh bags hang from hooks and are jammed into every crack and crevice.

Most skippers have a single-burner stove and meals are a freeze-dried pouch of something and water, eaten right out of the pot. It makes for less clean up. Hatfield ate out of a stainless steel dog bowl. It wouldn't rust, was strong and the contents were less likely to slop around. Snacks are anything that doesn't require refrigeration or heat: nuts, energy bars, candy, granola, trail mixes, cookies.

John Dennis carried a variation of freeze-dried fare, called Heater Meals, developed for the U.S. Navy. Each meal has a sealed packet of iron and magnesium and a pouch of salt water. When the water is poured into the iron and magnesium packet, it creates a chemical reaction that produces heat. In fourteen minutes or so, the meal is hot and ready to eat.

Heater Meals gave Dennis twenty-four breakfasts and twenty-four dinners for the first leg. The breakfasts were three pancakes, sausage, and syrup. The dinners were such things as turkey breast with gravy and mashed potatoes, or homestyle chicken and noodles in gravy.

Dennis also took dried nuts, fresh fruit, crackers, peanut butter, and long-life milk, which does not require refrigeration. Almost every lunch he ate canned fish – sardines or salmon – with crackers and cheese until it ran out. Other canned fare included Spam, soups and stews. He also carried granola and corn flakes; rice- or noodle-based dinners, with fish or meat added in. A little curry sauce spiced it up.

Dennis planned to drink one diet soft drink, one fruit juice, and two bottles of water a day, along with tea and hot chocolate. He carried forty-five gallons of water for cooking and the galley had one small non-pressurized alcohol burner. Dennis felt he ate well, but still lost weight because of the hard work handling the boat.

"I am now probably 20 pounds lighter than when I started," he noted as he neared Cape Town. "But I feel much more fit and with a very large drop in body fat. Five star cuisine? No. Adequate, yes."

Hatfield's partner, Patianne Verburgh, calculated his daily rations to the meal. To save weight, he did not carry canned food. For each leg, Verburgh had prepared ration kits based on his expected time at sea, allowing a 10 per cent margin of error. Hatfield's favourite staple was peanut butter cups, and he aimed to consume about five thousand calories a day, double the normal amount for a man of his age and size. He still expected to lose weight. Dennis, a larger man, planned on consuming six thousand calories a day.

Everyone had comfort food. Emma Richards liked Bird's Eye potato waffles. During the race she ate 120 packages of them. Tim Kent ate peanut butter and jelly sandwiches for most of the second leg, having found that the freeze-dried food he'd ordered through a camping supply firm in England was inedible. In South Africa he found a new supplier whose fare was so good Kent said that he looked forward to dinner, choosing among chicken Polynesian, sweet and sour pork, and spaghetti dishes. His favourite was beef stroganoff with noodles.

Brad Van Liew's strategy was to eat like a bear heading for hibernation in the months leading up to the race. "I just eat at will," Van Liew says. "It's actually kind of fun."

He is normally someone who has to watch his weight, but prior to the race he stuffed his six-foot, one-inch frame with anything fattening he could get his hands on. He left Newport weighing two hundred and forty pounds, about twenty-five pounds overweight. He lost ten pounds on the first leg and fifteen pounds more by the time he reached Cape Town. During the two Southern Ocean legs the sailors tend to maintain their weight. It is colder which makes their appetite stronger, and because they are down below for longer periods they use up fewer calories.

At sea there was sometimes something you rarely find on shore: an absolutely free lunch. As the fleet passed through the Doldrums and the trades on either side, there was often a flying fish or two lying on deck in the morning. Sometimes squid, too. They were attracted to the running lights on the boats.

Kojiro Shiraishi, aboard Class II *Spirit of Yukoh*, had his knife blades sharp and at the ready. He found three flying fish and two squid on deck one morning. He filleted them, seasoned them with salt and pepper, and sautéed them in olive oil. Simone Bianchetti landed a tuna and made some sushi. John Dennis was another flying

In 1994 at the age of twenty-six, Kojiro Shiraishi became the youngest sailor to circumnavigate the world non-stop and single-handed. He is pictured here in Newport before the 2002 race.
(Ann Harley)

fish fan. His technique was to fry them with a little bit of oil and lemon juice. Brad Van Liew regarded these creatures as deep ocean roadkill. He came on deck one morning to find *Tommy Hilfiger* wearing a flying fish garland. He hosed them off the deck and went below for an omelette with cheese, onions, salami, and potatoes.

Attitudes towards alcohol on board ranged from prohibition in Derek Hatfield's case, to vintage wines in the case of some of the European sailors. On his first circumnavigation in 1968, Sir Robin Knox-Johnston would go below from time to time to "check the level in his brandy bottle." He rationed himself to a bottle a week for the journey, and on one occasion was furious when a new bottle spilled, emptying his ration for the next seven days. In this Around Alone, sponsor Mumm's Champagne gave the competitors mini bottles for the special occasions of rounding the Horn and crossing the equator. Bernard Stamm and Thierry Dubois carried their own wine selections. One of Brad Van Liew's sponsors was Dry Creek Vineyards, a California winery. Dry Creek built a lightweight carbon fibre wine rack to store Van Liew's bottles at sea. He enjoyed them with special meals.

Emma Richards had stowed a bottle of "medicinal" rum on *Pindar*. Tim Kent had a couple of bottles of Miller beer (Miller was one of his sponsors) and the small bottles of Mumm's. Other than that, he was dry.

Personal hygiene is primitive at sea, but there is no one around to be offended by the sight and smell. The one good thing about the Doldrums was the torrential rain. It gave the skippers a chance to strip down and have a warm freshwater shower for the first time in weeks.

By the time the Open 60s entered the Doldrums, they were trading jokes about how ripe they had become. Thierry Dubois and Emma Richards were fast friends on land, and in Leg II they were sailing close to each other in a duel for second. As Dubois passed Richards, he claimed he could "smell a young blond English girl in the area." Richards replied that it was a lot better than being downwind of a Frenchman.

Racing sailors should have a toilet on board, but the rule is not enforced. Most forgo the luxury and use buckets. Some have both. *Pindar* was the only Open 60 with a toilet and perhaps not coincidentally the only boat with a female skipper. *Spirit of Canada* was one of the few other boats that had indoor plumbing. But the only way to get to the head on Derek Hatfield's boat was to crawl through a watertight hatch the size of a clothes dryer door. Once inside he would have to crab-walk over the exposed fibreglass bulkhead before, after a bit of manoeuvring, squatting over the toilet. It was too much for Hatfield. He rarely used it.

In 1990 the Australian David Adams was unfortunate enough to be using his toilet when his boat launched off a wave, during his first Around Alone race aboard *Innkeeper*. As the boat lurched, he grabbed the bowl. The toilet ripped away from the bulkhead and he and the toilet were slammed across the boat. Adams pried his behind off the bowl and hurriedly closed the seacocks to stop the compartment from flooding. "After that I had to crap over the side, which is fine in the tropics," he recalled in his book, *Chasing Liquid Mountains*. "But in the Southern Ocean you make sure you're desperate before you undo eight zippers to expose yourself to the cold – and the possibility of an icy salt-water douche."

Later, in the leg to Cape Horn, Emma Richards found the call of nature so problematic, she reduced her fluid intake. The ritual required that she remove her gloves with their rubber seals, take off her safety harness, and undo her jacket with its dry seals on the wrists and neck. Then she removed her foul-weather dungarees. The mid-layer jacket was next, followed by another mid-layer dungaree and three layers of thermal underclothes. The weather was so rough, she couldn't leave the cockpit, and so used a bucket there, knowing she was absolutely helpless if anything went wrong.

Tim Kent agrees that managing this simple act takes practice, and adds: "You know, you'd be surprised what you can do if you have to."

When it isn't raining in the tropics, salt-water showers are a way to keep cool. Both shampoo and dishwashing soap work up lather in salt water and when finished off with a freshwater rinse bathing this way is quite refreshing. In the Atlantic and Southern Ocean legs it's harder to keep clean as the skippers stay in their foul-weather gear for days at a time. Many sailors vacuum pack spare underclothes to keep them dry. Baby wipes are useful for clean up and baby powder is liberally used to reduce chafe.

Van Liew was very careful about staying dry. He has fair skin and gets salt-water boils pretty badly. As they can easily become infected, he frequently changes his clothing. Van Liew travels with two sets of foul-weather clothing so that he can always change into a dry one. Derek Hatfield did the same. He went to great lengths to stay dry and clean, changing often and using the heat of the engine block to dry damp clothes.

While they are at sea, the sailors sleep in snatches for four to six hours each day. Everyone's needs differ, everyone has a different pattern, but it is vital that they get their body's minimum sleep or the fatigue and fuzziness of thought can be fatal. The effects of sleeplessness are well known: irritability, difficulty in concentrating, headaches, and even hallucinations. Before the 1998 race Van Liew took part in a sleep study at the Harvard University Medical School. He learned that with four and a half hours of sleep a day, he could operate in the eightieth percentile of alertness. He took a forty-five-minute nap every four hours, using a kitchen timer to wake himself up. He admits that the regimen would not work on land because of the many noises and other distractions, but "at sea, I could do it indefinitely," he says.

Hatfield's nighttime regimen was similar. He would set an alarm for twenty minutes, wake up, check the boat's vital systems, and go back to sleep for another twenty minutes. After a few days he didn't need an alarm, having conditioned himself to wake up. Like Van Liew, he found it easy to do.

Tim Kent aimed for fifteen- to thirty-minute naps. When sailing near shore, he preferred to sleep by day and stay awake at night to monitor radar and avoid shipping lanes. The most comfortable spot on Kent's boat below decks was a "pipe berth," a hinged bed that could be adjusted to stay at a right angle to the heel of the boat. Kent slept outside on deck as much as possible. *Everest Horizontal*, like Simone Bianchetti's *Tiscali*, has a doghouse, a large overhang that extends from the hatch towards the cockpit. It provides shelter from wind and rain and allowed Kent to stretch out and watch the stars.

Even so, there were times when fatigue set in. The sailors saw or heard things they knew weren't there, but in a half-asleep, semi-lucid state, they weren't sure. As he rounded Cape Horn in 1968 the great solo circumnavigator Bernard Moitessier felt a voice calling him to the bow of his boat. He left the cockpit and walked to the bow of the boat as *Joshua* surged through the swells and the voice called him forward.

At one point in the 1986 race, John Hughes awoke to find himself sitting naked in the cockpit of the *Joseph Young* with his sleeping bag rolled neatly beside him. Hughes was travelling through the Bass Strait, which separates Australia from Tasmania. He hadn't slept in two days and was too scared to nap because of the proximity to land. The more tired he became, the more afraid he was that if he did sleep he would not wake up. Eventually he blacked out and when he awoke many hours later he was still sailing down the middle of the channel. To this day he has no idea what happened.

Brad Van Liew says he has come on deck a number of times to find the sails set differently with no recollection of having touched them. At other times he has climbed on deck because he heard noises and thought the boat was talking to him. He screamed at non-existent crew members demanding they reef sails because it was *their* turn and he was too tired. These hallucinations were more frequent when he was new to the sport. With experience they have diminished. "It's exhaustion more than anything else," he says. One night, while at the helm, Hatfield says he heard a voice calling to him from the cabin. He ignored it.

The continual banging and crashing at times made it hard for Kent to sleep on *Everest Horizontal*. When he did, his dreams incorporated the reality of being at sea. In one of them he was in a car with someone else driving. He yelled at the driver to stop hitting all the potholes in the road because it was shaking the car. He woke up to find the boat bouncing off the waves, trying to shake itself to pieces.

The fleet's passage through the Doldrums took them back across the Atlantic almost to the bulge of Brazil. The Doldrums are widest closest to the African coast and the sailors were trying to find the fastest way through the zone. One by one they crossed into the Southern Hemisphere and made a U-turn, heading east and south under sunny skies and steady winds in a high-pressure zone known as the South Atlantic or St. Helena High. This allowed the fleet to make a long angled ride to Cape Town, South Africa.

This leg of the race is won or lost by how well the yachts skirt the St. Helena High. If they cut the corner by not sailing close enough to Brazil, they can end up becalmed. As *Tommy Hilfiger* passed through the Doldrums and picked up the southern trades Van Liew was nursing a tired body. He had been too slow, too tired or both when, on November 6, in a classic Doldrums adventure, the winds had gone from dead calm to fifty-five knots in minutes. "It was one of the worst days of my sailing career," he says.

That day, hundreds of miles to the south, *Pindar*'s main halyard, the rope used to raise and lower the mainsail, snapped. Emma Richards had no choice but to climb the eighty-foot mast and fix it. "It was horrible, just horrible. Terrifying," she said later.

She started climbing in a fairly steady breeze of ten knots, but by the time she had reached the top, the wind was at twenty-five knots. The mast was swaying as much as twenty feet to either side. She was blown upside down in her climbing harness, twisting the gear, and was banged repeatedly into the mast, badly bruising her arms, ribs, and legs. Luckily she had donned a crash helmet, because her head smashed against the mast more than once. Richards managed to right herself, make the repair, and lower herself to the deck. She used every ounce of strength left to raise the mainsail, then collapsed, shuddering and in tears.

Three weeks and three days after the fleet left Brixham, *Tiscali* was towed out to sea from the Spanish naval base at A Coruña. Simone Bianchetti was at sea again, using Bernard Stamm's spare mast. The Internet firm Tiscali had bought new sails and the *Hatherleigh*, the fishing trawler owned by Emma Richards's patron, Andrew Pindar, had brought both mast and sails to Spain. Bianchetti set out in driving rain and thirty knots of breeze. He drove himself relentlessly, arriving in Cape Town with just two days to rest and reprovision before the fleet set sail for the Southern Ocean.

On November 13, the twenty-ninth day since the Brixham start, Bernard Stamm sailed into Cape Town to win the second leg of the race. Stamm's performance was remarkable. He had covered the 6,880-mile course in twenty-nine days and twenty-two hours. A year earlier, the fully crewed *Illbruck*, the winning boat in the Volvo Cup, had sailed much the same course, but had taken two days longer to complete it.

Stamm believes his tactics in the Bay of Biscay helped him to win. He had entered the eye of the hurricane after a horrendous passage, but when he emerged on the other side, the wind was just as strong but in a favourable direction, allowing him to extend his lead over the rest of the fleet.

That lead widened to 280 miles by the time he had passed through the Doldrums. As he tried to figure out where to catch the St. Helena High, Stamm hoped he would be able to latch on to it at the point where the system splits in two, with one portion moving south to Cape Town. It was this piece of good luck that had allowed Isabelle Autissier to win the leg by a five-day margin in the 1994 Around Alone race.

As it turned out, Stamm's lead shrank, but he still had enough of a cushion to beat Thierry Dubois in *Solidaires* by ten hours. Stamm tied up at the Victoria & Albert Waterfront marina to the cheers of a large crowd at about 10 a.m. on November 13. Emma Richards in *Pindar* arrived third. At the end of this month-long, hell-for-leather tilt from Europe to the tip of Africa the difference between first and third place over the 6,880-mile course was just seventeen hours. As Richards tied off at the dock, Stamm and Dubois were there to meet her. She put the boat in the hands of her shore crew and the three of them marched off for a "hungry-woman" breakfast of bacon, eggs, sausage, fruit, and toast washed down with fresh orange juice and tea.

Hatfield meanwhile was still stuck in the Doldrums, but running second in Class II to Brad Van Liew. When there was good wind and *Spirit of Canada* was moving well, he was in good spirits. When there was no wind, he was despondent. All he could think about was how long it would take to reach Cape Town.

After five weeks and three days at sea, Brad Van Liew had a day for the record books, setting a one-day record for a single-handed fifty-foot boat of 344 miles. It beat the existing record by eleven miles. "I've been blasting off in incredible wind, surfing faster than I probably should," he wrote. "The boat is capable of speeds that should really be controlled, purely to preserve the equipment on board."

Van Liew was less than one thousand miles from Cape Town. He arrived on November 27 after a passage of six weeks, two days, and three hours, finishing a day ahead of Bruce Schwab on the Open 60 *Ocean Planet*.

Tim Kent recorded his first taste of the Southern Ocean at the end of his sixth week at sea. The ocean proper was still far away, but some days when the wind blew from the right direction, it gave a hint of things to come. He noted that the water had changed colour, that the wind had a new feel, and the waves were bigger.

"Nothing can prepare you for the stark, windswept beauty of this place," he said. "The waves are huge, the wind is a physical force and albatrosses soar back and forth over the boat. The noise of the wind and waves is mesmerizing. The boat is flying and constantly awash; working on the foredeck, as I was this morning, requires you to be fully suited up because you are underwater all of the time."

Kent had dipped farther south than other boats, hoping to get a better angle for his approach to Cape Town. He was glad he had done so – it helped ease his fear of being down there. "I know this is just a taste of the meal that awaits," he wrote. "But, like any meal, the first taste lingers, and I find that this has a strange appeal."

On December 1, four days after Van Liew, Kent arrived in Cape Town to take second. Hatfield arrived just thirteen hours later.

On December 8 after seven weeks and six days, Alan Paris ghosted across the line in Cape Town, just twenty-two minutes behind John Dennis. The final few days had been excruciating for the two sailors. They had missed the system that had carried the other skippers to shore and had found themselves trapped in a zone of high pressure with very light wind.

Even so, they beat Simone Bianchetti, who arrived in Cape Town with just ninety hours to get ready for a restart.

LEG III

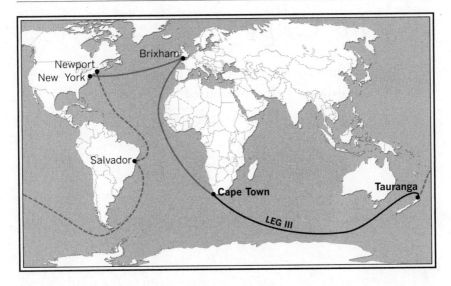

ROUTE: Cape Town, South Africa, to Tauranga,
New Zealand

DEPARTURE: December 14, 2002

DISTANCE: 7,125 nautical miles

6

The Cape Town Effect

**"I hate being frightened, but even more,
I detest being prevented by fright."**

– SIR FRANCIS CHICHESTER

THE CAPE OF Good Hope is the name given to the southern tip of Africa by Portuguese explorers. Bartholomew Dias named the peninsula Cabo Tormentosa (Cape of Storms) after his first rough rounding of the tip of Africa in 1488. In a burst of optimism, the name was later changed to Cabo da Boa Esperança (Cape of Good Hope) to signify that rounding the Cape meant that a sea route to the East was possible. In 1580, Sir Francis Drake sailed around the Cape and soon after his passage the Dutch East India Company established an outpost. It remained in Dutch hands until 1814 when it was ceded to Britain at the end of the Napoleonic Wars.

Cape Town grew up around the Dutch outpost and underneath Table Mountain, which rises 3,500 feet above the bay. Its flat summit offers a breathtaking view of the city below. Fifty miles out to sea sailors can see Table Mountain and have used it for centuries as a bearing. Within a short drive of the city are beautiful beaches, while inland lies South Africa's wine country. The city is a regular stop for Around Alone sailors and in 2002 the new V&A Waterfront Marina offered them easy access to pubs, restaurants, and shops.

The sailors used the time in port to prepare their boats for the next leg. Hatfield's mainsail was repaired, and most of the Open 60s exchanged their Atlantic Ocean sails for new, heavier ones. Brad Van Liew was able to replace his sails in Cape Town thanks to Honeywell, one of his sponsors, which covered the cost. The new sail was made from a Honeywell product called Spectra, which, Honeywell claims, is ten times stronger than steel even though it floats. It is also used in body armour, ropes, and protective gloves. Engines were overhauled, backup generators loaded on board, and instruments realigned. Because of the distance from the north magnetic pole, normal compasses are ineffective. Instead, southern sailors use gyrocompasses, non-magnetic compasses that use a motor-driven gyroscope to indicate true north.

There was a great deal of excitement as the fleet readied for departure, their anticipation mixed with fear. The Southern Ocean was what they had come for; the supreme challenge in the odyssey. For the next forty days they would pass through this ocean wilderness on their passage to New Zealand. At the end of this leg, they would know, as few people really do, the outer limits of their physical and mental powers. As they readied their boats, the sailors wondered whether they would be able to cope with the worst conditions on the planet. Could they manage the fearful knowledge that for weeks on end they were beyond rescue? If they needed to be rescued, the closest help would be their fellow sailors who would be facing the same dangers and risking disaster themselves.

John Dennis had been nicknamed "Pops" by Emma Richards for his outgoing nature, boyish enthusiasm, and fatherly concern. Some race observers had wondered whether Dennis's age and diabetes would be a liability for him, but he had proved in the first leg that he could do it, arriving in Brixham fourth out of six in the Class II fleet despite having an older and slower boat. Although he had faced emotional and physical challenges in the second leg, his diabetes had not been a problem for him. He had finished the second leg last, but in good spirits.

In Cape Town he spent most of the time with his daughter, Stephanie, and his wife, Penny. They had flown from Toronto and were there on the dock to meet him.

At Bayer's suggestion, Dennis spent some time while in Cape Town speaking to groups of diabetics as part of his deal with the drug company. Bayer provided another $10,000 (U.S.) to make repairs to the boat and the supervision of the repairs was left to a professional. "We've got a really good group of people here and the boat is not in bad shape," Dennis said. "We know exactly what we have to do and fortunately all the parts are here in the city."

While Dennis took his mind off the race, Hatfield tended to the small details of his refit. He had pushed hard in the second leg and missed coming in second by only eleven hours. He had sailed dangerously close to the line, hand steering when the others were using

Derek Hatfield and Patianne Verburgh make last-minute adjustments
to the *Spirit of Canada* in advance of the final safety check in
Newport, Rhode Island. *(Adam Mayers)*

their autopilots and sleeping less than he might to stay at the helm.

"It only takes one misstep and that would be it," Hatfield
admitted. "If you fall off, you're not going to get back on."

He did not let up on shore. For each of his ten days in Cape
Town, Hatfield and Patianne Verburgh spent fourteen hours on
their boat. They removed every item and sorted them into two
piles: necessary and unnecessary. Unnecessary was left behind. The
rod rigging that holds up the mast was inspected. The rod was
coated with a blue dye so that hairline cracks would be visible.
Since Hatfield could not afford thirty thousand dollars for a new,
heavier, mainsail, the old one was reinforced by a local sailmaker.
Every inch of the rope was inspected for chafe. Sheaves and
shackles, fittings and blocks were all examined for cracks and signs
of fatigue. The engine was overhauled and lubricated, a leaking

transmission was repaired, filters and belts were replaced. Along with the other boats, *Spirit of Canada* was hauled from the water and the bottom cleaned.

Raymarine, a leading manufacturer of marine electronics and an Around Alone sponsor, gave Hatfield two heavy-weather autopilots to cope with the Southern Ocean pounding. They were installed, checked, calibrated and Hatfield took the boat out to test them. He spent hours poring over weather maps and talking to veterans like Brad Van Liew about tactics.

Hatfield's financial problems were never far from the surface. Not knowing whether he'd have enough money to finish the race wore him down. "I have sold everything I have; used all my savings and I am borrowing money to continue," he said. "I think about that every day. It's a constant rattle."

The shortage of money meant that, like Dennis, he'd be sailing without a backup generator and heater, equipment others in the fleet saw as essential. It meant saving each of the 120 plastic, 1.5 litre water bottles on board, refilling them, and carrying them back to the boat. Skippers with money invested in desalinators, which allowed them to carry only the compulsory minimum amount of fresh water – a weight-saving measure. They made the rest as needed.

Other skippers provisioned with high-calorie supplements, electrolyte- and energy-replacement drinks, fruit juices, milk, coffee, and tea. Hatfield carried water, Tang, hot chocolate, and a powdered cinnamon drink. These were the realities of a shoestring budget. He simply didn't have the resources of Brad Van Liew's $1.5 million campaign or the big European entries' $2 million-plus.

Van Liew was in a class of his own, romping home in Leg II four days ahead of Tim Kent and Derek Hatfield. That gave him a full two weeks in Cape Town with his eight-month-old daughter, Tate, and wife, Meaghan. He spent some time carrying out his obligations to his title sponsor, Tommy Hilfiger, and with a five-person shore team, he spent only two hours a day on his boat.

He saw this Around Alone race as the next step in establishing a professional sailing career. An articulate and passionate ambassador for the sport, he is also a pilot and enjoys car and motorcycle racing. He is also a self-confessed adrenaline junkie — a guy who likes to live on the edge. In Newport, Van Liew had talked about the Southern Ocean, which he had sailed alone before, with equal parts fear, respect, and excitement.

"The tough thing about sailing the South is to gauge the addiction," he said. "The birds are beautiful, the sea is beautiful and everything is intense. It's a total rush. But you pay a heavy price." He paused before adding: "But obviously not heavy enough, because I'm going back."

Van Liew considers sailing his occupation and his boat his office. His job is to pull ahead of the boat in front of him and then the one in front of that. He and Hatfield are of the same mind when it comes to attitude and focus. Both view the race as a military campaign. They study tactics, gather intelligence about the opposition, develop strategy, plan for contingencies, and then follow through. They understand the physical and mental demands of their sport.

"If you're going to do this right, you have to be focused," Van Liew says. "I can't count how many times people have asked me what I think about and what I read. Do I look at the stars when I'm at sea? They're missing the point. The stars? I don't need to know about the stars."

With her spinnaker flying on a downwind run, *Tommy Hilfiger* is a beautiful sight. Brad Van Liew set a speed record on the approach to Cape Town, travelling 344 miles in twenty-four hours. *(Billy Black)*

Van Liew knew *Tommy Hilfiger* inside and out. He had spent a year refitting the former *Magellan Alpha*, stripping the boat down and rewiring it so that he would know what each connection was for, that it was properly soldered, watertight, and easy to get at. He had a good working knowledge of every mechanical system. In a weight-saving exercise he standardized all the bolts so that he would have to carry only four wrenches with him.

In Cape Town, he calibrated his electronic systems, tuned the autopilots, worked with satellite equipment, and downloaded weather files. Typically, he spends a day and a half before each start plotting weather scenarios as his crew "drill and hammer all around me." He says, "I have that luxury because I built the boat, and if anyone has a question about a system, they can ask me."

In his spare moments Van Liew wondered about the Cape Town Effect, a seeming law of Around Alone sailing. In virtually every running of the race, the Cape Town Effect sees one or more competitors leave port, only to face a mechanical problem that forces them back. The problem fixed, they would set sail again and something else would go wrong. Finally, they would return to port and give up.

In 1994, the Cape Town Effect claimed Simone Bianchetti. In 1998, it hit former U.S. Marine George Stricker, who broke his boom a few days out of Cape Town. He fixed it, but by then was nine hundred miles behind the last boat in the race. Still, he set off again and returned a day later reporting a fuel leak. He fixed that and set off a third time, now more than twelve hundred miles behind. In a gale, he broke the gooseneck fitting, which attaches the boom to the mast. He retired in despair, saying: "This race is not for me."

These stories were part of the lore, talked about quietly by the veterans as they looked around the marina and wondered who would be next.

"It's really, really tough to leave Cape Town," Van Liew says. "The Southern Ocean is an entirely different experience than anyone has ever had on a boat. It's a mind-blower. You have a knot in your gut the whole time you are down there because there is no place like it on the planet. It's unbelievable. Nobody's seen anything like it until they've seen it."

Within a week, the fleet would see for themselves.

At noon on December 14 the fleet crossed the starting line in the shadow of Table Mountain and headed out to sea. They turned their bows south towards Antarctica and the heart of the vast, empty ocean at the bottom of the world, waters that have been feared and respected by sailors for centuries.

Derek Hatfield had been in Cape Town just two weeks when he sailed out of Table Bay, past the infamous prison on Robben Island where Nelson Mandela was held for years. Race day was beautiful, with the temperature in the high twenties (low eighties Fahrenheit), a cloudless sky and a light breeze tickling the flags. Hatfield had been up since 5 a.m., fussing with last-minute tasks. He was ready, but two things worried him; the cold he would be facing and his lack of backup equipment.

Hatfield's big lesson from winter sailing on Lake Ontario was the effect of sub-zero temperatures on the body's ability to perform simple tasks. In the cold, fingers quickly became clumsy and unresponsive and the mind cannot process information quickly or think clearly. He knew that he risked becoming too befuddled to notice the failure of an important part or the chafe of a line. Such a slip could prove fatal.

The solution was to stay warm and dry, but Hatfield did not have the means to do so. He had arranged for a diesel heater to be airfreighted to Cape Town, but it had been held up in customs. His best efforts to get the unit released had got him nowhere, so now he was setting sail without it. Until *Spirit of Canada* reached New Zealand, his only sources of heat would be a single-burner stove and his engine. He expected to get by. "The middle three weeks are going to be cold and miserable, but I guess you grin and bear it," he said stoically.

Hatfield's other gamble was more dangerous. The cardinal rule of ocean racing is redundancy, so that when one system fails, another is available. Short of cash, he had agonized about spending $1,500 for a backup generator to charge his batteries should his engine fail. At the last minute he had decided to buy one, but the only available model was too big to fit on the boat. So it was down to his engine. Should it fail, his batteries would eventually die, which meant that he would not be able to use his telephone, receive e-mails, or download weather reports. His chart-plotting software and Global Positioning System (GPS), which told him where he was and how fast he was moving, would be useless. Perhaps worst of all, there might not be enough power for the autopilot. This would force Hatfield to steer manually for twenty-four hours a day straight, which would be impossible in the stormy Southern Ocean. The only means of determining his position would be by shooting the sun with a sextant, a skill that each sailor was required to have under race rules, but few practised.

His only other source of power would be the solar photovoltaic panels on his coach top. He wasn't exactly sure how much electricity they would generate, but he knew it would be far less than farther north where the sun was more directly overhead. Hatfield greeted these possibilities with a shrug. "You just have to bite the bullet," he said. "The Southern Ocean is what you come for. I'm ready."

7

Baptism

**"The sea, among its many qualities,
is an unerring discoverer of weakness."**

– DEREK LUNDY, GODFORSAKEN SEA

*T*HE SOUTHERN OCEAN is like no other place on the planet. Made up of the southern portions of the South Pacific, Indian, and South Atlantic oceans, it is frightening in a big boat and at times utterly terrifying in a small one. Nobody goes sailing alone there for fun. Death is very close in these waters: a missed handhold, a moment's inattention, being on deck at the wrong time. The cold is damp, penetrating, bone-chilling; a good night's sleep is impossible. But the Southern Ocean is the allure of the race. The few who sail there single-handed are explorers and adventurers eager for a taste of the wilds at the end of the earth.

The Ocean's northern edge is 360 miles south of the Cape of Good Hope and the Antarctic continent lies about twelve hundred miles farther south in the Screaming Sixties. This ocean has a point that is the farthest from land of any place on Earth, about 1,660 miles equidistant from Pitcairn Island, last refuge of the *Bounty* mutineers, and Cape Dart on Antarctica.

In the Roaring Forties, the cold water circling Antarctica mixes with the warmer waters from the north. The intersection of the two bodies can create wild and unpredictable weather: fog, thunderstorms, hail, snow, and driving rain. Sailors experiencing the Southern Ocean for the first time are surprised that the air temperature can be in the balmy mid-twenties (mid-seventies Fahrenheit) with a breeze from the north and then in minutes drop ten or fifteen degrees (twenty or thirty degrees Fahrenheit) when the wind shifts and comes from the south.

It is a wild, beautiful, and desolate place, filled with glorious sunrises and breathtaking marine bird life. It can also be ugly, grey, and bleak, making a person feel as alone and insignificant as one can possibly feel. There is nothing of man's footprint there and the sailors pass through it without a trace. They are inconsequential, trivial, and unimportant. It takes a lot of courage to cast the lines off in Cape Town and point your bow south. Everyone knows at some point they're going to get walloped and that they will have to face whatever must be faced alone.

The trick is to head south and then east, hitching a ride on the prevailing westerlies that flow around Antarctica. So after leaving Cape Town, the boats head south for two or three days and then turn. The other option is an angled descent, which is slower. The frequent storms are like booster rockets, packing high winds that carry the boats along at tremendous speed.

Satellite-based weather forecasts predict what's coming and give the skippers time to prepare their boats and make a little extra hot chocolate or more one-pot stew. The limitation of the forecasts is the lack of local conditions. There are few ships to speak of and no land nearby, so the all-important local readings are unavailable. The computer models can only offer a guess at the intensity of the low-pressure systems and often miss by a lot.

The farther south the boats go, the shorter the distance to New Zealand, because the shape of the earth narrows. So the experienced sailors like Stamm and Dubois dove deeply south. They would brave intense cold and the possibility of ramming icebergs to gain time and distance. The less experienced and more cautious, stayed farther north.

The waves are huge in the Southern Ocean because the winds are constant and there is no land to interrupt their motion. Often called Ocean Himalayas because of their size, some may be half a mile or more between crests, with a wave height of forty feet. Novices are often petrified when, on a relatively calm day, they look over their shoulder and see a huge green wall about to engulf them. Instead the boat rides to the top of the swell and gently down the other side.

Below fifty degrees south, low-pressure systems form and collapse in a continuous cycle of bad weather. Seasons here are meaningless. The difference between summer and winter is often just a few degrees in temperature and an extra day of calm between storms. The wind typically blows at between thirty-five and forty-five knots for two or three days, builds up waves of fifteen to twenty-five feet and then quiets. But sometimes it just keeps blowing, and the waves get bigger and bigger. Brad Van Liew believes the largest wave ever measured – an astonishing 120 feet – was off the Kerguelen Islands, which the fleet passed at Christmas.

The trick is to stay on the north side of the storms. This puts the prevailing wind squarely behind the boats, allowing them to travel at incredibly high speeds. If the sailors make a tactical mistake and end up on the south side, the ride becomes an uphill slog with

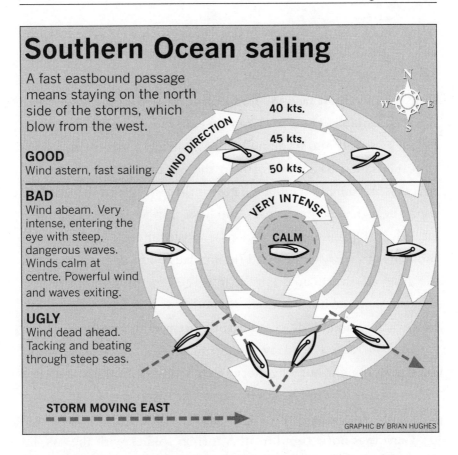

Southern Ocean sailing

A fast eastbound passage means staying on the north side of the storms, which blow from the west.

GOOD
Wind astern, fast sailing.

BAD
Wind abeam. Very intense, entering the eye with steep, dangerous waves. Winds calm at centre. Powerful wind and waves exiting.

UGLY
Wind dead ahead. Tacking and beating through steep seas.

40 kts.
45 kts.
50 kts.

WIND DIRECTION

VERY INTENSE

CALM

STORM MOVING EAST

GRAPHIC BY BRIAN HUGHES

the wind and sea in their faces. Between storms, the wind drops to twenty to twenty-five knots and the seas calm down to ten feet or less. The difference between here and that other stormy ocean, the North Atlantic, is that the systems come through more frequently, with greater intensity and less of a break between them. Any one of the weather systems can go from a common Southern Ocean blow to a storm with winds of sixty knots, just below hurricane force. On land at these speeds, a person weighing one hundred pounds or so, will fly.

Sailing here is as big a psychological challenge as a physical one. The emptiness and sense of aloneness gnaw at the skippers, who are constantly fighting depression. Thinking about these conditions

sent Donald Crowhurst into his fatal collapse in 1968. The Englishman had wagered everything he had on the race, but once he set
sail from Plymouth, he knew he was unable to do it. At the same
time, he could not face the humiliation of withdrawing. What to
do? He couldn't go forward and he couldn't go back. Crowhurst
deluded himself into thinking he had come up with a perfect solution. He sailed back and forth in the South Atlantic for several
months, planning to rejoin the fleet for the last leg home. He would
slip in near the end of the pack and hope nobody would pay much
attention. Crowhurst radioed false position reports, until in a
moment of clarity, he realized the implausibility of his deception.
He jumped overboard. His boat was eventually found in the
Doldrums. Crowhurst had left behind him hundreds of pages of
notes cataloguing his descent into utter despair and finally madness.

In 1998, Mike Garside was so terrified by the anticipation of this
leg that he sought out a hypnotist to help give him the confidence
to leave Cape Town. He says it was so effective he was able to roar
out of the gate and really "put my foot down and give it hell."

Garside is not a timid man. A former soldier with the SAS, he
was wounded during Britain's covert war in the East African sul-
tanate of Oman in the late 1970s. He then went into magazine publishing, and after making his fortune by taking his company public,
he spent $1.7 million mounting his campaign aboard *Magellan
Alpha*. He and Brad Van Liew talked each other through the worst
parts of that 1998 race and have become close friends.

He says that, for the rookies, the initial fear is of the unknown.
They have long heard the stories told by veterans and read the many
first-person accounts of solo sailors, and they are enough to scare
anyone. But the only way to overcome the fear is to dive into it.
Most sailors quickly get used to the Southern Ocean's greyness,

desolation, and huge seas. Then, he says, "It becomes satisfying. It is a place to find yourself."

Tim Kent was the first to feel the storm's cold breath. The low-pressure system was building when the fleet left Cape Town, but during the first forty-eight hours of the third leg the winds were light and the sky clear. Last-minute repairs delayed Kent's departure by almost a day, but within a dozen hours of setting sail on Sunday, December 15, *Everest Horizontal* was moving at a brisk seventeen knots. He soon reefed the mainsail to keep the boat on an even keel. Some twenty-four hours later, he had reefed the main twice more and had replaced the big Southern Ocean genoa at the front of the boat with a tiny storm jib. The sky had faded to grey and then premature night. Kent shivered as he looked over the stern. It was as "dark as the inside of your pocket," he said.

By the evening of Day Three, the wind was a sustained thirty-five to forty knots and Derek Hatfield was enduring the ride of his life. He had not seen conditions like this in the worst moments of his transatlantic crossings, not even in those first few nasty days in the Bay of Biscay. In the dense, damp Southern Ocean air, the wind shrieked in the rigging.

By midnight on Monday, the barometer had fallen off a cliff, plunging from 1020 millibars to 972 within a few hours. The speed of the drop in air pressure indicated how quickly the storm had developed and how violent the wind would be. At first the rain fell in fat drops, the size of grapes and as hard as gravel. They bounced off the deck and hurt when the wind drove them into Hatfield's face. Soon they became a torrent.

The boat was swept up the swells by the wind and, at the top, the waves curled and broke over the deck, pitching her down the other side. In the trough, the roar stopped for a moment, then returned, as the boat rose up the back of the next wave. Hatfield went below and ran through his checklist again. Anything that might move had been lashed tight and stowed. On deck, the mainsail was reefed to its third set of cringles, reducing the size of the boat's biggest sail by 80 per cent. He set a storm sail up forward; a tiny patch of reinforced fabric.

Hatfield put on his safety harness. He was waiting, although he wasn't sure for what. Sailors recognize the sounds their boats make and are reassured when they hear them in the right sequence and at the right pitch. But the noises he was now hearing were new and terrifying. They might mean something awful, or nothing at all. Hatfield sat facing the stern with his back to the navigation station, locked his feet around the base of the tiny galley, and gripped the handholds on either side of the sink. The muscles in his arms, legs, and lower back were soon in agony from being permanently clenched as he braced himself against the boat's awkward movement. In conditions like this both Tim Kent and Emma Richards wore a bicycle helmet to avoid head injuries, but not Hatfield. His cabin was much smaller than theirs, and he figured he wouldn't go very far if the boat tossed him around. He turned frequently to watch his instruments, each time noting with relief that the auto-pilots were working well, keeping him on a straight course and helping the boat set a new speed record.

By the small hours of Tuesday, the seas were as tall as a two-story house. The wind was a sustained forty-five knots, and the foam on the wave crests was being blown sideways. The air was now so thick with water it was difficult to breathe while facing into the wind, or do much else on deck for that matter. Hatfield crawled out to check the lines for wear and tear one handhold at a time, blinded by the spray. The boat slid up to the top of each wave and as she passed over the crest she was momentarily suspended as the wind lifted and twisted the stern. Then she fell, nose forward, surfing for a few hundred feet into the trough. Every once in a while, a rogue wave slapped the boat hard and the hull shuddered from the impact. In the cabin, whenever she started to roll, Hatfield's feet would leave the floor and he would end up walking on the cabin wall. Then, when all seemed lost, the keel would bite, bringing the boat upright.

In some gusts, *Spirit of Canada* drove off the top of a wave so quickly, the boat buried her nose in the wave ahead. The water would stream over the cabin dome, turning day into night for Hatfield, strapped inside. On deck, the huge scuppers choked on the deluge and were unable to drain all the water away. Then would come a respite in a trough, and the boat rose again. All through the night, Hatfield wondered and worried, unable to eat, too anxious to sleep. Would this first encounter with the Southern Ocean be his last? Would a freak wave catch the boat and spin it like the chamber of a revolver, the force of the rotation shattering the mast and shredding the sails, ending his quest just five hundred miles into this leg of the race?

Hatfield, like the other sailors in the fleet, faced this life-threatening storm with questions, but still calmly. The danger made him feel much more alive, heightening his senses. As author Derek Lundy says, deep-ocean sailors are not afraid in the same way other people are. They are capable of enduring fear for long periods and are able to function in spite of it. When the seas are really bad, they know they may capsize but they keep going anyway. In an interview before the race began, Lundy said he believed that Hatfield had the right combination of skills, including the ability to stay cool and analyze problems while under great stress.

As the storm peaked, Hatfield kept a watchful eye on his instruments. He monitored critical systems and mentally played out the what-ifs and what-thens. He was awed — and thrilled — by the power of the ocean and filled with pride in his small boat. He had helped build this worthy vessel, and now during her first real test she was exceeding his expectations.

At the start of Leg III, John Dennis set an easterly course along the coast, rather than diving south as most of the fleet had done. He had tried to use his Iridium phone, one of two telephone systems on board, but found that it wasn't working properly. Dennis was initially unconcerned, believing the problem was being caused by a satellite shadow. When the phone's reception didn't improve by the evening of the first day, Dennis went looking for the cause. He found it at the base of the antenna. The antenna had been moved to a different part of the stern in Cape Town. When the coaxial cable was reconnected, the work had been done with solder and electrician's tape, instead of a proper connector. The connection was weak, almost dangling.

At midday Sunday, the next day, Dennis put in to the small port of Struis Bay to make repairs. He told race headquarters he expected the delay to be short.

Struis Bay is a small fishing village and the harbour is only five feet deep, far too shallow for Dennis's eleven-foot keel. He anchored in the unprotected bay and went ashore to arrange for parts. He felt the wind pick up and when he looked at his boat in the bay he was startled to find it had moved. The anchor was dragging and the wind was pushing *Bayer Ascensia* onto a sandbar. He hastily arranged a ride out to the boat in a dinghy and set a second borrowed anchor. The line parted. Another anchor was set. The rope attached to it broke too. Dennis hailed a nearby fishing boat and *Bayer Ascensia* spent the night tied to the stern of the trawler.

Monday and Tuesday passed. On Wednesday, Dennis moved his boat to Mossel Bay, a larger community a few miles down the coast, where he purchased the part to connect the coaxial cable for a few dollars. He figured he'd be back at sea by ten that night, the fourth day since the restart. "I'm a few hundred miles behind, but I'm going out there to get my miles back," he said.

By then, Derek Hatfield was less than five hundred miles away, sailing in winds that touched fifty knots in gusts. He was mentally spent and his body was bruised from being slammed around the cabin. He felt out of control as the boat surfed in spurts faster than twenty knots. All he could do was sit below and watch. It was so rough that he couldn't go on deck. To stay comfortable as the boat pitched and rolled, he lay on the cabin floor, wedged in such a way that he stayed in one place. And he worried.

Kent weathered his first Southern Ocean storm with the same sense of foreboding. A month later, the same conditions would hardly trouble him at all. But this was the first kiss, a wild ride he'd remember forever.

Just before dark on Day Three, Kent's heart fluttered when he noticed that the battens at the top of his mainsail had ripped out of their pockets and were threatening to poke a hole in the sail. Battens are yardstick-like carbon fibre or fibreglass extrusions used to stiffen the sails along their back edge. They help the sails maintain their shape. Kent unfurled a storm jib and struggled to lower the mainsail in winds that gusted at fifty knots. It took half an hour and he was so exhausted by the time he'd finished that he collapsed in the cabin and slept.

When he woke, a close inspection of the mainsail showed that the damage was worse than he'd expected. The pocket for the second batten looked like "it was attacked by hungry dogs." The top batten was in pieces. There was nothing Kent could do. It was blowing too hard. The wind was roaring between thirty-five and sixty knots all day. The motion was violent, and he was wearing his crash helmet to avoid injury should he be whacked on the head.

On *Tommy Hilfiger* Brad Van Liew had also collapsed from exhaustion. "Last night I simply put racing behind myself," he wrote. He had taken only one decent nap in four days and could barely see straight. Unable to stay awake any longer, he left the autopilot to it and fell into a deep sleep.

The big boats were enjoying the blow and blasted south at breakneck speed, *Solidaires* and *Bobst Group* locked in a tight battle for first. Dubois headed east, while Stamm headed more to the south. Unlike Leg II, when both had gone easy at the start, this time they both pushed hard in the early stages, in the hope that after establishing a lead they could hang on to it until New Zealand.

By Day Five, the winds were down to about twenty-five knots and the seas were slight. The fleet used the break in the weather to clean up the mess. They knew they might not get another chance.

John Dennis was still in Mossel Bay. He didn't leave Thursday night, but set sail Friday morning, six days and about twelve hundred miles behind the tail end of the fleet, a vast physical and psychological gulf. With no hope of catching up en route to New Zealand, Dennis would be more alone than anyone else in the race. He would have to endure whatever lay ahead without any hope of help from the other sailors should something go badly wrong.

At about 10:30 p.m. Friday evening, just twelve or so hours after setting sail, Dennis turned on his engine and heard the high-pitched squeal of metal on metal. Some bearings had seized and it took several hours to free them. He decided he could not continue and turned back to Cape Town. It was over. John Dennis was not going to sail around the world.

"I'm so drained, I don't have any tears left," he said. "It is a dream and I know now I am never going to achieve it. I'm devastated."

"Cape Town always grabs somebody," Van Liew said. "It takes huge *cojones* to walk up to the precipice of this leg and step off."

That fearful first week was a refining fire for the Open 40s and 50s. The Open 60s had faced their test in October. This storm, with gusts in the fifties, put the smaller boats through a similar trial. Only Van Liew had sailed these waters before, and in his view the storm was "nothing really dangerous and we have to be thankful for that." For the others, with the exception of the Japanese skipper Kojiro Shiraishi, it had delivered the worst conditions they had ever seen. Surviving it lifted their spirits and pegged their confidence bar one notch higher.

For the Class of '02, the first Southern Ocean buster had come early and hard. But three days later they would face a far tougher test.

8

The Roaring Forties

**"In survival conditions – Force 10 and upward,
the only possible point of sail will be running. In fact,
due to the strength of the wind and the height of
the seas, you will run no matter what."**

– TONY MEISEL, NAUTICAL EMERGENCIES

AS THE NORTHERN Hemisphere celebrated the shortest day of the year on December 21, 2002, the summer solstice descended on the Around Alone fleet. But the longest day in the southern latitudes did not bring them sunshine and warmth. Instead it handed them the warning that a strong depression was on its way, one that in all likelihood would be worse than the first. The heart of this massive, spinning storm was about six hundred miles off. It would cover them for almost three days.

One week and a day into the leg, Derek Hatfield was about 1,600 miles from Cape Town and 1,000 from the Kerguelen Islands. He was in second place behind Brad Van Liew and took advantage of the lull after the first storm to clean up and recover his equilibrium. He was jubilant that he had survived. He had managed his fear and the boat had performed well. On the other hand, this was only the beginning and the fleet was entering the part of the race that Derek Lundy calls "the heart of the matter" – the days of hard sailing through treacherous waters.

For the few people who dare race in these around-the-world marathons, the Southern Ocean legs make up about half of the 27,000-mile course. That is about three months of sailing if nothing goes wrong. But for 40 per cent of the boats something does go wrong and where they come to grief is often here. Of the thirteen starters in this race, two – John Dennis and Patrick de Radiguès, who raced only the first leg – had already dropped out. By all rights, another three would be gone before it ended.

The other legs pose challenges and are dangerous, but not in the same way. The sailors are usually more familiar with the waters and the weather is less severe. As Lundy writes in *Godforsaken Sea*: "When they sail into the Southern Ocean, the sailors enter a realm of contingency: wind and sea conditions there can destroy even the best boat and the skipper unlucky enough to encounter them."

Hatfield felt he was doing well, all things considered. The going was drastic and hard core and not for many people, to be sure. It was cold and windy, and the conditions were constantly changing, which meant that he was always on the move, easing this line, or tightening that one, taking in sail or letting some out. What sleep he got was in fitful naps between tasks. Yet, he felt the journey ahead was manageable.

He was enjoying himself. Fear and excitement are the flip sides of the same coin, as every amusement park operator knows. Dry mouths and thumping hearts at the top of the roller coaster give way to exhilaration at the bottom when the ride ends safely. The difference is that the roller coaster offers fear without harm. It is a thrill: the loss of control, the rough-and-tumble of being thrown around, the heightened senses of sight, hearing, and smell. All of it is fleeting, lasting a few minutes. But in the Southern Ocean, the storms are continual and relentless. They can last for weeks at a time. People like Hatfield and Van Liew are capable of enduring fear for long periods and functioning well in spite of it. What would terrify a weekend sailor doesn't even make them blink.

The urge to seek out danger is present in all these sailors, or they wouldn't do what they do. In Newport, before the race started, Brad Van Liew described being at a wedding and meeting old friends who, like him, had trained as pilots. It reminded him of the career he'd walked away from – a fate, he figured, that would have been worse than death. He couldn't wait to get back to Newport to prepare for his second crack at the Southern Ocean. He was already looking beyond the race to his next challenge. "When your adrenaline meter is pegged this high, what do you do?" he asked. "Where do you go from here?"

Gales offer a sense of exhilaration in their early stages and when they have passed, elation, but otherwise they are miserable experiences, says K. Adlard Coles, whose *Heavy Weather Sailing* remains the bible for offshore sailors. The book was published almost forty years ago, and its insights into how to survive at sea are still relevant despite advances in communications, electronics, and boat design. Coles says the difference between a gale and what sailors call a survival storm is that in a gale, with winds of around forty-five knots, the skipper and crew are still in control. They take whatever measures they think best to navigate and adjust course. In a survival storm, when winds are over fifty knots, or even gusting to hurricane strength, the wind and sea become the masters. You hang on, and whether you live or die may come down to pure luck.

On Midsummer's Day in the Southern Ocean, December 21, squalls were boiling over the horizon in fitful gusts threatening to knock *Spirit of Canada* down. Hatfield hurried on deck and reduced his mainsail, a twenty-minute job, only to watch the black clouds blow harmlessly by. He spent another twenty minutes of hard labour hoisting the sail again. Some hours later another squall threatened. Tired and frustrated, Hatfield left things as they were and went below. Within minutes the boat was knocked flat and he was thrown across the cabin. That's how it is alone at sea: a moment's inattention, the wrong decision and the sea pounces.

As the day wore on, the squalls became more frequent and the wind speed started to climb. The sky had become a sullen, mid-winter grey, a forbidding low ceiling. Hatfield reefed the mainsail one more notch and noted that, without a heater, despite layers of fleece, it felt like a December in Toronto. It was cold enough to snow, but instead it rained, a bone-chilling wetness that seeped through his foul-weather gear. When he went outside to change sails, or check things over he got wet and had to undress and dress again: fleece, foul-weather pants, jacket, safety harness, hood, gloves. Then he'd go back on deck, into the icy spray and biting wind and crawl, climb, tighten, adjust, and tie. Then, soaked again, he'd go back inside. Everything was wet, inside and out.

All through the weekend the winds gusted and settled back like an incoming tide. With each passing hour the wind speed blew stronger, to thirty-five knots then forty, past forty to forty-five, a sustained forty-five knots, gusting at fifty. The waves now twenty-five feet, and every once in a while thirty feet. In a matter of hours, the barometer fell from 1018 millibars to 992. Hatfield knew the instrument was right, but prayed that it wasn't, because what it told him made his heart race: the approaching storm was moving quickly and packed very strong winds.

The cold air he was in was overtaking a warmer system in front and sliding underneath it. As the warm air climbed, the pressure at sea level dropped. This pressure difference is what the barometer was recording.

That Saturday afternoon Brad Van Liew was about three hundred miles ahead of Hatfield and reported that the wind had increased to forty knots. Conditions were rough, but for a veteran who had seen worse, they were okay. "Textbook Southern Ocean," Van Liew said.

Alan Paris, who was several hundred miles behind Hatfield at the tail end of the fleet, caught the storm first. He reported fifteen- and then twenty-foot waves. A couple of hours later, he was surfing *BTC Velocity* to a new speed record of twenty-two knots. The front third of his boat was shooting over the top of the waves like a submarine breaking the surface, plumes of water erupting on either side of the mast. If he was afraid, Paris didn't show it. It was "awesome stuff," he wrote.

Then things fell apart. *BTC Velocity* was going so quickly, she exceeded the speed of the wave that carried her and she shot forward then slowed down. In the vulnerable moment while she waited to catch the next wave, a cross-sea smacked her on the beam, knocking her over.

Meanwhile, Kojiro Shiraishi on *Spirit of Yukoh* had his hands full with engine troubles. The engine impeller, a small, multibladed rubber fan that forces seawater through the engine to cool it, was worn out. He was having other problems with the engine as it wasn't starting easily. This meant he couldn't use it to pump water ballast from one side of the boat to the other to keep the vessel stable. And if his engine woes weren't bad enough, Shiraishi had also cracked a tooth. As he huddled in his sleeping bag, he listened to his boat howling and thumping and noticed that a moaning sound made by his keel in earlier legs was no longer there. He was going too fast.

Tim Kent was playing catch-up after his late start. He had passed Paris and was not far behind Shiraishi. With a triple-reefed mainsail and a partially rolled storm jib, Kent was fine until late Saturday when the wind increased to the mid-fifties. Kent decided it would be prudent to roll up the jib entirely and sail with just the triple-reefed mainsail. It was that kind of storm.

Everest Horizontal hit a new speed record just shy of twenty-six knots and by 10 p.m. that night had passed *Spirit of Yukoh*. Then Kent got the fright of his life. He roused from a nap to the beeping of an alarm. He jerked awake and tracked the noise to a battery power warning light. Kent wasn't worried because he had two more backups. He switched to the second bank of batteries, but the power was low there. He switched to the third system. It was dead. He was on the verge of panic.

Before he could decide what to do, his autopilot failed, releasing control of the boat. *Everest Horizontal* took the path of least resistance, gybing through the wind with a jolt that Kent feared might break the boom at the mast. He donned his foul-weather gear, went up on deck, and pulled the boat back onto the right tack. Then he took all sail down and let the boat drift. He needed time to think.

Kent traced the problem to a loose ground wire. It had prevented the alternator from charging his batteries. The immediate problem was how to start the engine as no combination of batteries had enough power to do it. Kent feared his race was over. Open boats need electricity to run computers, GPS, radar, wind instruments, and the all-important autopilot.

There was one last chance – a fourth backup. Kent had installed ten solar panels in Brixham. They had worked well in the tropics on the leg to Cape Town. He hadn't paid much attention to them since then, figuring that the angle of the sun and the constant cloud would make them of limited use. But now they were all that stood between him and disaster. He turned everything off, made some breakfast, and waited. Four and a half hours later he tried the batteries. There was just enough power to get the engine running. It was, he said, "a lovely, wonderful, fantastic sound."

The electronic systems on board Open class boats are as complex and temperamental as they are sophisticated. Sailing instruments now tap into satellites orbiting the earth, transforming life aboard. The days of sextants and mechanical logs are long gone (although sailors keep them on board as last-ditch backups). Sailing today has become a matter of push-button analysis of wind direction and speed, location and course heading, of Internet downloads and streaming video. Sailors are bathed not in the glow of kerosene lamps but of LED displays. Autopilots steer the boat using computerized brains that "learn" how the boat behaves. Some of the systems are so complicated that few cruising sailors know all of their functions. Digital cameras take videos that are e-mailed around the world via a wireless connection to the Web. Desalinators turn salt water into pure water, while CD players provide background music and DVD players show recent films.

To keep everything going, the skippers must generate power, balancing supply against the demand of their instruments and equipment. They must store power and understand how much spare juice their batteries can hold. They must also have a working knowledge of the various components so that when things fail – as they invariably do – they have some idea of how to fix them.

When Brad Van Liew bought *Tommy Hilfiger*, he stripped it down and rewired the boat so he would know where every wire went, what it did, and where it was connected. As Tim Kent discovered, something as simple as a loose wire can be catastrophic. Van Liew was able to isolate failures quickly, and since most of the problems occurred at the least convenient times, he saved precious minutes in finding a solution.

Sometimes the problems aren't obvious. On the first leg, Kent's autopilots were faulty and nothing he could do seemed to solve the problem. It took a diagnostic in Brixham to determine that the cause was incorrect wiring.

The insatiable demand for power makes electricity management an important factor in boat construction. Most Open 60s have three two hundred–amp absorbed glass mat (AGM) batteries and sometimes four. The advantage of AGM batteries and gel cel batteries is that they are vacuum-filled with an electrolyte the consistency of candle wax. Because they can't spill, you don't have to worry about battery acid and they can be mounted in a variety of positions. However, they are usually double the price of lead-acid batteries.

Each battery on an Open 60 weighs about one hundred and fifty pounds. Hatfield had three, one to start his engine and the other two to run his equipment. Van Liew had six, five to run his equipment and the sixth to start his engine.

The average cruising boat with refrigeration needs about 110 amps a day. An Open 60, whose skipper is downloading weather maps from the Internet, talking to shore crew, and sending video back to shore via satellite, can use four hundred amps a day. Van Liew reckons that each day he was using 250 to 300 amps and running his engine three times for an hour at a time to generate the power. He had four GPS units doing various tasks and on standby as backups and four satellite phones. In the Southern Ocean his autopilot could be on for twenty hours a day, drawing five amps an hour, or 100 amps a day. Hatfield figures he used two hundred amps or less per day. He was scrupulous about turning off equipment when not in use and he had few high-draw electrical devices other than his autopilot and computer.

Sometimes engines fail, so, in the spirit of backups and redundancy, most boats carry small generators, and more and more also have solar panels. Single crystalline cell (SCC) solar systems do well even when the sun is low and when the sky is cloudy but bright, as it often is in the Southern Ocean. *Spirit of Canada* had five panels hooked up in series. On paper, each panel can generate twelve amp hours a day, but that is under ideal conditions. Even so they were a valuable, renewable energy source for the entire race as they produce enough energy to start an engine in a pinch. They are quickly becoming essential equipment. Van Liew had a solar system on *Balance Bar* in 1998, but on *Tommy Hilfiger* he installed instead a small gasoline generator as a backup. With hindsight, he believes it was the wrong choice. If there's a next time, he will go solar.

By midnight Saturday, the waves were rolling in one after the other, rumbling like a freight train down the track. On deck, spindrift stung Hatfield's face and eyes. *Spirit of Canada* strained up the swells and fell off the other side into the troughs. Every five minutes or so a wave bigger than the rest would pick the boat up and turn her sideways. For a moment the rudders would be useless and the boat would teeter precariously. Then she would drop like a sack of cement tossed off a roof, landing with a thud on the back side of a wave. It felt like driving a car into a wall at twenty-five miles an hour, every few minutes, for hours on end. As the boat buried her bow, jets of icy water cascaded down the deck and over the coach top, filling the cockpit waist-deep before washing over the transom and through the scuppers.

Many of the sounds that had frightened Hatfield during the first storm were familiar now: the groans of the boat as it rode up the wave front, the shriek of the wind, the silence on the other side. But now he could tell something was wrong. The boat was rising, but her attitude wasn't right. The noise was somehow different, or maybe it was the lack of noise. The wind was gusting to fifty-five or sixty knots, and above the noise he could hear something coming. It was the sound of a wave breaking.

Hatfield grabbed the handrails on either side of the navigation station and waited. The whole thing was over in five seconds, maybe six. The boat was knocked on her side and the mast touched the water. The boat quickly popped upright.

The damage wasn't as bad as it could have been. The wind vane at the top of the mast was gone. The lazy jacks – a system of lines that catch the sail as it is brought down – had been torn away on one side. The worst of it was that the impact had broken his Satellite-C receiver, his prime means of communication. If his backup Iridium system failed, Hatfield would be very much alone.

At just about this time and place in the 1994 Around Alone, Isabelle Autissier met disaster in the second of her attempts at a solo circumnavigation. The conditions were similar, the storm about as bad. The difference was that Autissier was unlucky. As the sailors will tell you, often this is what it comes down to. Hatfield lost his wind vane, Autissier lost her mast.

Autissier is one of the most accomplished sailors in the world, a woman whose achievements have made her a national hero in France. An engineer and marine science professor who took up racing for "self-improvement," she has sailed to the edge of endurance four times in the Southern Ocean in two Around Alone races and two Vendée Globes. She has only made it through twice. After her last experience she won't sail there alone again.

Brad Van Liew regards Autissier as one of his mentors. She explained her decision to him simply. She told him the first time she sailed in the Southern Ocean, in 1990, she was very afraid, but enjoyed it. She finished that Around Alone in seventh place. She returned a second time in 1994 and felt confident. It was in the first leg of this race that she beat the nearest boat by five days to Cape Town. Her victory created a sensation and Autissier was mobbed when she arrived. On the next leg, she broke her mast and put in to the Kerguelen Islands to repair it. She set sail again. About 1,200 miles south of Australia calamity struck again, when a rogue wave rolled her boat over and peeled off the top of her boat. The Australian Navy had to rescue her.

Autissier came back a third time in the 1996 Vendée Globe. She was disqualified in that race when she put into port for repairs, but finished anyway. Autissier entered the 1998 Around Alone because, as she told Van Liew, after her second race, "I understood the easy and the hard." She was rolled over again and rescued this time by a fellow competitor. That was her last trip. The Southern Ocean had beaten her.

9

The Deep South

**"In the pit of my stomach where the butterflies are
afraid to go, I know I'm knocking on death's door.
Oh, Tony, what a mess."**

– TONY BULLIMORE, SAVED

THE FLEET PASSED the Kerguelen Archipelago in a week-long
procession between Christmas and New Year's. The Kerguelens,
equidistant from Africa, Antarctica, and Australia, were the first
land sighted in almost two weeks and would be the last until the
fleet reached New Zealand. The main island is named after Breton
captain Yves Kerguélen who discovered it in 1772. Kerguelen
Island has a jagged fjord-like coast that's free of icebergs and an
interior covered with glaciers. It is 85 miles across at its widest
point, and surrounded by nearly three hundred smaller islands.
Captain James Cook dubbed it Desolation Island after his visit
there four years after Kerguelen.

The weather on the Kerguelens is typical Southern Ocean
fare: Rain and snow fall for about three hundred days a year and

gale force winds blow continually from the west. Because the islands lie on the edge of the zone where the cold Antarctic water mixes with the warmer waters of the Indian Ocean, there is an abundance of marine and bird life: penguins, petrels, albatrosses, and a variety of terns and gulls. There is also the Kerguelen cabbage, as edible as any you buy at the grocery store.

Louis XV of France believed that a southern continent had to exist to balance the weight of the Northern Hemisphere and commissioned Kerguelen to find it and lay claim to its riches in his name. Kerguelen discovered the islands on February 12, 1772, but was unable to make landfall. On his return to France, he gave the king an exaggerated account of the island's potential and Louis XV commissioned a second expedition. Kerguelen set sail in October 1772 with a fleet of three ships and again failed to set foot on the island, although the captain of a sister ship managed to get ashore. After a survey the captain concluded: "This region is as barren as Iceland, and even more uninhabitable and uninhabited." The king was not amused and Kerguelen was imprisoned for the next sixteen years.

The sealers were the next to discover the islands. Americans arrived in 1791 to find the coast so thick with seals they could barely walk between them on the beach. Within twenty-five years the colonies were virtually wiped out. Whalers followed. They set up factories to render blubber into oil that was shipped back to Europe and North America. During the Second World War the Germans used the islands as a base for their submarine and surface commerce raiders. Since 1949, a French scientific community of between fifty and one hundred people has lived on the islands. The amenities now include a hospital, restaurant, library, and movie theatre – and the resources to repair racing sailboats such as Isabelle Autissier's.

As the Open 60s passed the islands, they managed to get ahead of the worst of the storm that had blanketed the Open 40s and 50s.

Some of the sailors participated in a science experiment aimed at tracking the movements of sea creatures in these waters. When *Pindar* passed to the north of the Crozet Archipelago, about nine hundred miles to the west of the Kerguelens, Emma Richards dropped an Argos beacon in the water. Via satellite, students at a school in France would track the beacon's movement through the ocean as part of an oceanography class. On *Hexagon*, Graham Dalton participated in a similar project for a French oceanography program called Argonautica. Dalton was helping scientists track the movement of leatherback turtles, the largest turtles on earth. A full-grown adult can reach up to eight feet long and weigh as much as two thousand pounds. Leatherbacks feed on jellyfish in the middle of the ocean and come ashore once a year to lay their eggs. Many of the turtles in the archipelago had been tagged. Dalton dropped a tracking beacon in the water that would receive signals from the turtles' tags and transmit them to the scientists by satellite.

Brad Van Liew's experience passing the Kerguelen Islands a few days before Christmas was miserable. The waves were rolling in one after the other, it was freezing cold, and the weather was giving him no rest. His diesel heater was leaking and there was condensation everywhere inside the boat. "Any normal person thrust into this situation would just go down below and hide in the bunk to cry," he said.

As that weather system passed, the wind shifted from northwest to southwest and gradually faded to fitful, squally gusts. The swells were still huge, with the top four or five feet rolling white water. The change in wind direction meant that eventually the boats would have to alter course.

There are two ways a boat can change direction either by tacking or gybing. Tacking moves the bow through the wind and is safer because the boat is easier to control as the boom pivots around the mast. In boats with sixty- to eighty-foot masts, the force applied by the swinging sail area is huge. On Hatfield's *Spirit of Canada* the mainsail is fourteen hundred square feet. The sails are so heavy the sailors can barely raise and lower them even with winches. If the boom should swing uncontrollably from one side to the other, it would kill anyone in the way.

A series of ropes connected to pulleys on a steel track are tightened and released at critical moments to slow the speed of the boat and control the force of the pivot. This also ensures that the gooseneck fitting that attaches the boom to the mast doesn't snap. To help Emma Richards perform this manoeuvre, *Pindar* had been retrofitted with a "coffee-grinder" in the middle of its mainsail track. This double-handled winch made it easier for her to raise and lower the sail.

Gybing is more dangerous than tacking because it takes the stern of the boat through the wind. The boom doesn't pivot in a controlled arc, but swings wildly from one side to the other. If a gybe is uncontrolled, the boom speeds through its arc and snaps the gooseneck, becoming a lethal projectile that tears the sail from the mast and may break the rod rigging. Another possibility is that so much force is exerted on the boat by the swinging of the boom that the momentum knocks the boat over in a crash gybe, where the mast touches the water.

Gybing is a harum-scarum manoeuvre even when done with a full crew in moderate winds and seas. To do it solo, in gale force winds, with the boat pitching and tossing, is petrifying. The first step is to make sure everything below is tied down or stowed. Next the water ballast has to be shifted to centre using a hydraulic pump. On deck, the mainsail is reduced by taking in reefs. This slows the boat, making it easier to control. Step four is to centre the keel, so that the boat remains stable.

Then comes the tricky part. The jib is rolled up, leaving the mainsail to drive the boat. The boat loses speed, becomes lethargic, and starts to wallow. The skipper then winches the main towards the centre line of the boat. Almost simultaneously he has to adjust the running backstays, the lines that run from either side of the mast near the top to each corner of the stern. If the wind is blowing over the port, or left-hand side, of the boat, the port back stay is winched tight to absorb the tension of the sail while the starboard stay is slackened off. As soon as the boat moves onto the opposite tack, the starboard stay has to be tightened and the port stay loosened off. Once the manoeuvre is executed the sails must be set and trimmed to the new course.

"It's a very fine balancing act," Van Liew says. "A gybe at 30 knots takes forty-five minutes at least."

The small boat sailors celebrated Christmas as they raced towards the Kerguelens. The sun came out and the wind moderated. They spoke to friends and family by phone or chatted via e-mail, opened presents on the boat, and also talked to each other. The North Americans treated themselves to hungry-man breakfasts of sausage, eggs, and potatoes, if they had them. Later they dug into their goodie bags for treats of Christmas pudding and mince tarts. The Europeans sat down to a dinner of hors d'oeuvres, followed by pasta, fruit, and chocolate, washed down by wine. Each sailor celebrated with one eye on the weather, noting that another storm was brewing on the horizon.

"It was business as usual here," Derek Hatfield said on Christmas Day, adding that all the Open 40s and 50s were on a northeast heading so that they would be on the north side of a low-pressure system expected to arrive the following day. Hatfield was tired. The continual banging and crashing was making life inside barely tolerable. He was staying warm enough without his heater by wearing layers of clothes and running his engine, which warmed the cabin. Even so, it was permanently damp below.

Conditions were so benign for Tim Kent he wondered if he would ever pass the Kerguelens. In a Southern Ocean rarity, he was almost becalmed. "I was hoping for a nice day for Christmas, but this is not what I had in mind," he grumbled.

Kent decorated his navigation station with a garland and the stuffed animals given to him by his daughters. He ate a breakfast of scrambled eggs and sausage patties polished off with orange juice and apple sauce. On Boxing Day, still in calm waters, he attended to housekeeping chores, filling his fuel tanks and topping up his water bottles. It was a dreary, rainy day.

Christmas was a time of reflection for race leader Bernard Stamm. "We're really lucky with the weather," he said. "The wind is down to 30 knots, and the temperature has risen. In the boat, it's about 9 degrees C [48 degrees Fahrenheit], whereas yesterday it was still only 2 degrees [36 degrees Fahrenheit]. I'm privileged to be spending Christmas where I am. The view is magnificent. When you don't have much more than what is strictly necessary for a long period, anything at all can become the world's most beautiful gift."

Stamm's Christmas dinner included an appetizer of crabmeat, followed by ham with pasta and mushrooms, and fruit salad and chocolate for dessert. He washed it down with a fine Burgundy.

At the back of the fleet, almost sixteen hundred miles behind Stamm, Alan Paris's Christmas was a crisp and clear day with temperatures from seven to nine degrees Celsius (upper forties Fahrenheit). The wind was a light ten knots from the southeast and the waves only two to four feet. On Christmas Eve Paris had sailed south to avoid the bottom edge of a low-pressure system. Since he couldn't get above it to hitch a ride, he decided to get out of its way.

Kojiro Shiraishi on *Spirit of Yukoh* was several hundred miles in front of Paris and still having engine troubles. "Dear Santa Claus," he said. "All I want for Christmas is . . . a Yanmar impeller."

Eleven hundred miles ahead of Paris, Graham Dalton and Emma Richards felt alone yet not lonely, cheered by the sunny skies. Simone Bianchetti had the worst of it. He was pushing hard to the south to make up for time lost on the second leg when he was dismasted and put into A Coruña. He paid the price on Christmas Day when *Tiscali* was knocked on her side. Bianchetti was asleep in his berth and "had a traumatic wake-up," as he put it, when the boat lurched in a fifty-knot gust. He was thrown across the boat as it broached.

On deck, the rigging was tangled around the mast. He managed to untangle it as the boat popped up, only to be hit by a second gust that knocked it down again. It took thirty minutes to get the boat moving. Bianchetti was rewarded for the risk he'd taken. He gained ground on *Hexagon* and *Pindar*, moving into third position in Class I.

John Dennis had the worst Christmas, limping back to Cape Town, feeling lonely and defeated. He slipped into the deserted Royal Cape Yacht Club on Christmas Eve. He had been assigned a vacant slip and given a number to call if he wished to have Christmas dinner with a family, but he chose to spend Christmas Day on the boat alone, reading cards from his family and mourning what had happened.

"I don't think I'd make very good company right now," he said in a telephone interview.

Tiscali's life raft was
stowed on the transom
so that, if the boat
turned turtle and the
skipper was able to
escape via the hatch, he
could easily get at it.
(James Robinson Taylor)

Spirit of Canada romped through the Roaring Forties. After safely
passing through three major storms, Hatfield felt good. His self-
confidence was high and he was able to relax slightly and savour
some of the things he had come to see. December 29 was a perfect
sailing day, with the sun shining and glistening on the water. The
wind was blowing at twenty-four knots from the northwest and
Spirit of Canada was broad reaching effortlessly at ten to fourteen
knots. Every few minutes as the boat surfed down a wave, water
and spray covered the deck, but with the wind from the north, it
wasn't too cold. The water temperature had risen from 9 degrees
Celsius to 15 degrees Celsius (48 degrees Fahrenheit to 60 degrees
Fahrenheit) as he sailed north. He spoke to Tim Kent who was less
than fifteen miles away and felt comforted to know he wasn't alone.
Hatfield saluted the pace set by Stamm and Dubois. "Incredible,"
he wrote in his log. "Ah, to have an extra twenty feet of waterline."

New Year's Eve found the fleet moving north towards the Tasman Sea. Brad Van Liew was about one thousand miles south of Australia, not far from where Autissier met her final disaster in the 1994 race.

The weather was warmer, the sea moderate and the wind manageable, quite different from the conditions Autissier had faced eight years earlier. Van Liew celebrated, he said, "on the patio at sunset," with a glass of wine. "Not a big celebration, but a good one."

Aboard *Tiscali* Bianchetti was locked in a battle for third place with Emma Richards on *Pindar*. Both were sailing at a latitude of fifty-two degrees, where the temperature was below freezing. They were just twenty-eight miles apart. Bianchetti was less than three hundred miles from the drifting Antarctic pack ice and was startled to spot a growler, a piece that had broken off an iceberg. Richards had a nerve-wracking twenty-four hours after her temperamental autopilot put the boat through a crash gybe while she was in a forward locker. The boat was lying on a forty-five-degree angle when she stumbled on deck. Almost immediately, a huge wave lifted the boat and it gybed back on course. Richards waited for the sound of tearing sails or a snapped mast, but she was lucky. *Pindar* sprinted away.

The Open 60s were starting to converge on the virtual gateway, a waypoint in the course they had to keep to their south as they passed. This would ensure they stayed safely away from pack ice. The race committee had set the mark at latitude 46 degrees south between longitudes 105 degrees east and 120 degrees east to accommodate the Australian government's concern that the sailors stay within range for any emergency search and rescue.

A second waypoint had been set off Cape Reinga, the northern tip of New Zealand. The boats were required to leave this mark on their starboard side. This meant they had to sail around the

North Island rather than through the Cook Strait that separates the country's two main islands. It made their course longer but eliminated the chance that tired sailors became shipwrecked sailors. Safety first.

The New Year's Eve storm failed to live up to expectations and passed by as just another few miserable days. Stretched out across the vast ocean, the fleet rang in 2003 in different time zones. Bernard Stamm was on his approach to the Tasman Sea and spoke for everyone when he said it was just another day at the office.

"Every day is ruled by the rhythm of the waves, the winds, night and day," he said. "I am going to rummage in my food boxes as there must be some nuts or some fruit salad – freeze-dried of course – left to eat. Also I have a little bottle of champagne – not bad! My resolutions are simple – for nothing on the boat to break or to suffer any kind of breakdown, and to look after myself, to keep within my limits, so I can go all the way."

Emma Richards was still having problems with her autopilots and on New Year's Eve again crash gybed *Pindar* while broad reaching in thirty-knot winds. Each gybe made her more anxious but there was nothing she could do. She was tempted by her mini bottle of Mumm's, but decided it would be prudent to keep her wits sharp.

By New Year's Eve Alan Paris was under the same sunny skies as Hatfield and the breeze was light. Of all the sailors, he had spent the most time at sea – just 14 days on land out of 142 since the start of the race – and was finding the lack of time on land hard to take. Even though he was the consistent "back marker" in the race, with little chance of changing his position, he had no regrets.

Tim Kent's thoughts followed a similar path. He had now completely transformed from being a Great Lakes sailor to a solo circumnavigator. The adventure that had begun in his imagination was now a reality.

"I get the bruises and the cold toes, but we all get to live this adventure together," he said. "In just a few months, it will be over. And twelve months from now I will be wondering how the year slipped away so quickly."

10

Halfway

**"I find that the harder I work,
the more luck I seem to have."**

– THOMAS JEFFERSON

BY ITS THIRD week at sea since leaving Cape Town, the wear
and tear on the fleet's mechanical and electrical systems began to
show up. Sails tore, battens broke, and autopilots failed. A boom
vang snapped, pumps leaked, engines failed to start, shackles and
sheaves broke, and high-tensile rope parted like twine. Along with
the deterioration of their boats, the sailors experienced a physical
and mental decline. The storms wore them down. They were tired,
sleep deprived, cold, and depressed.

On New Year's Day, Bernard Stamm was only 1,900 miles or
eight days from Tauranga on the North Island of New Zealand, the
end of this leg of the race. He was due south of the island of
Tasmania and about 250 miles ahead of Thierry Dubois on *Solidaires*.
Brad Van Liew had 3,200 miles to go, a little over two weeks. He was

about 750 miles south of the southernmost point of Western Australia, Cape Leeuwin. Still to the south and west of Australia, Derek Hatfield had about 3,800 miles to sail before he reached Tauranga. Stamm and most of the Open 60s would have a month in New Zealand to rest and recuperate, Hatfield about half that.

In every leg of the race fatigue was hardest for the skippers of the small boats. Because they couldn't sail as fast as the Open 60s, they spent more time at sea. This meant facing more storms – and more opportunities for things to break. In this leg, they had no choice but to keep going. There was nowhere to land for thousands of miles.

The longer the boats spent at sea, the less time they had in port to make repairs. As well, the smaller boats tended to have smaller budgets, so when their skippers were onshore there was less time for them to rest as they had to do repairs themselves. The local yacht club usually arranged billets, otherwise they slept on their boats.

Van Liew says that the small boat skippers sail a different race. Their level of fatigue is higher because they have fewer days onshore. Also, he says, "Your odds of something happening are greater if you're out there twice as long." Even if they had the same budgets as the Class I sailors and could afford the costly communications time for updated weather files, as they would still be at sea for far longer, they would not be able to download the forecasts as frequently.

But the smaller boats do have some advantages. They are cheaper to repair because they have smaller rigs and the forces applied to their critical parts are weaker than on the Open 60s. This reduces wear and tear. But overall, the sailors in the forty-footers would rather be at sea in a bigger boat.

"The whole thing gets tiring," a weary Hatfield said during the middle of a thirty-hour storm in early January. "There's no sunshine, just day after day of strong wind. There's motion all the time.

It wears you down. I don't recommend people do this in a small boat. It's a tough game."

It got tougher for Hatfield on December 31 when he made a frightening discovery. The boat had become sluggish. Despite high winds it wasn't moving well. He came down into the cabin after a time on deck and heard the sound of water sloshing in the middle watertight compartment. When he investigated, he found that it was filled with about eighteen inches of water, probably a hundred gallons. He got out a small hand pump and drained the water into his toilet and then overboard. He kept at it for three hours until he realized that the water was coming in as fast as he could pump it out.

A closer inspection revealed two leaks. One was a hole in the main bilge line. That was easily repaired. The other was a leak in one of the daggerboard trunks. Each board slid through the boat through a slot in the deck. Inside the boat there was a formed lip on the hull and underside of the deck and a rubber sleeve was attached to the two extrusions. One of the sleeves had split and every time the boat took water on deck — which was more or less continuously — it drained inside.

Hatfield found a tube of marine adhesive, which cures when exposed to water to form a rubbery, extremely strong seal. After three tries he managed to reduce the flow to a small leak of about five gallons per hour. "It's amazing what you can do with a tube of 5200 and a roll of duct tape," he said.

He had also broken three of his sail battens, which he had to repair or risk doing more damage. It wasn't dangerous work, just exhausting. The first job was to take down the 145-pound main-sail. The pockets were hand stitched, so he opened them, installed new battens, and muscled the main back up.

Next, his computer failed. Hatfield suspected it was a victim of the constant pounding of the ocean. This also highlighted the difference between a well-funded and a no-frills campaign. Brad Van Liew's computers were supplied by Panasonic, another one of his sponsors. They were the same heavy-duty waterproof models used by the U.S. military. Hatfield's two computers had been donated by one of his supporters. They were off-the-shelf equipment from an electronics store. He couldn't fix the one that had died, so switched to his backup. After three hours setting up all the waypoints and communications, he got back to racing.

Alan Paris was also finding that duct tape and marine adhesive were his best friends. Duct tape worked for temporary repairs, but epoxy putty was the clear winner because it could be applied to wet or even underwater areas. It is pliable for the first ten minutes then hardens like steel. No one should go to sea without it, was Paris's view.

He faced a serious test when a starboard stay that supported his mast parted. The good news was that by then he was only one hundred miles from Hobart, Tasmania, and the repairs took less than a day.

Tim Kent's biggest challenge was when he fired up his Yanmar engine to charge his batteries and it banged to life, filling the cabin with smoke. He suspected an exhaust manifold gasket was to blame, but it was worse than that. The injector for the middle cylinder was shooting exhaust into the boat. When he contacted his shore crew, he was advised that the engine would still get him to New Zealand, which it did, but the clouds of smoke were so bad he couldn't stay below. By the time he arrived in Tauranga, the joke was that he had become an "All Black," a pun on the name of New Zealand's famous rugby team. The interior of the boat was covered in soot and had to be steam cleaned.

Emma Richards ripped her mainsail in half during a squall. Since the boats did not carry spares – they were too heavy to carry and almost impossible for one person to hoist, she spent several days sewing it back together. Wearing gloves made her hands too clumsy for the task, so she sewed bare handed, taking a break every hour or so to warm up. When she'd finished, her hands were a mass of pinpricks from forcing the needle through the thick material.

Hatfield's confidence that 5200 would do the trick proved overly optimistic when, a few days later, the split in the dagger-board sleeve reopened. He had run out of ways to repair it. The tubes of marine silicone were gone, and the tear in the rubber was such that nothing else he had on board would fix it. The boat was not in danger of sinking, but something had to be done with the hundred gallons of water an hour that came in. For twenty minutes an hour for the rest of the trip, Hatfield pumped. He figured the exercise helped him lose four or five pounds.

The Open 60s all made port between January 8 and 16. Stamm rounded Cape Reinga on the northern tip of New Zealand in the teeth of a gale the night of the seventh. The wind was blowing from the southeast at thirty to thirty-five knots and Stamm was forced into steep seas to safely round the cape and turn south to the Bay of Plenty and Tauranga. In the process, all his communications equipment died; his hull started to delaminate as the layers of fibre-glass and carbon fibre separated; his mainsail was torn; and one of his tillers was smashed. Even so, he broke another speed record, shaving two days off the old one. For the third time this race, Stamm arrived first, making the 7,125-mile trip in twenty-five and a half days, for an average speed of 11.6 knots per hour.

Stamm said later that he had expected the approach to Tauranga to be "just a formality." The problem was that, even as the wave heights increased to twenty-five feet, the distance between them hardly increased at all, so the boat was severely pummelled by both the wind and the sea. Stamm had a 450-mile lead over Thierry Dubois, so he reduced his mainsail to the third set of reefs. Then, when the sail began to tear, he took it down. *Bobst Group* was so heeled over, it was impossible for him to stand up inside without holding on. Suddenly the boat went right over on its side. He suspected a steering problem. When he opened the compartment, he could see that the piece of metal that connected the tiller to the rudder had sheared off. Stamm was temporarily frozen with fear. He had lost his steering in the middle of a gale near a rocky shore. "I had to do something very quickly," he said.

In short order, he drilled holes in the rudder stock, put screws partially in and fixed it all in place with pieces of strong Vectra line which he cut off from one of his sails. While all this was going on, Thierry Martinez, a sailing photographer, flew over the boat in a helicopter. He and the pilot saw *Bobst Group* drifting in heavy seas, with no one on the deck. They circled the boat and were relieved when Stamm emerged from his cabin. A short while later, Stamm safely rounded the cape and blasted down the coast with four reefs in his mainsail and a small jib. The visibility was so poor that he saw the finish line only about three hundred feet before he crossed it. As he turned the boat into the wind to take down the mainsail, the tiller fell off in his hands.

A frustrated Thierry Dubois was second for the third leg in a row. "Yet again victory has eluded me," he said gloomily. "I am always just one step behind."

Dubois was the most experienced sailor in the race, but his passage had been tough. He had turned east rather than south after leaving Cape Town, crossing the Agulhas bank and taking an early lead. It was a short-lived lead though. Stamm headed south where he picked up the strong westerlies and quickly pulled into first place.

Dubois had experienced gear failure since before he rounded the Kerguelen Islands. His lightweight air reacher and new large gennaker had blown out, the south magnetic pole caused havoc with his autopilot, and to top it all off, one of his rudders snapped off. "No collision, no explanation," he said later. He arrived a day and a half after Stamm.

Graham Dalton on *Hexagon* took third and Simone Bianchetti on *Tiscali* was fourth. Bruce Schwab on *Ocean Planet* was fifth and Emma Richards with her tattered mainsail came in last of the Open 60s.

Brad Van Liew was the first of the Open 40s and 50s to arrive, having sailed a remarkably fast and problem-free leg. He finished in thirty-two and a half days for an average speed of 9.1 knots, more than 1,000 miles ahead of Tim Kent.

Van Liew felt tired and the boat needed work, but he thought that the passage had not been extraordinarily dangerous. For him, the Southern Ocean hadn't lived up to its reputation. "We experienced lots of big weather, but no really, really dangerous weather," he said.

Kent limped toward Tauranga with continued engine problems. Using the engine became so unpleasant he shut down most of his electrical systems and relied on solar power alone. He managed to rise above it with a sense of humour and even composed a song.

On top of old smokey,	The cabin is filthy,
Still banging away,	The decks are all tracked,
Sits my poor old sailboat,	My food all tastes oily,
Becoming quite grey.	My face it looks blacked.

The smoke it is pouring,
From hell down below,
It's making some power,
How much I don't know.

On top of old smokey,
I'll be glad to dock,
My eye is just watching,
The GPS clock.

My hands are all grimy,
My clothes are all shot,
My pillow's disgusting,
There's little that's not.

I want a hot shower,
A nail manicure,
A thick steak with french fries,
And cold beer for sure!

On January 23, after five weeks and four hours at sea Kent arrived in Tauranga, beating Derek Hatfield by just ten hours. His average hourly speed had been 7.6 knots. He felt a huge sense of accomplishment and said that he was enjoying the developing camaraderie among the sailors. Whenever things had gone wrong, he said, his spirits had been lifted up by a note his ten-year-old daughter had left on the boat. It read: "Daddy this is your dream and you will finish."

"I had to keep remembering it," Kent said. "It's true this is not an ordeal, it's an adventure, and it's the best one I have ever had."

The last weeks had been tough on Derek Hatfield. He had been living without heat for almost a month. The only warmth came from his engine, which he kept running only long enough to recharge the batteries. The cold had added to his general fatigue, and each storm had taken a little more energy and left his reserves that much closer to empty.

At the end of the first week of January, a Southern Ocean gale had pushed *Spirit of Canada* to a new speed record of 25.1 knots.

But the same wind had made the sea so rough he'd found it impossible to sleep for thirty hours as the boat surfed down wave after wave. From start to finish it took four days for the system to pass, which seemed like forever to Hatfield. The waves were the biggest he had seen, some forty-footers. "Real monsters," he called them.

On January 22, Derek Hatfield crossed the line in third place. His average hourly speed had been 7.5 knots, just one-tenth of a knot slower than Kent, whose boat was ten feet longer. His performance showed just how skilled and tenacious he was. Halfway through the race he stood third overall, just one point behind Kent. Few observers would have predicted that at the outset.

Hatfield felt a sense of accomplishment, but as was often the case, he found it hard to express how he felt. "There's no way to describe it, really," he said. "Dramatic. Extreme. You can't go down there and treat that ocean lightly or it will do you in."

It had been a lonely voyage for him, frightening at times but often exhilarating. It had taken him to the limits of his abilities and tested him. He had been challenged and had become a better sailor for it, aiming higher and achieving more. Now he had arrived safely. He was 60 per cent of the way home, long past the point of no return. Yet even as he rested for a few days in the calm waters of the Tauranga Bridge Marina, in the back of his mind, he knew that what lay ahead promised to be tougher.

Kent was equal parts awed and worried. "The power of the storms we saw was just unbelievable," he said. "When you're triple-reefed, surfing at 30 knots, you wonder: When it gets worse than this, what will I do? That's the thing I keep wondering about. What happens when the wind is blowing 80 knots? What am I going to do then?"

LEG IV

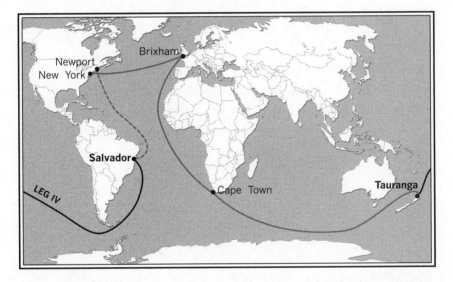

ROUTE: Tauranga, New Zealand, to Salvador, Brazil

DEPARTURE: February 9, 2003

DISTANCE: 7,850 nautical miles

11

Playing Catch-Up

**"I could feel myself not far from death.
I had passed the first threshold of descent.
It is that knowledge that led me to say, much later, that I
had returned from the kingdom of the dead."**

– RAPHAËL DINELLI, RESCUE FROM BEYOND
THE ROARING FORTIES

EUROPEANS SETTLED NEW Zealand in the middle of the nineteenth century. It followed a treaty with the Polynesian Maori in
1840, in which the Maori ceded sovereignty of the islands to
Queen Victoria. The native people thought they were retaining
territorial rights, but a series of battles over the next thirty years
ended with their defeat and subjugation.

New Zealand has about four million people living on the two
islands separated by the Cook Strait. With ten thousand miles of
coastline, New Zealand is home to a huge sailing fraternity.

The Around Alone stopped in Tauranga, rather than Auckland,
because the America's Cup, which ran from February 15 to March 2,
2003, had laid claim to the larger and better-known port. Tauranga
is a popular resort town on the eastern coast of North Island,

surrounded by miles of white sandy beaches, with mountains just inland. Mount Maunganui serves as a landmark for sailors approaching the harbour. Inside the sheltered bay there are two marinas with room for more than one thousand boats. The city is home to New Zealand's boat-building industry and offers all of the related marine services.

Bernard Stamm, who had plenty of time on his hands, visited Auckland to look over the America's Cup fleet. He spent three days as a guest of Team *Alinghi*, the Swiss entry in the match series. (They crushed host New Zealand 5 – 0 to become the first European team to win sailing's oldest trophy, and the first from a landlocked country to win.) From a trial boat that follows the fleet during the races Stamm watched a tune-up race. He drew comparisons between the two types of racing, the one wide open and solo, the other a team effort with as many as sixteen crew on board, competing in short, intense sprints. The boats are built of the same materials, rigging and sails are similar. America's Cup boats are seventy feet long while the biggest Around Alone boats are 60s. America's Cup sailors were puzzled when Stamm referred to his sleek *Bobst Group* as a "truck." He was amused by their reaction. What he meant was his boat was tough enough to stand up to the Southern Ocean, even though, at twenty thousand pounds, it was three times lighter than *Alinghi*. However, the America's Cup boats can't manage more than eighteen to twenty knots, while Open 60s exceed thirty knots at times.

The big difference in design reflects their use. America's Cup boats are built to sail around a course that is usually triangular, with each leg giving a different point of sail – upwind, beam reaching, and downwind. The boats have thin, sheer lines. Open boats are pizza-shaped wedges, with wide, flat bottoms. They sail best downwind, which is why the Around Alone and Vendée Globe courses circle the world from east to west. The prevailing winds are behind them most of the time.

During the layover, Stamm had time to reflect on the tactics that had helped him win Leg Three by a convincing one-and-a-half days. It began with the decisions he made immediately after leaving Cape Town. Thierry Dubois chose to hug the coast of South Africa and go more east than south, the most direct route to New Zealand. A second option was to set a more southeasterly course to angle down into the Roaring Forties, pick up the westerlies and hitch a ride along the succession of low-pressure systems. This was the tactic favoured by Brad Van Liew, Tim Kent, and Derek Hatfield, as well as some of the Open 60s.

Stamm chose a third option. He sailed south by southwest – away from his destination – knowing that he would be well off the lead initially. But by the third day out he had picked up the westerlies below 40 degrees south. He made a left turn and soon he was blasting along. By the end of the first week, he was running neck and neck with Dubois, far ahead of the other boats.

As the fleet prepared for the first big storm, Stamm faced more decisions. He could position himself to the north of the system and avoid the worst of it, stay his course, or head for the centre of the low-pressure area to take full advantage of the wind direction on the far side. He chose to head for the centre, but as the rest of the fleet headed north, he wondered if his decision was sound. What did they know that he didn't? The first rule of racing is to cover the fleet, or at least stay within striking distance. He turned north too, he says, "as much to keep an eye on the others as to keep moving." After twelve hours, he couldn't find any reason to continue north, so changed direction and headed into the heart of the storm. Once he had scooted out through the eye, he picked up the strong winds on the far side. He was ahead of Dubois and he never let go.

By the time the fleet reached the Kerguelen Islands, Stamm had a 250-mile lead over his rival. He did not know about Dubois's gear failures, particularly the loss of the light air sail. This made sailing more difficult for Dubois once the fleet climbed into the calmer and warmer Tasman Sea for the final sprint to New Zealand. For the last few hundred miles, Stamm had a 450-mile lead, which allowed him to relax a little.

There was plenty of work to be done as the fleet prepared for the Horn. The boats were all hauled out and their keels, rudders, and daggerboards inspected and cleaned. The delaminated hull on *Bobst Group* was fixed. Masts came down and were dye-tested to see if the fittings had any cracks.

When Tim Kent hauled *Everest Horizontal*, he was alarmed to find that the keel bulb was slightly off-centre. The boat had been dragged over a rock on its way into the harbour, nicking the bulb, and he suspected this had also caused the twist. He consulted the boat's California designer, Jim Antrim, who was confident there was no major damage. After filling and faring the bulb and adding a new coat of bottom paint, *Everest Horizontal* was relaunched.

Simone Bianchetti took down and returned Bernard Stamm's spare mast, replacing it with one that had been built for his boat in Australia and shipped to Tauranga before he arrived. Derek Hatfield repaired his leaking daggerboard trunks, installed the ESPAR heater and a charger/generator backup system that had been held up in South African customs but now had been shipped on to New Zealand.

There was also time for fun. Brad Van Liew's wife had joined him, and the couple invited Tim Kent over to their rented house

Tim Kent repairs *Everest Horizontal*'s keel bulb in Tauranga, N.Z. The bulb scraped rocks while under tow and was slightly misaligned.
(Everest Horizontal)

to watch the National Football League Super Bowl between Tampa Bay and Oakland. Because of the time difference, they had taped the game. Kent was an avid Green Bay Packers fan and was astonished to realize it was the first football game he'd seen that season. He'd missed the whole thing, as he had not been able to figure out how to listen to the games on his SSB radio.

Some of the skippers took a good break from the sea – in the air – when they tried parachuting from twelve thousand feet, with the first eight thousand feet in free fall. Simone Bianchetti liked the sensation so much, he did it a second time. Brad van Liew went glider flying, and Emma Richards took flying lessons. Meanwhile, back on the water, Graham Dalton took local schoolkids out for a spin on *Hexagon*.

Thierry Dubois spent his time in Tauranga visiting schools, to raise awareness about children's rights, a cause close to his heart.

Amnesty International was among Dubois's sponsors, and at every stopover he asked children to design a logo or image with a human rights theme. The winning design was painted on his genoa. These diversions provided a much-needed mental break for the sailors before the start of the next leg.

On February 9, 2003, Prime Minister Helen Clark, and thousands of other New Zealanders, watched the fleet set sail on the longest leg of the race. The route would take them around Cape Horn, about 4,800 miles to the southeast, which was about two weeks of fast sailing for the Open 60s. Then it was another 3,000 miles to Salvador, Brazil, halfway up the other side of the South American continent. This stretch would take the lead boats another two weeks. The Open 40s could need as many as twenty more days to complete the leg.

For the first five days, the fleet rocketed southeast under the umbrella of a high-pressure system. The leaders were able to scoot along at fifteen knots an hour, with fifteen to twenty knots of breeze coming more or less from behind them. It was proof of the effectiveness of the Open designs, and they managed 350-mile days. The pleasant conditions were caused in part by El Niño. This meant that parts of the tropical Pacific Ocean were warmer than normal, producing rising, moist air. The effect often gives the Pacific Coast in Canada and the U.S.A. a wetter winter than normal, while eastern North America gets a mild one. It also affects currents along the coast of Chile, forcing the colder, stormier Southern Ocean weather to stay farther south than usual.

Still, the nagging worry for the sailors was reports of ice. The one-hundred-and-fifty-foot French trimaran *Geronimo* had spotted an iceberg and growlers at 54 degrees south, directly in the path of the fleet and some 120 miles northwest of the Horn, which lies at 56 degrees south. *Geronimo* was vying for an around-the-world speed record and the Jules Verne Trophy. Her skipper reported seeing the ice in relatively warm water, which meant an iceberg was breaking apart. The growlers that trail after big icebergs pose the worst risk to small boats. They are difficult to spot by radar or by the naked eye. They float on the surface, and in the huge waves they look very much like white foam. A piece of ice no bigger than a basketball can snap a rudder off. It is so cold this far south, even in the summer, the sailors don't spend a lot of time on deck. If you're going to smack into something, the odds are that it is when you aren't looking.

The ice becomes less of a danger closer to Cape Horn, because nearshore currents keep the bergs out to sea. The trick for anyone sailing this route is to angle the descent to the Horn by going more southeast than south to skirt the edge of the ice. That was Van Liew's tactic. He had been here before and seen what could happen. "I'm sailing in an uninsured boat and I've got a baby girl, so it's not a tough call," he said.

The movement of the ice pack changes over time. It grows in one spot and sloughs off a piece somewhere else. Since 1998, scientists have been watching an iceberg called A-38, which is one hundred miles long by thirty miles wide, the size of Prince Edward Island. A-38 broke off the Ronne Ice Shelf in the Weddell Sea, south of the Falkland Islands in the Atlantic. Pieces have been spotted off the Falklands and farther east as the ice drifts with the west to east flow of the current.

The fleet was briefed about the ice pack before leaving New Zealand, but as Sir Robin Knox-Johnston says, tracking ice is as much art as science. Satellite images taken by the U.S. National

Oceanic and Atmospheric Administration (NOAA) in February 2003 showed big bergs at 60 degrees south, 240 miles south of Cape Horn. One chunk was six miles long, and growlers could be trailing bergs for ten to twenty miles. Knox-Johnston said, "The information is not complete. None of us knows exactly where the bergs are lying, and that's giving us a problem." This "not knowing" explained the two waypoints set for the leg. The fleet would have to keep to the north of both these points to keep clear of the ice.

The rule of thumb is to pass pack ice on the upwind side. That way you stand the best chance of avoiding growlers, as the wind will be blowing the chunks away from your boat. That's the theory anyway.

Derek Hatfield's luck ran out just two days into the leg. He informed race headquarters he was returning to port for emergency repairs.

Hatfield had installed new batteries in Tauranga, but had not had the money to load test them. Load testing draws current from the battery to check that it works. He had assumed that new, high-quality batteries would be fine, but within hours of leaving Tauranga, he found that when he turned his engine off after charging them, a power surge blew out his critical systems.

First his computer, the brains driving his navigation system failed, so he couldn't send or receive e-mails. Then his satellite phones failed. Then his GPS unit went and with it the ability to know his location, the boat's speed, and how hard the wind was blowing. Hatfield figured that the batteries were dropped at some point before installation and damaged internally.

None of these failures was cause for alarm. Hatfield was resourceful. He knew that he didn't need sophisticated electronics

to sail around the world. Sir Robin Knox-Johnston had circum-
navigated in 1968 without much of anything. E-mails, weather fax,
telephones, and the Internet were all luxuries. All you needed was
a sextant and charts and Hatfield had both. Hatfield's plan was to
sail on – a decision he'd later regret – but then his autopilot stopped
working too. "When the pilot gave up I knew I was done," he said
later. "You can't do it without them."

It took him twenty-six hours to get to Napier, New Zealand,
which is about a five-hour drive south of Tauranga. He steered by
hand the entire way, dozing at the helm in fitful snatches. Every
hour out took him an hour to get back, adding to his time for the
leg, and he also incurred the mandatory race forty-eight-hour
penalty for putting in to port. It took him thirteen hours to install
and test the new batteries and to replace burned out components.
He was overwhelmed by the help he received from the equipment
supplier Raymarine and from the shore crew.

He was back at sea by Day Four, but was now more than one
thousand miles behind the leaders. Alan Paris in *BTC Velocity* was the
nearest boat and Paris was four hundred miles away. A week later, on
Day Eleven Hatfield was 1,400 miles from New Zealand and about
2,600 from the Horn. He had halved the gap between himself and
Paris to just 200 miles. The weather was sunny and warm. Perfect
conditions.

The fleet stretched out across the Southern Ocean for about
two thousand miles, with the lead boats just six hundred miles from
Cape Horn. While Hatfield was basking in the sun, Emma
Richards, who had sailed these waters a year earlier on a crewed
boat, was once more feeling the icy grip of the south.

"This is the Southern Ocean I remember," she said. The waves
were mountainous, coming from varying directions, masses of
rolling white peaks. It was blowing so hard she spent six hours at

the helm waiting for a lull in the wind so she could turn on the autopilot and drop the staysail. *Pindar* was flying with a triple-reefed main. Even that felt like too much for winds that were gusting to fifty knots.

Each time *Pindar* surged forward, the wave behind the boat would throw it nose first into the one in front. Before the rudders could bite, she would hear a massive roar and look over her shoulder to see white water about to bury the boat. It was frightening, and the only thing more terrifying was sailing under these same conditions at night in the pitch black with only the sounds of the waves to offer a clue to what was coming. Richards was so spooked by steering in the dark she switched on the autopilot and went below. There, in the confines of the cabin, there was light, a warm sleeping bag and other reassuring things, including a kettle, a hot cup of tea, and dry clothes.

Brad Van Liew was not far away from *Pindar* and reported that the wind was "jumpy," swinging from thirty to fifty knots. He was exhausted. The unpredictable wind speeds made for tough navigation and a sleepless night. Like Richards, he sensed an otherworldly feel to the night. *Tommy Hilfiger* was roaring along at twenty knots, "sailing on the edge," Van Liew said, with two reefs in the mainsail.

In these conditions the worst can happen. The sailors can't prepare for anything because they are below decks and it is so dark they can't see out of their windows. That night, the wind veered from west to south and *Tommy* crash gybed. Van Liew was thrown across the cabin as the boat went in an instant from heeling on the starboard side to lying flat on the port side. The boat was pinned there, because the canting keel, which had been set to counterbalance the force of the wind, was now helping to keep the boat flat.

Van Liew immediately released the keel to its centre line position and was in such a rush to free his boat, he went up on deck without foul-weather gear. He was wearing his safety belt, and clipped a line onto it once he was in the cabin. He started to rescue the boat by releasing the lines. This would spill wind from the sail and let the boat pop up. In the middle of doing this the wind increased, the sky opened, and down came a deluge of hail and rain. The sails were slapping and the ropes were flogging with a lethal force, tying themselves in a knot. Van Liew's normally agile hands became numb and a wave that hit the side of the boat drenched him from head to toe, a cold-water bath in near freezing temperatures. He didn't care. Fear is a great motivator. He struggled on, and two hours later, *Tommy Hilfiger* was sprinting south again. As Van Liew said later, "It was just another day in the Southern Ocean."

Derek Hatfield meanwhile was purring along at ten to twelve knots in a gently rolling sea. Every day in light air was a blessing, even if it was unnatural for the Southern Ocean. He had a good idea of what was going on ahead and wondered when it would be his turn. "I'm eager to get around the Horn and out of harm's way," he said. "It's a bit of good luck really, that you get through unscathed."

It was Sir Francis Chichester who started this insane modern urge to sail around the world alone. In 1967, Chichester brought the *Gipsy Moth IV* back to Plymouth, England, after sailing alone around the world, and declared that the only challenge left for single-handers was *non-stop* circumnavigation. It was seen then as an almost impossible achievement, but in early 1968, London's *Sunday Times* came up with a prize of five thousand pounds sterling and a trophy called the Golden Globe. The race was on.

The rules were simple. The boat had to set out from a port in the Northern Hemisphere between June 1 and October 31, 1968,

Sir Robin Knox-Johnston won the first around the world challenge in 1968. Here he is pictured with Emma Richards in Newport before the race.
(Ann Harley)

and return to the same port, having rounded the three great capes: Good Hope in Africa, Leeuwin in Australia, and the dreaded Horn. The voyage had to be completed without outside help or any replacement fuel, food, water, or equipment once the boats set sail.

By today's standards, the boats that were entered in that first race were hopelessly slow and appallingly ill-equipped. The difference was equivalent to that between tin cans tied to a string and cellphones that can send and receive e-mail and photos. The fleet comprised modified cruising boats of between forty and fifty feet, most of them with full keels and heavy canvas sails. There were no furling headsails with lines leading back to the safety of the cockpit. The sailors had to go forward to the bow as the boat pounded through the swells and unclip the old sail, stuff it down a hatch and put the new one on. The journey took about eight months, compared to three to four months now for the Vendée Globe. E-mail, the Internet, and emergency position beacons were a generation away. There were no backup generators or solar panels, and the only electronics on board were knot logs that measured boat speed. Single sideband radios with a range of between nothing and a few thousand miles, depending on the weather, were considered state-of-the-art communications.

Nine mariners set sail in 1968. Five withdrew and a sixth, Donald Crowhurst, committed suicide. Three rounded the Horn, but only one finished the race. It took him 312 days. That was Robin Knox-Johnston, a merchant seaman. He had no idea he had won until he tied up in Plymouth, as his radio had broken some weeks earlier.

The one thing that hasn't changed since 1968 is the toll taken by fatigue. The tools for coping are different, but the sleeplessness, the constant physical struggle with the boat, the need to stay alert, are all the same. Most sailors attempt a routine, because time at sea has always been measured by a checklist of tasks. Routine focuses the mind, wards off depression, and offers comfort. Each day is a round of eating, sleeping, tending to the boat, and repairing things. If the Doldrums are a place where the sailors suspend routine, the Southern Ocean, where the wind blows hard and generally from the same direction, is where the routine takes over.

Everyone has a sleep management plan. Most favour taking short naps whenever conditions allow. Hatfield used a kitchen timer to wake himself up from naps of half an hour or so, but no longer than an hour – unless he was so exhausted he passed into a deep sleep. He would wake just long enough to cast an eye over key instruments, listen to the sound of the boat, and then he'd nod off again. If the wind or sea changed dramatically while he was asleep, alarms would sound.

Most skippers build a routine around meals to give order to the day. Brad Van Liew got up at dawn and had a bowl of granola and a cup of coffee. He ate dinner just after sunset. This could mean six p.m. when he was near the equator, or eleven p.m. during the passage through the Southern Ocean. The rest of the time he would snack to keep up his energy.

Between meals a skipper might spend three hours a days analyzing weather and looking for the fastest, safest route through the current system. If conditions permit, they spend some time talking to shore crew and family, journalists and sponsors, and checking the race Web site. Talking to people drives away the loneliness. Most of the skippers had commitments to send e-mail newsletters to the thousands of fans around the world who had signed up to receive their latest reports. As well, they had to write for their own Web sites and the Around Alone site.

For about two to three hours a day, the skippers turned their engines on to charge batteries. Lines and deck fittings were checked for chafe and wear. Constant attention is paid to the sails. If there was time they read a few pages of a book, caught a few minutes of a movie or simply sat, as Kent often did, under his doghouse watching every wave roll under his keel.

In this stretch of ocean the loneliness can grab you when least expected, often at night. It can be unnerving. Mike Garside says that while sailing here he suddenly became aware that he was passing through the most desolate place in the world. He was an infinitesimally puny speck of life in waters that were as far from land as you can be. It was where others, many of whom were better sailors than he, had perished or nearly perished. "It is a terrifying place," Garside says. "It is so very, very isolated. If something happens there is no way anyone can help you except another competitor."

In 1998, Isabelle Autissier came to grief along Dead Man's Road, as clipper sailors named these waters. Her boat rolled over and she was unable to right the vessel by shifting her canting keel because her mast was still intact and acting like a keel. Within hours of death, she was rescued by Giovanni Soldini, who went on to win the race. This helped her decide to put single-handing in the Southern Ocean behind her.

In 1996, Montrealer Gerry Roufs, a close friend of Autissier's, disappeared here during the Vendée Globe. Roufs, aged forty-three, had crewed with her aboard a record-breaking New York to San Francisco trip. He had given up practising law to sail full-time and had been a member of Canada's Olympic sailing team between 1976 and 1983. Roufs was ranked as a contender who could win given the right conditions and was running second when he disappeared.

Parts of Roufs's boat were later washed ashore on the Chilean coast near Cape Horn. Derek Lundy speculates that Roufs was either washed overboard, or the boat was knocked down and he became entangled in debris and drowned. "That could happen to any one of these guys in any race," Lundy says. "They know that when things are really bad that it may come down to luck. The boat may right itself after a knockdown, but you have to be inside to survive."

During this leg, smart sailors stay below most of the time, reaping the rewards of their investment in a diesel heater. In the 1998 Around Alone, Garside kept his heater running most of the time and took an extra ten gallons of fuel for that purpose. He jokes that he sailed most of the Southern Ocean below decks wearing only a T-shirt and shorts. He would taunt Van Liew (who hates cold weather) about how warm and dry he was. He knew that Van Liew's heater wasn't working and that he was cold, wet, and miserable most of the time. "This time he made damn sure that he had a new version of the heater I had on board," Garside says.

There is no point sitting at the helm in freezing weather unless your life is at risk. Often, all that's needed is to lift your head out of the hatch once in a while, look around, and slam it back down. Only the most driven of skippers sit on deck, steering manually. They do so because human hand-eye coordination is about 10 to 15 per cent better than the best autopilot. On the other hand, human decision making deteriorates quickly in the freezing cold. But when the winds are constant and the seas are predictable, a pilot can keep the boat going in straight lines for a long time.

Christophe Auguin, who has won three consecutive around-the-world races, used to say that the only time he touched the helm in the Southern Ocean was in and out of harbour at the start and end of the leg. Tim Kent followed another rule of thumb: Above forty knots and below eight knots focus on preserving yourself and the boat. In between, sail hard.

When the skippers do go on deck during this leg of the race, it takes them longer to do everything. It takes longer to put on and take off damp weather gear, longer to clip on the safety harness and visually check the lines, fittings, and sails. Everything hurts. By the end of the second leg of the race, John Dennis said his hands felt like hams. Cuts and bruises do not heal with constant salt-water soaking.

Muscles ache all the time because a boat at sea is always in motion and the skippers are lurching from one handhold to another. Sometimes the lurches threaten to pull your arms out of their sockets, as Emma Richards said after the Bay of Biscay storm. The constant clenching and unclenching of muscles sends the skippers in search of places where they lie still and relax. John Dennis and Thierry Dubois both resorted to sleeping in sail lockers at different times. Tim Kent would wedge himself under his overhanging doghouse. Derek Hatfield would find a spot on the cabin floor.

As the fleet headed farther south, the lagging boats caught the storms first, as the weather systems rolled from west to east. For a time this allowed them to gain ground. Then the boats in front of them caught the wind and accelerated, widening the gap again.

In the early days, Bernard Stamm was in front and he was not about to play it safe. He veered far to the south, luring the experienced Dubois and the less experienced Dalton, to follow him. They were headed into Iceberg Alley, a place that Van Liew described as being full of "boat-shattering chunks of frozen water."

By the twelfth day of the leg, *Hexagon* was blasting along at twenty-eight knots. Graham Dalton wasn't able to spend much time on deck because it was so cold and the large waves breaking over the boat made it dangerous. Instead, he spent hours at the navigation station, watching his instruments, particularly the radar alarm. If any object – most likely ice – passed within its range he would be alerted in time to steer around it. Of course, he knew it would miss smaller or submerged pieces. The radar was unable to sense them.

Dalton was feeling edgy, and more so after Bernard Stamm sighted a berg. From that point on, ice was never far from Dalton's mind. "Every strange noise or bump increases my stress levels," he said. His nervous system was pumping out so much adrenaline, his brain would not switch off long enough for "even a short burst of relaxed sleep." The greater the danger, the greater his fatigue, the greater the risk of a catastrophe. This is always the case in these races. Even the wild and unstoppable Simone Bianchetti, who celebrated his thirty-fifth birthday on February 20, the eleventh day out, was unnerved enough by the prospect of ice to move more to the north. But Stamm was fearless, eating up the miles at a ferocious pace. On Bianchetti's birthday, he was just 1,800 miles from the Horn. During the previous twenty-four hours, he had covered 419 miles for an average speed of 17.5 knots.

Stamm said that the conditions that day were ideal for the better part of sixteen hours as he surfed down the huge waves. He seemed almost indifferent to a surprise sighting of an iceberg in thick fog. He thought he was dreaming when he first saw the three-hundred-foot berg, thinking that his radar would have picked up an object that large. But the fog cleared and he watched the berg for five minutes until it disappeared from view. Luckily he was on the upwind side, so that any debris would drift away from him. He also believed that the worst risk of ice was over. Still, sleep was out of the question, but stress didn't break his resolve. He kept the pedal to the floor. Man and machine were racing at the edge of control.

The fleet was illustrating the paradox of single-handing: These skippers are the best in the world, the most skilled, the most conscious of safety, and the most prudent, yet they sail in a manner that is about as unseamanlike as it gets. Sailing is about being careful, minimizing risks, and safely getting from A to B. It is about keeping watch and getting enough rest to stay sharp and alert. When the weather is bad, you don't set sail, you stay in port. If you get caught out in a blow, you shorten sail, not pile it on. On a crewed boat, a system of watches ensures that fresh eyes are always on the lookout. In this race and the others like it, the opposite is true. The skippers are exhausted and to get some sleep they turn their boat over to an autopilot. The pilot can more or less keep the boat on a straight course, but it cannot avoid something in the way, whether it's land or an iceberg.

Tim Kent was scared witless by the prospect of hitting ice and knew he should be on the constant lookout. But it was too cold to stay on deck. Down below, he knew he was flying blind because the radar wouldn't pick up the ice. In Leg II Thierry Dubois had curled up in a ball in a sail locker as *Solidaires* hurtled through a hurricane. And, in 1998, Brad Van Liew found a small place to hide in the back of his locker as he waited and wondered whether he would survive another hour. None of these decisions suggests prudence.

Derek Lundy notes that most collisions, knockdowns, and dis-mastings occur when the skippers are below. But there is no other choice. It is a condition of single-handed sailing that the boat is fre-quently on its own. Without a second person to stand watch, single-handers must rely on the soundness of their vessel, the latest advances in technology, and good, old-fashioned dumb luck.

12

To the Horn

**"I'd never seen it but of course it was the Horn.
The great rock sphinx, the crouching lion
at the bottom of the world."**

– DAVID HAYS, MY OLD MAN AND THE SEA

~~~~~~~~~~~~~~
~~~~~~~~~~~~~~

SIR FRANCIS DRAKE may have been the first European to see the Horn in 1578. Queen Elizabeth I had sent Drake's *Golden Hind* and two other ships, the *Marigold* and the *Elizabeth*, on a voyage of discovery and plunder. They raided the Spanish Main in the Caribbean, turned south down the length of South America and rounded Cape Horn to the Pacific. They were in search of the Manila gold ship that voyaged once a year from the Philippines to Chile and on to Spain, laden with spices from the Orient and treasure stripped from South American gold mines. There is some debate about whether Drake saw the Horn or not. The weather was terrible and he had only crude instruments to measure his location. He noted there was nothing to the south of his position, which could mean that he was not at the Horn, but at the Diego Ramirez

Even on a calm day, Cape Horn is a bleak and forbidding sight for sailors rounding the tip of South America. *(Andrew Prossin)*

Islands, fifty-six miles farther west. Or, it could have been the Horn itself, a small island, about five miles long and about a mile across, part of the Hermite group, an archipelago in Southern Chile.

In 1616, Willem Schouten became the next European to sail these waters. He named the rocky promontory Cape Hoorn after his hometown in Holland. Schouten was on a mission of commerce, trying as Drake was, to find a way to the Pacific that avoided the Spanish-controlled Strait of Magellan, which lay just to the north.

Rounding Cape Horn from the west is always difficult (though generally easier than approaching from the east). At the Horn the waves are treacherous because the water becomes shallow quickly. One hundred miles offshore the ocean is three miles deep. Ten miles from the Horn it is only three hundred feet. Waves that have been driven east for thousands of miles with nothing to stop them rise as they hit the continental shelf. This creates steep, short waves that often come simultaneously from different directions. Compounding this danger is the fact that the vast expanse of the Southern Ocean is trying to squeeze into the Drake Passage, the six-hundred-mile gap between the Horn and the Antarctic Peninsula. This greatly increases the water pressure.

Another reason for worry is that the South American landmass adds a new variable. Wind is funnelled down the spine of the Andes and spills into the Drake Passage, often in a different direction from the prevailing westerlies. These winds are known as williwaws and can come with a thirty or forty-knot punch. Sometimes the only warning of one is a flattening of the top of waves or strong ripples on the water. These winds can strike ships well offshore, knock them down, and sink them.

Bernard Moitessier was the first to round the Horn in the 1968 race that Sir Robin Knox-Johnston won. The French adventurer was enchanted and inspired. He felt spiritually connected to the sea and overcome by the conflicting emotions of fear and satisfaction. One wonders, when reading about his feelings in his book, *The Long Way*, whether Moitessier, like Donald Crowhurst, had lost his mind.

On February 4, 1968, as Moitessier neared the Horn, he had been at the helm for almost forty-eight hours straight. The conditions were cruel – storm force winds and a steep, short breaking sea. He was soaked, half-frozen, and hadn't eaten much in two days. He knew he was on the edge of disaster and that he should shorten sail. Instead he left the cockpit and moved forward to the mast to feel *Joshua* surge through the swells. He clung to the mast watching the spray running off his staysail, later describing them as "pearls you want to hold in your hand, precious stones." The wake running behind him, he said, was "like a tongue of fire."

Moitessier moved farther forward and held on to an inner stay, closer to the bow. He felt the impulse to move up farther, but he resisted, knowing that it would be utter madness to be that exposed. So there he stood, in the middle of the night, as his boat forged through the deep swells at the bottom of the world, in a storm of apocalyptic proportions.

"I feel no fatigue, no weariness, the way after a long, strenuous effort of swimming the mind begins to float above the body," he wrote later. "Memories of my childhood rise up. I shoo them away. They come back, go away easily when I ask them to leave me alone with the Horn tonight."

He knew he should shorten sail and slow down, but at the same time, he says, "I felt the thing I want to hear further, still further, is the great luminous wave where one could swim forever." How long he stood on the cusp of madness, he doesn't say. Eventually he woke from his trance and returned to the cockpit, holding "tight to the boat and [my] sanity." Had Moitessier continued on to Plymouth he would have won the race. But something in the days following this epiphany made him change plan. He kept going east, past the Cape of Good Hope for a second time and on to the South Pacific, where he remained for several years.

Eighteen years later in a 1986 solo race, Canadian John Hughes rounded the Horn on the forty-two-foot *Joseph Young*. Hughes was a master mariner, though not really a sailor, and the only magic he felt was that each mile brought him closer to safety. The sea was violent, creating dangerous breaking waves. He found the motion inside the boat was nauseating.

Hughes had been dismasted a week after leaving Australia, which was where the leg to Cape Horn began in that race. He was too stubborn to quit, so he had rigged a new mast from two spin-naker poles and continued. He says he would not make the same decision now. Hughes spent forty-five days with this jury rig. The weather was particularly bad that year with winds so strong they pushed his battered boat to 150-mile days. About one thousand miles from the Horn, Hughes was down below when he heard a hissing. He thought it was his cassette player on its last legs. He glanced up through the slightly opened hatch and saw a wall of water with a breaking crest tumbling towards the stern. The water buried *Joseph Young*.

The impact threw him to the floor. The noise was incredible. Hughes wondered if the boat was going down as he curled up in a ball to shield himself from flying tools, and books. Seconds later, he managed to stand up and with hands clamped on the companionway ladder waited for the killing blow. It didn't come. He had been spared. Recalling that night, Hughes says, "I'm not religious, but you felt there was something bigger than you out there."

A week later Hughes was about sixty miles from the Horn. Conditions were so rough he had been steering non-stop for twelve hours. Finally, he was too exhausted to continue and switched on the autopilot. He went below, tied himself to the settee, and tried to sleep. He had noted in his log he would be rounding the Horn in the middle of the night. He couldn't have cared less.

He awoke to a feeling of being vaulted through the air, as if he was in a car that had gone off a cliff. It was dark so he didn't have any visual cues. The boat was rolling. Rolling, falling, banging. He didn't know whether he had hit something, ice maybe, or run onto some rocks. Everything that wasn't bolted down was flying.

He says that the noise was like being inside a garbage can that someone was beating on with sticks. It seemed like it lasted for a long time, but in reality it was all over in about thirty seconds. The boat rolled through 360 degrees and righted itself. Hughes struggled to his feet and waded through broken glass and ankle-deep water mixed with diesel and food. He was almost too scared to go on deck and check the damage. If his jury-rigged mast hadn't survived, he was finished.

Somehow Hughes summoned the strength to look and to his amazement the rig and sails were still there. The tiny storm jib was being flogged, because the rope that tied it off to a cleat was torn away. So were most of the hanks – the clips that attach the sail to the forestay. But that was the extent of the damage.

To this day, Hughes isn't sure what happened. He speculates that at the top of a wave his autopilot was overpowered and for a moment the boat was drifting. It took the path of least resistance, which was to turn gradually with its bow into the wind. In the middle of this manoeuvre it was hit by a wave. The boat broached and was knocked on its starboard side. As it swung upright, a second wave landed and rolled it through the full 360 degrees.

"I was lucky," Hughes says. "Very lucky. People seem to have a problem about a couple of hundred miles west of the Horn. It's a different place."

Benign weather doesn't last long in the south, and by the time the fleet was twelve hundred or so miles from the Horn, three to four days away, depending on the boat, foul conditions had reasserted themselves and things on board began to break, even though every inch of the boats had been inspected in New Zealand. The fleet had been at sea for more than one hundred sailing days. Repeated knockdowns and crash gybes had put enormous stress on fittings and fixtures. Even the best equipment has a breaking point.

The first near disaster came when a forestay on *Everest Horizontal* parted. The sound, an ominous banging of a heavy metal object against the side of his boat, woke Kent from a restless sleep. He dressed, went on deck, and what he found was more chilling than the waves trying to force their way into his foul-weather gear.

Where the drum for the furling equipment for his big genoa attached to the deck at the bow, a pin had wiggled loose and the unit had become a seventy-foot writhing snake. The only thing holding thousands of dollars of equipment to the boat was a piece of light rope in the drum used to roll up the sail. The furling unit was part of a stay that helped support his mast. Luckily he had three others. Because he was sailing downwind, the pressure was pushing the rig forward and so there was less stress on the others. If the wind swung around, the weight shift could cause the rig to collapse. Kent had the choice of lowering the unit to the deck and cutting the whole thing away, or finding a way to secure it and buy some time.

As the boat pounded through the green swells on that moonless night, he decided to buy time. He found a spare shackle and tied a piece of rope to it. Like a cowboy wrestling a steer to the ground, he picked the right moment and pounced. He clipped a shackle to the bottom of the flailing unit and ran the rope through blocks to the cockpit. He used a winch to crank it tight. That kept the stay and the furling unit rigid.

Shaking with exhaustion, and with disaster temporarily averted, Kent went down below and collapsed. He reasoned that the middle of the night was not the time to deal with a problem of this magnitude. It was better to get some rest. Remarkably, he was able to sleep, dreaming of solutions – none of which he used.

At dawn, he could see that the temporary fix had worked. But now it was clear that the damage extended to the top of the mast, where a fitting joined the stay to the mast. The only thing holding the furler to the mast was the rope that raised the sail. The system was beyond Kent's ability to repair. He worried that if the rope broke, the unit would become a steel whip that could kill him or punch a hole in the boat. He had to get rid of it.

Kent stopped the boat's motion by dropping his mainsail. He eased the rope holding the unit, and since the wind was coming from behind the boat, it blew the unit off the bow. Next he crawled forward, cutting the line that held the unit to the deck. He unclipped the shackle holding the headstay in place. The unit whipped back and forth, smashing into the side of the boat and sending chunks of paint and carbon flying. Kent crawled back to the cockpit and eased the rope at the top of the mast. The device fell over the side and as soon as the drum hit the water, the movement became more controllable again. Kent cut it loose. "It was gone. Just like that," he said. His final act was to run a genoa halyard to the bow and tension it off with a winch to act as a temporary forestay.

Behind Kent, Kojiro Shiraishi on *Spirit of Yukoh* was knocked down by a wind shift that caused a crash gybe. He lost all the instruments at the top of the mast. Without them he had no information about wind speed or wind direction. This could be dangerous. With the wind blowing directly astern, slight wind shifts could lead to knockdowns or worse. Shiraishi had spares, so he decided to climb the mast even though the seas were running fifteen-foot waves and the breeze was at twenty-five knots. He phoned the race officials first. They were worried and asked him to call before he began the ascent and call again when he came down. Shiraishi clipped on a safety harness, donned a crash helmet, and with two lines, using a device similar to those used by mountain climbers, he hauled himself up the mast.

Among Shiraishi's many accomplishments is climbing mountains, so he knew what he was trying to do. The feat was made more difficult by the fact that his boat was one of a few in the race that had a wing rotation mast. This meant that it did not have spreaders for the final ten feet or so. At the top there are no side stays or forestays. Each time he lost his grip the force of the boat's motion smashed him like a rag doll against the mast.

There are two types of rig used by racing sailors. The traditional rig is a fixed mast with stays on each side and at the bow and stern. These points of attachment keep the mast flexible but well supported. It means that the mast can be lighter, because there is more lateral support. The other type is the wing rotation mast. It has less support but also less compression. The masts weigh up to 50 per cent more because they gain their stiffness through the structure of the tube. Rigging from the top of the mast to the deck supports them.

Spirit of Yukoh and Bruce Schwab's *Ocean Planet* both had wing rotation masts, but the majority of new Open boats use fixed masts. Most sailors believe that the weight advantage of a fixed mast out-weighs the efficiency and aerodynamics of a winged mast.

The other drawback, as Shiraishi found out, is that the wing rotation mast offers precious little to hold on to. He hung on with one arm, while he unscrewed the fixture that had held his instruments with the other. He took the wrecked pieces apart, installed new ones, and reattached the fixture, all in near-zero temperatures, while swinging like a human metronome sixty feet above the ocean. The repair took two hours.

Some five hundred miles behind Shiraishi, Hatfield was sailing in a different sea. As Tim Kent repaired his broken forestay and Shiraishi climbed his mast, Hatfield was still cruising along in what he dubbed the *Spirit of Canada* high. Such are the extremes of the Southern Ocean. By Day Fourteen of the leg, Hatfield had been flying his light-air spinnaker for four consecutive days.

From the start of the leg Brad Van Liew had been in his customary place at the head of the small boat fleet and had caught up to the slowest Open 60s. He had a 375-mile lead over Tim Kent, and his weather was the tough stuff Emma Richards recalled.

But then, on Day Ten, *Tommy Hilfiger* was knocked over. The following day Van Liew faced a sustained fifty-knot wind. It kept blowing, and by Day Thirteen, the barometer was dropping and the wind carried the bite of Antarctica. Van Liew's hands and feet were cold. The waves were building, and behind him Tim Kent was making his repairs. Bad as they were, Van Liew was surprised the conditions weren't worse. Four years earlier he had almost died in the same spot and had talked to Mike Garside by phone on the hour every hour, each of them making sure the other was still alive.

On February 25, Day Sixteen of the leg, Van Liew was about five hundred miles from the Horn. The previous twenty-four hours had been severe with gusts to sixty knots. He had watched anxiously as the barometer dropped "like a homesick rock." The low-pressure system parked itself directly overhead, and the sunny skies and light winds in the eye of the storm gave him some false hope. Luckily, the depression wasn't as bad as it had been four years earlier. This system moved quickly and the seas only got to twenty-five feet or so – about the height of two double-decker buses. After the eye had passed, it was uncomfortable and rough, with lots of thumping and banging, but it was not deadly. Still, it caused him four days of misery.

Three days later, after three weeks at sea, Brad Van Liew was first in the small-boat class to round the Horn. "It wasn't like 1998," he said with relief. "It wasn't that deadly, but it was boat-breaking ugly."

Van Liew was now six hundred miles ahead of Tim Kent and fifteen hundred miles ahead of Hatfield, who had begun to catch some of the bad weather he had expected much earlier. On the nineteenth day into Leg IV the temperature on deck on *Spirit of Canada* was 7 degrees Celsius (45 degrees Fahrenheit). It was rough, with big rollers, thirty-knot winds, and driving rain squalls. The wind would rise and fall, forcing Hatfield to go through the tiring routine of raising and lowering sail every few hours. He was spending six to eight hours on deck at a time, more than any other skipper. He thanked his good sense in buying and installing the heater. "I'm feeling good," he told a journalist, "but I'm anxious to get out of the Southern Ocean."

13

The Summit

**"Cape Horn! What a vast and terrible cemetery
of seamen lies under this eternally boiling sea."**

– VITO DUMAS, ALONE THROUGH
THE ROARING FORTIES

*T*HE SKIPPERS PASSED the Horn one by one, paying homage by
word, or deed, as they did so. For them, it was the equivalent of
climbing Mount Everest alone. It was what they had set aside
careers, loved ones for and, in some cases, spent all they owned to
achieve. Even the professionals paused to savour this brief moment
of satisfaction.

For more than three and a half months they had sailed alone,
covering two-thirds of the globe, enduring fear, loneliness, and conditions they could not adequately put into words. Most had come
close to death at least once or twice as the result of a slight mis-
judgment or missed handhold. They had experienced weather that
is continuously the worst of anywhere on Earth, and had passed by
the spot that is the farthest from any land on the planet. They had

sailed through waters where veteran sailors had perished, simply because their luck had run out. They had seen waves that rose higher than their masts and had withstood the roaring winds that played spine-chilling tunes in their rigging. At the height of some monstrous storm, in the dead of night, when they were at their weakest and most vulnerable, they had huddled in a berth or wedged themselves in a small corner and listened to the unholy sounds, wondering which system might fail, what would they do if it did, and if they'd survive. But they always managed to contain the fear and get up when they had to and do what had to be done.

The point of enduring the fatigue and sleep deprivation and sub-zero temperatures was to see this mist and storm-enshrouded pile of rocks that had been cursed by European sailors ever since Schouten and Drake first rounded it. Cape Horn sits like a jagged brooding sentinel guarding the narrow passage of water between the world's two greatest oceans. The skippers were comrades by now, sharing a bond with the greatest mariners who had ever lived. One by one they were rewarded, gaining admission to the club, joining the 100 or so others in history who have done the same thing: sailed around this rock alone in a race and survived.

Bernard Stamm was the first to round on February 23. Stamm's pace from New Zealand had been a whisker short of suicidal. He had pushed hard and fast, setting a tempo that only Thierry Dubois was able to match, although Graham Dalton and Bruce Schwab tried for a while.

Stamm's rounding in fourteen and a half days matched the pace set by the fully crewed Volvo Ocean Race leaders earlier in the year. During the two weeks since leaving Tauranga, he had averaged 310 miles a day and a speed just shy of thirteen knots an hour. Emma Richards who was tracking *Bobst Group*'s progress said, "I continue to watch in amazement, no, fascination, as Bernard keeps clocking massive average speeds." Richards had sailed a slower, safer race and Stamm was more than three days ahead of her. Around Alone Web site correspondent, Brian Hancock, wrote, "Stamm has blown the doors off everybody. Only a major breakdown can stop him now."

As Stamm rounded the Horn, the wind was gusting sixty knots and *Bobst Group* laboured under reduced sail. The seas were "monstrous," he said. The boat was surfing at twenty-one knots, had passed the Horn and was turning northeast for the Strait of Le Maire, the strip of water that separates Staten Island from the Argentine mainland, when a huge sea picked up the twenty thousand-pound boat and flicked it on its side. *Bobst Group* skidded down a wave and smashed into a trough. Stamm heard a sickening noise as his keel cracked in two places. His boat and his life were now in danger. At that moment he had to overcome the debilitating fear that his keel was so badly damaged it might fall off, sinking the boat or turning it over. He found that the upper part of the keel inside the boat where it swung on its pivot was badly damaged. "I've got a big problem," he said.

Bobst Group Armor Lux has a fifteen-foot keel below the water-line with a 3,500-pound bulb. It isn't much heftier than *Spirit of Canada*'s keel, which is eleven feet below the waterline with a 2,750-pound bulb. *Bobst Group* has another five feet of the keel inside the boat. A series of blocks and tackle move an arm, canting the keel from side to side. The sudden impact had put so much pressure on this mechanism that the lever arm inside the boat snapped off. Stamm could no longer move the keel from side to side or even easily lock it in a centre line. He stabilized the device using ropes and pulleys, but without inspecting the keel below the boat, he had no idea how bad things were. He reduced sail and spent the night thinking about what to do. Eventually, he decided to put into the Falkland Islands, which lay about four hundred miles to the northeast. He would incur a forty-eight-hour penalty, plus the time ashore, to fix the problem.

Less than ten hours behind Stamm, Thierry Dubois had pushed hard enough to stay close. His strategy was to keep up and once they rounded the Horn, pour it on for the finish in Salvador.

Dubois was cheerful on February 24 as he passed the Horn and celebrated his thirty-sixth birthday. He was pleased that after his many mishaps passing through the Southern Ocean he had finally made it. The passage was stormy, but a break in the clouds created a spectacular light show. Dubois drank a little champagne, raised the bottle in a tribute to the sea that had allowed him safe passage, and dug into his goodie bag. He found a CD with songs and messages from family and friends that kept him laughing all day.

In a poke at the reckless pace set by Stamm, Dubois said, "To win you have to finish. This leg in particular demands a vigilant and careful handling. But my heart goes out to my friend."

Dubois now held the lead for the first time in the race and realized this meant he could win. Going into the leg, Stamm had a two day, eight hour lead. That was cut to eight hours because of the forty-eight-hour penalty incurred by Stamm for his Falklands stop. If Dubois could win this leg by eight hours the two would be even going into the final stretch. While Stamm and Dubois were friends, Dubois was exasperated by his defeat in each of the previous legs. While in Cape Town he had put together a collage he called The Ultimate Fight and posted it on his navigation station to remind him that Stamm was the man to beat.

Behind the leaders were Graham Dalton on *Hexagon* and Bruce Schwab on *Ocean Planet*. Both boats had been wounded in their approach to the Horn and were in need of repairs.

On paper, *Hexagon* was the fastest boat in the fleet, a new boat built for this race. The skipper, however, had the least ocean going racing experience of any of the sailors, aside from Tim Kent. Every experience was new, and so where seasoned skippers might let up a little, he kept the pedal down, where they would pour it on he sometimes hesitated. The steep learning curve put a lot of stress on his boat. In many ways it was like putting a Formula One race car in the hands of a new driver.

Dalton had broken a mast on the way to Newport back in September. On each leg, he had experienced some sort of gear failure. Now, in his enthusiasm to keep pace with Stamm and Dubois, he went over the line again. About 750 miles from the Horn, *Hexagon*'s boom snapped during a gybe in high winds. He later said there had been nothing out of the ordinary in the manoeuvre.

Dalton took the usual steps to gybe the boat. He rolled up the jib and pulled the mainsail to the centre of the boat, which slowed the sixty-footer down and reduced the load on the sail and the spars. He switched off the autopilot so he could hand-steer through the gybe and picked the right moment in a wave trough, which provided shelter from the wind. He didn't realize right away that anything was amiss. There was no loud noise, but he noticed that the blocks at the end of the boom were sitting at an odd angle. He glanced along the bottom of the sail and saw that it was sitting strangely too. His boom was broken.

The boom had settled into a V-shape, with one end resting on the deck and the break in the middle pointing toward the sky. This made it hard to reduce the sail and move the boom enough to lash it down. Then the mainsail got stuck and didn't want to come down. It eventually did, but Dalton found it hard work to control hundreds of pounds of flapping material.

With the mainsail out of commission, Dalton sailed *Hexagon* hard under its big jib alone and the boat was soon moving at sixteen knots in forty knots of wind. He was still in third place.

Dalton made arrangements to meet his shore manager in Ushuaia, Argentina, just 100 miles north of Cape Horn and about three sailing days away. His ground crew would bring a carbon fibre sleeve, essentially a splint that could be riveted and glued onto the old boom.

About eight hours after Dalton's bad news, *Ocean Planet* was almost overwhelmed by a rogue wave while skipper Bruce Schwab was taking a nap. Schwab had been in a deep sleep and was so groggy on waking he realized too late by the boat's motion that the autopilot had lost control and his boat was headed for a crash gybe.

As soon as he understood what was happening, he scrambled out of the cabin, but before he could reach the tiller, the thirty-five-foot boom swung around and crashed into a runner, a wire rope that runs from the mast to the stern corner of the boat on each side. The force was so great that the boom snapped where it hit the runner. Where the runner went through a pulley on deck, the block exploded. A cleat was ripped out leaving, Schwab said, "a good sized hole." Several hours later he was still cleaning up the mess. He resumed under headsail alone and decided to put into the Falklands. It was his second broken boom of the race.

On *Hexagon*, things kept getting worse. On Day Fourteen, as Stamm was rounding the Horn, *Hexagon* was battling towards land in sixty- to seventy-knot winds from the north. The strength of the wind meant that *Hexagon* was fighting to stay upright and not be forced over on her side. If Dalton turned south that would put the wind more behind him and provide a more comfortable and safe ride. It would also send him to Antarctica. Without his mainsail he wouldn't be able to claw his way back north and make the rendezvous in Ushuaia.

He could only hope the front moved off quickly. Down below he could feel the boat shudder with each impact with the waves, and through the portholes, all he could see was whitewater. As the day wore on, the storm did not abate. Dalton had not been able to go on deck and worried that he had not securely lashed the broken boom to the deck. Still, he was not about to go out and check, realizing that the risk of being swept overboard was so high that it was not worth it.

During that night, the weather eased, which is always the most dangerous time. The wind dropped, and the boat slowed down and now lacked the power to drive through the enormous waves. But the adrenaline that had kept Dalton going for thirty-six hours was gone. With the wind a steady thirty-five knots, he fell into an exhausted sleep. Minutes later, his world turned topsy turvy. A breaking wave had rolled *Hexagon* on her side. Dalton hung briefly upside down before *Hexagon* slowly swung upright again and he was buried under a volley of loose equipment. The deep pockets that hang beside the navigation station emptied out and the bucket that was wedged deep into the sink came loose. He guessed that the boat had been just shy of a 180-degree roll. Dalton searched vainly for his glasses and a flashlight in the mess. He could find neither. He was afraid to look at the conditions on deck, fearing that would be even worse than in his cabin. But he had no choice. He found that the force of the rollover had torn the boom free of its lashings and broken it. A piece had swept down the deck like a battering ram and had smashed into one of *Hexagon*'s twin steering wheels. The impact drove the boom through the spokes, locking the wheel and preventing the autopilot from working. The good news was that the mast was still standing.

Dalton freed the boom and lashed it down again. Then another problem surfaced. A piece of rope had wrapped itself around his propeller. He was without a mainsail and now couldn't use his engine in the narrow Beagle Channel once he rounded the Horn. If the wind and current were against him, the potential for shipwreck was high.

Dalton exhibited enormous self-control in the face of these terrifying conditions. He was calm, resolute, and positive. He considered himself lucky in a strange way, because if the mainsail had been up when the wave hit, he would almost certainly have lost the mast.

The wind was still blowing at fifty-five knots as Dalton neared the Horn on February 25. He put up a staysail to slow *Hexagon* down as the boat was being driven perilously close to the shore of the island. He was unable to raise his shore crew on the radio to let them know he was in peril, but a Russian survey and passenger vessel heard his transmissions and acted as an intermediary. The ship relayed his coordinates to his shore crew and stood by *Hexagon* as the boat rounded the Horn. In the midst of this, the rope used to roll up his largest headsail broke. The sail unrolled and within minutes had lashed itself to shreds.

Simone Bianchetti passed the rock a few hours later, overtaking *Hexagon* although they did not pass within sight of one another. It was an emotional moment for Bianchetti as he reminded himself of the many boats that had tried and failed to do the same thing. He saw this moment as the closing of a door to the south. "[It is] a sign you have done a good job [and] brought your boat through safely." It was his second rounding, and just as thrilling as the first. "There are some things you never get used to," he said.

Dalton was not far away repairing his boom and later described in his log the terrifying sequence of events of the previous day. They had been, he said, the most dangerous he had faced in the race. Only his seamanship and cool head had saved his life.

Dalton finally got through to his shore crew just south of Navarino Island, about fifty miles northeast of the Horn. Twenty hours later he found a safe anchorage near the tip of the island of Tierra del Fuego. By then, Dalton was, he said, "exhausted, disorientated and staggering." He collapsed for a few hours then went straight at the repairs.

The boom was easy to fix by riveting a sleeve on to the two broken parts. The rope was removed from his propeller and his wheel repaired as best could be done under the conditions. He was back in the race within twenty-four hours.

Even with a broken boom, Bruce Schwab rounded the Horn the following day in fog, drizzle, rain, and hail. "I can't imagine what this place must be like in the winter," he said.

On February 27, after two weeks and four days, Emma Richards rounded for her second time, the first time alone. She described the experience as every bit as good as she imagined – better. Her final memory of the Southern Ocean was surfing on perfect waves in thirty-five-knot gusts of wind, with two reefs, at her highest speed yet – thirty-two knots. She opened her bottle of champagne and toasted her safe passage. The rain stopped, the wind died, the sea flattened out, and sun came through the clouds. It was a glorious moment.

Brad Van Liew's rounding – also his second – held none of this sense of wonder. He wanted to get out of the Southern Ocean in one piece and into the lee of South America. There, the wind would diminish, the sea would turn green again, the waves would moderate, and he could make good time up the coast. Four years ago on his first rounding, he had been wide-eyed and strung out. "My adrenaline meter was maxxed out and I was at full throttle absorbing it all," he says. This time it felt like a job.

He rounded on February 28, Day Nineteen of the leg, and didn't even see the rock. He was a few miles away, with squalls keeping him busy. Visibility was poor. He felt only relief.

Van Liew had been sailing quite close to *Pindar* and had encouraged Richards to sail a conservative leg. She had pushed *Pindar* as hard as she felt prudent and kept a more northerly course than the other 60s, refusing to take the bait when Stamm pushed south into the ice. Van Liew thought her caution wise and Stamm's tactic questionable. "I was surprised that Bernard dragged himself so far south," Van Liew says. "Anybody can do it. But the odds are that if all of us jump down to 60 degrees south somebody will whack a piece of ice. Luckily that didn't happen."

A year earlier Tim Kent had never sailed on an ocean. Now he was savouring the experience of a lifetime. On the night of March 2, Day Twenty-one of the leg, he had less than 100 miles to go. Like Moitessier before him, he felt a sense of inner peace, even though it was a squally night with gusts to forty knots. Just before midnight, the sky cleared and Kent sat on deck under the protection of his doghouse roof. He often did this, capturing the sights and sounds of the journey. He had seen conditions like that so often now they had become familiar.

The moon broke through the cloud and lit up the sky. Lines creaked and groaned, and he listened to the sound of the wake flowing by at fourteen knots, the rhythmic whine of the autopilot. A month ago he would have shuddered with fear. Now he contentedly watched the stars. "I sit and watch the miles roll away and ponder the idea of doing this again," he said.

At midmorning, as *Everest Horizontal* surfed down wave crests at twelve knots, there was the Horn, about six miles off his beam to the north, drenched in a sliver of sunshine. Kent felt that God had touched the sky so that the light could act like a beacon, guiding him safely on his way.

"These are hallowed waters," he said. "I feel honoured and lucky to be on a boat this safe, in weather this good, on an adventure this grand."

On March 3, after three weeks and a day at sea, Kojiro Shiraishi passed the Horn for his second time. He was pleased to be able to see it. The last time he was over ninety miles away.

On March 7, Day Twenty-six, Alan Paris in *BTC Velocity* rounded. The wind had been building all that day, gusting to fifty knots. The waves churned in the shallow waters and came at him from three different directions. He was knocked down twice, once while he was on deck, safety harness on, luckily, reducing his sail. It was blowing a good fifty knots. He heard a roar and all of sudden he was looking at the water

Paris was only 100 miles ahead of Derek Hatfield. Earlier, Hatfield had radioed the fleet to tell them that the hydraulics on his keel had failed. Paris worried about his friend and sent a message to race headquarters that he was going to slow down in case Hatfield ran into trouble.

"It just seems the right thing to do," Paris said.

14

Where Heroes Flourish

**"Courage is not the lack of fear.
It is acting in spite of it."**

– MARK TWAIN

AFTER THREE WEEKS and three days at sea, Derek Hatfield was still two days shy of Cape Horn. He had pushed harder, hand-steering longer and carrying more sail than was sensible, until exhaustion forced him to engage the autopilot. He had asked Brad Van Liew earlier in the race what it took to win. Van Liew's answer was to steer for an hour beyond the time when most other people would have given up. The misery would yield extra boat speed, because the human eye and hand can adjust that much faster than the best autopilot.

Throughout the previous week, Hatfield had become more anxious as *Spirit of Canada* had ambled along. The sea and the wind were no longer benign, but they were certainly not deadly or even as bad as they had been after Cape Town. It was only a matter of time and math. Small boats were slower and spent more time at sea. They were in harm's way the longest. "I'm just waiting for the hammer to drop," Hatfield said.

On March 5, like a space shuttle leaving orbit and descending to Earth, *Spirit of Canada* locked on to its course for Cape Horn. The boat was in the fast lane of the great Southern Ocean highway. It could neither slow down, nor pull over. To the left was the jagged, rocky coast of Chile. To the right, Antarctica. Behind, there was only current and huge seas. Straight ahead was the only way.

The weather fax showed a series of tight concentric circles centred more or less on top of Hatfield's position. The circles were pressure gradients, their tightness indicating that a violent storm was brewing. The map was filled with arrows, like a dartboard. Every arrow had four, maybe five feathers, each one representing ten knots of wind. The least he could expect was forty- to fifty-knot winds. Closer to the centre of the weather map were red triangles, beside the arrows. You don't see them very often on a weather map. "The little triangles, they're 55, 60," Hatfield says. "When you look at that, it gives you a chill."

This system was likely to peak in thirty-six hours, a weather bomb of near hurricane force winds. That day of indecision before turning back to New Zealand was costing him now. Had he turned around even twelve hours sooner, he would have rounded the Horn before this monster had time to strike.

It was too late for regrets, and Hatfield is not the sort to second-guess his decisions. He had made the call and that was that. Now he had to turn his full attention to what lay ahead. The forecast called for conditions to ease Thursday, build again Friday, and peak Saturday at sixty knots. By Saturday Hatfield hoped to be well beyond Cape Horn and in protected waters. As he hunched over his navigation station while whitewater broke over the dome, Hatfield realized that he couldn't have written a worse scenario. With a stoic sort of fatalism, he readied for the storm. "There's no other place to go, of course, so you forge ahead and hope for the best," he said.

By the late afternoon, the waves had built to twenty-foot swells and were rising. Driving rain mixed with hail pelted the boat, banging and clattering on the deck, stinging Hatfield's face. He donned goggles to protect his eyes. On land, the wind at this speed sets large trees swaying and sings through telephone wires. In the dense, damp Southern Ocean air, it makes an eerie shrieking sound.

Hatfield had been in this kind of weather many times during the last few months. A forty-knot wind was average in the Southern Ocean. So as the conditions deteriorated, he had time to go through his checklist. He lashed down everything on deck that could be tied and checked and rechecked it. In the cabin, he stowed containers of diesel and water, food, tools, utensils and other loose equipment. He reduced the mainsail until it was as small as it could get and ran up the small scrap of storm jib that *Spirit of Canada* carried to lend stability.

The boat's angle to the wind was creating problems even though the wind speed was manageable. A wind blowing from behind at fifty knots pushes a boat along at a speed of fifteen knots, but coming from an angle it packs the full fifty-knot punch. It tried to push the boat sideways as it swept up the swells.

As any sailor will tell you, it's not wind that's the worry but waves. A thirty-foot wave with a mile-long train is easy to handle – the boat rides up one side and down the other. A thirty-foot wave with a short cycle and breaking foam is another thing altogether. It crushes boats and kills sailors.

Late Wednesday afternoon Hatfield downloaded an updated forecast. It showed the system accelerating, not slowing down. It would overtake him in twenty-four to thirty-six hours – before he could get around the tip of South America. As he pondered this unhappy piece of news, he sensed that the boat was behaving sluggishly. He cast his eyes around the boat and saw a streak of orange move at the edge of his vision. The top of his keel was painted orange and it was visible through a glass plate. The keel shouldn't have been moving, since he had locked it at thirty-degree angle to the windward side of the boat to keep the boat flat in the water.

Hatfield unscrewed the plate to take a closer look. The keel was flopping back and forth like a pendulum. It shook the boat and he felt the vessel shudder as it was thrown from side to side. If this motion continued, the keel could rip a hole in the hull and send the boat to the bottom of the ocean.

The hydraulic system that moved the keel was shot. Hatfield had noticed a small leak a week after setting sail from New Zealand for the second time. He had kept going, because he was already so far behind. He had not been able to find the source of the leak and had been adding hydraulic fluid every day or two. He had long since run out of hydraulic fluid and now, hoping against hope, he filled the cylinder with diesel fuel, figuring it was not very flammable and might work. But, as soon as the slightest bit of pressure was applied, the fuel poured into the ocean. The cylinder was useless. Hatfield used lengths of his strongest line to lash the keel in the vertical position. It was all he could do for now.

That evening he called Patianne Verburgh in Halifax. They agreed he could not continue and after some debate agreed to meet in the Falkland Islands. It was more or less on the race route and unlike Ushuaia, Argentina, it was English-speaking. Verburgh would bring spare parts to fix the hydraulics.

By the early hours of Thursday, March 6, the wind was inching toward the mid-fifties. In a small corner of his mind, Hatfield started to doubt that he would get around Cape Horn safely. The storm was overtaking him with a wind and wave combination few experience. Fewer still live to describe it after an encounter in a boat his size.

That morning, the forecast was revised again. It called for sixty knots by late Thursday, gusting to eighty maybe overnight. Sixty knots is a Force I hurricane, eighty knots Force II. On land, there would be severe damage. At sea: visibility close to zero, the air thick with driving spray, waves crests blown into froth, the horizon lost from sight behind the swells.

Brad Van Liew had seen similar conditions in the same spot in 1988. The waves were deeper from trough to crest than the height of his seventy-five-foot mast. That's the height of a seven-story building. He says it was the most frightening of all his solo sailing experiences. He was afraid, not of the waves themselves, but because there was absolutely nothing he could do. The raw power of the sea made his enormous skills pathetically inadequate. "I had no idea how big the waves were, how strong the winds were, it was all off the meter," he says. "I had a little bunk, a cubbyhole down the back alley of the boat. I went in there and waited. I don't even like to think about it."

Hatfield was two hundred miles from the Horn, less than twenty hours from its protection. When a gust caught the boat at the wrong time at the top of a wave, the impact hurled the vessel sideways and it would hang for a moment. Inside the cabin, Hatfield's feet would leave the floor. When all seemed lost, the keel would bite, bringing the boat back up. Where other skippers might have trusted their boats to the autopilot, Hatfield felt he could do better steering by hand. If you can't rest, you might as well work, he reasoned. He was barely in control of *Spirit of Canada*, too busy steering to be afraid, or perhaps keeping busy to keep the fear at bay. "When you see a 50-foot wave with the top 10 feet breaking you really don't want to sleep," Hatfield says. "There's some fear factor there, believe me. It keeps you awake."

If he could get past the cape and turn northeast, putting the island between him and the conditions, he thought, the waves should be more manageable.

That evening the damaged keel forced Hatfield to slow down. Because he could not use it as a counterweight, he had to take down the mainsail completely. By midnight, the world had dissolved into sensory chaos – the unearthly moan of the wind, the deafening roar of waves, spray filling the air, driving rain that pounded, numbed, and stung. Nature was shaking with rage at the southern tip of South America.

Even so, *Spirit of Canada* was making nine knots an hour and surfing at twelve knots down the back of the waves. Hatfield was eighty miles from the Horn. The wind was a sustained sixty knots and it was all he could do to alter course slightly one way or the other. With the wind squarely behind him he was all right. Then it shifted slightly to one side and the impact overpowered him, pushing the stern sideways. The boat spun on its keel and tried to turn the bow into the wind, seeking the path of least resistance.

Part of the way through the turn, the boat lay at right angles to the sea and was at her most vulnerable. Each time it tried to right itself, she was knocked down time and time again. It took enormous physical strength for Hatfield to pull the tiller toward him, pushing the rudder in the opposite direction and turning the boat back on course. He lost count of how many times the boat was knocked over, how many times the mast touched the water. Each time, the thin strands of rope holding his keel in place creaked and groaned, but held firm.

The wind chill put the temperature close to 0 degrees Celsius (32 degrees Fahrenheit), and in the dark, visibility was only a few yards. There was nothing to see except shades of grey and black. The tops of the waves were blown sideways hard enough to blind the naked eye. Hatfield sat hunched on the port side of the cockpit with his back to the wind, feet braced on the lip on the other side, listening to the sound of water behind him.

The rogue waves were the ones to fear most. Unlike the others, they sounded like surf breaking on the shore. He had about fifteen seconds between hearing the sound, glancing back to judge its speed and size, and reacting. Like a surfer, he had to steer across its face. They rose like a wall, curled at the top, and fell with enormous force. He could only hope he was far enough ahead that when the top fifteen feet of the fifty-foot wave collapsed, it didn't break on top of his boat. "You have to try and avoid the curlers," Hatfield says. "They are the killers."

Spirit of Canada and its skipper had passed into the place where, as Derek Lundy says, heroes flourish. Hatfield was beyond the realm of his experience, engaged in a struggle for survival. He was sailing through the kind of weather that a racing sailor might experience once in a lifetime, and rarely when alone. The sole objective was to survive another minute, and then another, until the wind stopped howling and the waves diminished and the glow of dawn painted the sky pink once more.

As dawn broke on Friday, March 7, Hatfield saw a red light winking ahead to his right about two and a half miles away. He had been at the helm for almost twenty-four hours and was so exhausted he could barely think, so he was not able to comprehend immediately what his eyes were telling him. As the realization sank in, fear squeezed the breath from his lungs. He would later say this moment was the most terrifying in his life. "It still makes me shiver thinking about it," he says.

Hatfield knew he was looking at the glow of a lighthouse. But if this was the Horn, the lighthouse should be on his left, not his right. If it was the Horn, it meant he was driving towards assured destruction, for to the left there could only be the jagged shards of volcanic rock. Driven by hurricane force winds, he would be dead very quickly, joining the thousands of others who had perished here.

Hatfield wasn't sure what to believe. His eyes told him he was at the Horn and about to die. His instruments said he was sixty miles away. Which was right? He had figured his course would carry him well south of the cape. There was a chance that the wind had shifted and he had been driven closer to shore, but that would mean his instruments were wrong. Was that likely? For the past 100 days and 21,000 miles they had been bang on. On the other hand, everyone had problems in the south. Compasses don't work well, as the north magnetic pole is at the other end of the world. Mike Garside had been knocked down twenty times in twenty-four hours near this spot because his gyrocompass couldn't keep a correct course. An error of sixty-odd miles across thousands was nothing, except when it meant the difference between life and death. Hatfield was paralyzed.

"I looked at the light in disbelief," he says. "I didn't know which way to go. The seas are running 25 feet. It's blowing 50 to 60. I'm starting to panic, thinking over and over: How can there be a lighthouse there? Why is it there? I'm dead, if I'm going in behind and onto the rocks. I'm dead. The chance of me hitting the rocks, getting off the boat and up on to shore are basically nil to none."

Over the next fifteen to twenty minutes, the red circle of light drew closer as *Spirit of Canada* surfed barepoled towards its fate. The light transfixed Hatfield, and he wondered as the boat bore down whether these were his last minutes on earth. He tried to change course and sail towards the light in the hope that as he got closer, he would be able to see it more clearly and manoeuvre around it. But try as he might, he couldn't do it. The wind and wave combination was such that as he altered his course the waves threatened to capsize his boat. When collision seemed certain, the light slid by and receded into the night. He was still alive.

Hatfield switched on the autopilot, ducked below, and for the first time in thirty hours looked at his charts. The answer was immediately obvious. He had passed the Diego Ramirez Islands, a small chain of rocky outcrops, exactly where his instruments said they were, thirty miles west of the Horn. His indecision had saved his life.

15

Hatfield's Hurricane

**"Below 40 degrees south, there is no law;
below 50 degrees south, there is no God."**

– SAILOR'S PROVERB

HATFIELD FELT MORE tired than he believed possible. His confusing and frightening approach to the lighthouse had drained the last reserves of adrenaline. He could either give up, set the autopilot, and wait for whatever was going to come, or he could keep steering. He decided to steer.

For the next ten hours, Hatfield's luck held and his skill prevailed. Sitting with his back to the wind, flinching from the impact of hail that stung like buckshot, he listened for the sound of a breaking wave above the roar of the wind. It was a breaker that had nailed John Hughes in 1987 and probably swept Gerry Roufs overboard in 1996. Sometime around midday he passed the Horn, though he couldn't see it. He turned *Spirit of Canada* northeast, hoping that the lee of the islands would afford him some protection from the elements. But, even in these more sheltered waters, the seas were still horrendous.

Alan Paris had rounded the Horn at about eight-thirty p.m. the previous evening in weather that was bad and getting worse. Still, the winds were manageable and he took the time to call and wish his friend luck. Paris had made a similar call, all those months ago on a June afternoon, as Hatfield set off down Lake Ontario. Paris knew about Hatfield's keel and was worried about his safety. His was the only boat close enough to mount a rescue, and so he had slowed down.

By early afternoon Friday, Hatfield figured he might just make it. He was thirty miles past the Horn but, ominously, the wind continued to pick up. Desperately tired and hungry, Hatfield snuck below to warm up and swallow a can of Boost. The high-energy drink had been his sole source of nourishment for almost two days. Then he turned on the Yanmar diesel engine to charge his batteries. His alternator had been giving him trouble, possibly because it was getting wet. Mindful of the circumstances that had sent him back to New Zealand, Hatfield wanted to make sure he had plenty of electricity. He let the engine run.

After just a few minutes below, Hatfield went back on deck. He had just sat down and hadn't even clipped on his safety harness when he glanced over his shoulder and heard, then saw, a wall of water coming at him. It was topped with ten feet of curling white foam. As Hatfield watched it overtake him, he thought that being killed by this wave would be a pity, because it wasn't as big as some of the others he'd seen earlier. "It was just pure bad luck," he says. "When I heard the wave I knew I was in trouble. The front was pure vertical. And the noise. It was deafening."

Hatfield had no time to react as the stern was lifted, the bow pushed straight down and for a moment, the boat stood on its nose.

The tiller was ripped from his hand and he was thrown headlong into the doghouse roof. Then he hit the lip as the boat moved past vertical and rolled on its side, throwing him to the starboard side of the boat. He grabbed a lifeline.

The rollover seemed to take forever, even though the event from impact to recovery lasted only twenty seconds. It was so rapid he didn't have time to take a breath. The boat hung for a moment, frozen, graceful. Then it dove back into the water, the bow splitting the sea, twisting and rolling. Then *Spirit of Canada* fell on top of him. He could see nothing, only hear the rush of water, followed by the muffled sound of explosions. The mast, made from some of the strongest materials known to man, had disintegrated. Hatfield clutched his lifeline, suspended in the cold, dark liquid and felt nothing as his boat broke up all around him. The sounds were unbelievable, he said later: a gurgling followed almost immediately by a blast, muted by the enveloping green water.

Just as quickly as it dove, the boat sprang upright, rocking wildly back and forth without its stabilizing mast. Hatfield lay there, stunned. Slowly the sounds of the storm returned, the keening wind, the awful whistling rush of the waves. He was in shock and his mind struggled to engage. A terrible thing had happened, but as he lay among crushed stanchions and twisted, knotted ropes that's all he knew. In front of him the mast was leaning drunkenly over the side of the boat.

Had Hatfield been below, he would almost certainly have been seriously injured. Everything that wasn't bolted down became a lethal projectile: fire extinguishers, cans of fuel, hammers, screwdrivers, pots, pans, cutlery, the Honda generator, the anchor, anchor chain, rope, bolt cutters. Objects that were bolted down were ripped away. The seat in front of the navigation station had smashed into the cabin top, even though it was secured with two-inch screws. But Derek Hatfield was unhurt.

The boat wallowed and another rollover seemed likely. Hatfield knew he must do something. Even a small piece of the mast could punch a hole in the hull, sending the boat to the bottom. He willed himself to move. He had to, otherwise he would die.

He crept forward on hands and knees to take a look at the damage. There was only one piece of the mast left, a ten-foot chunk attached to the mast step. The forehatch had gone, had been torn away, and water had filled the hold. Stanchions all along the port and starboard side were crushed, but otherwise the boat seemed okay. The first thing he had to do, he knew, was to cut the rig away, to get rid of what remained of the mast before it battered a hole in the hull. He was less worried about the hatch. Even though water was filling the compartment, that alone could not sink the boat. He had to find bolt cutters.

He opened the hatch and a cloud of acrid smoke billowed out. Water and flying equipment had smashed into the navigation station, starting electrical fires. In the haze, Hatfield could barely breathe. He was shocked by the damage but then realized he could hear the sound of the diesel engine still chugging away. He broke the seal and engaged the engine in forward. He had manoeuvring power at least, some ability to turn the boat more head-on to the waves, reducing the likelihood of another rollover. The little 18-hp Yanmar engine that he had started just before the rollover continued to run all that day and the next, until it was shut off Saturday at midnight.

It was time to tell the world what had happened. Important telephone numbers were written on the coach top above the now ruined navigation station. The first number to call is manned twenty-four hours a day in Southampton, England. When that phone rings it says that the person on the other end is facing life-threatening peril. Hatfield could not reach the number. He's not sure whether he dialled it correctly in his confusion. He called Patianne's cellphone, a number he knew by heart.

At 11:45 a.m. local time that Friday, Patianne Verburgh was in a desperate hurry to make her connecting flight, dashing through the terminal at Hartsfield-Jackson International Airport in Atlanta. Her plane from Toronto had touched down on time and she had just twenty minutes to make the connecting flight to Santiago, Chile. Verburgh was on her way to the Falkland Islands, carrying the spare parts for *Spirit of Canada*'s keel hydraulics. Just hours after talking to Hatfield on Wednesday, she had booked a flight to Toronto from Halifax. Thursday evening she had the parts. Friday morning found her en route to South America.

As she shouldered her bags and headed to the departure area, her cellphone rang. A disembodied voice could be heard over the wind and water. "It was hard to hear because of the noise, but I knew right away it was Derek," Verburgh said. "He said: 'The worst thing has happened. I have been dismasted.'"

16

Survival

**"You gain strength by every experience
in which you look fear in the face. You must
do the thing you think you cannot do."**

– ELEANOR ROOSEVELT

BEFORE SHE TOOK up sailing Patianne Verburgh had been a paramedic. She had arrived at the immediate aftermath of innumerable car accidents and fires and seen first-hand the wounds people inflict on each other on purpose or by accident. Now she stood transfixed in Hartsfield Airport, listening to Derek Hatfield in the middle of his hurricane.

She could tell a lot about Hatfield's physical state by his mental state. He was lucid, not slurring his words or babbling. He seemed to grasp what had happened and be able to make decisions. She peppered him with questions, keeping him focused on the small details of survival. What do you see? What do you hear? How do you feel? What should you do first?

"I heard a man trying to hear himself speak above the noise all around him," she says. "He didn't sound panicked, he didn't sound irrational, he didn't sound like he was in shock. Very methodically we went through what had to be done."

The conversation was short because Hatfield could not charge his phone. Once the battery died he would be unable to contact the outside world. Every other piece of communications equipment on board was a smouldering ruin.

Verburgh hung up and made two calls in quick succession. She left a message for a travel agent with instructions to change her flight. She would not be flying to the Falklands after all. She needed to get to Ushuaia, the most southerly city in the world, where Hatfield was heading. The other call was to the emergency number Hatfield had failed to reach. Then she hoisted her bag and ran to catch her plane.

Halfway round the world in Southampton, England, it was 4:53 p.m. local time. In the office of Clipper Ventures, the company that runs the Around Alone race, a cellphone rang. The phone had been switched on for all 173 days of the race, but this was the first time it had rung. A man answered it, listened quietly, thanked Patianne, and hung up.

He went to another phone and called Sir Robin Knox-Johnston, chairman of Clipper Ventures, to let him know what had happened. His second call was to Salvador, Brazil, where Kelly Gilkison was preparing to welcome Bernard Stamm and Thierry Dubois who were about to finish the fourth leg of the race.

Gilkison acted as part race organizer, part fixer, part crisis manager, and sometimes all three. In an emergency, her job is to decide what needs to be done and then pull out the stops to make it happen. She had a quick conversation with Verburgh and for the next hour tried, without success, to reach Hatfield. As a precaution Clipper Ventures called Maritime Rescue-Co-ordination Centre (MRCC) in Falmouth, Cornwall, and alerted them to the dismasting. MRCC Falmouth is the international co-ordinator for maritime accidents and it would fall to them to organize a rescue through the Chilean or Argentine coastguard.

Around Alone boats carry two pieces of equipment that enable race officials and rescue services to keep track of them. One is a transponder, a simple tracking device similar to the units dropped in the ocean to track sea turtles. It transmits a continuous signal, allowing race officials to pinpoint its latitude and longitude and track each boat's progress. The information is updated three times a day and copied to the race map, which is posted on the Around Alone Web site.

The second piece of equipment is an emergency position indicating radio beacon (EPIRB), a small transmitter that sends out distress signals as digitally encoded bursts of information about the vessel's identity, location, and nature of the alarm, via satellite to MRCC Falmouth. Most recreational sailors who venture off shore carry EPIRBs.

The Around Alone fleet had the most sophisticated type of EPIRB unit, which operates on a radio frequency of 406 MHz, which means that a satellite receives the signal and stores it if it is out of range of a ground station. It later retransmits the signal. As well, the satellite can locate the boat within a few hundred yards.

Hatfield had two EPIRBs. One was attached to the boat and would automatically engage if immersed in water, indicating the boat was sinking or in serious trouble. The other unit was manual and could be triggered if the first one failed or if he was forced to

abandon ship and get into a life raft. Neither of the EPIRBs had been
triggered, which was a good sign. But in a precautionary step, race
officials started hourly polling of his transponder. Gilkison couldn't
reach Hatfield because he was stabilizing the boat. After Patianne
Verburgh hung up, he set to work cutting away his broken mast. In
the chaos below decks, Hatfield had been unable to find the bolt
cutters carried on board for just this purpose, so he did the job with
a pair of needle-nose pliers and a hammer, the only tools he could
find. It took him forty-five minutes to pull the pins that held the
rod rigging to the deck, cut away the tangled ropes, and let the
stump and sails sink to the bottom of the sea.

All the while, the storm was at its worst and Kelly Gilkison was
trying to reach him. It took her an hour.

"He was running on adrenaline," Gilkison says. "I just let him
know he wasn't alone."

As Verburgh and Gilkison worked to help get Hatfield to shore,
about 100 miles to his south, in the teeth of the same hurricane,
Peregrine Mariner was slowly moving north in an effort to come to
his aid. The 383-foot steel-hulled Russian scientific research vessel
was returning from Antarctica with 100 passengers on board. The
weather was so bad the best speed the ship could make was a little
more than four and a half knots an hour.

The boat was under charter to Peregrine Adventures, an
Australian travel firm, and the man who leads *Peregrine*'s Antarctic
cruises is an engaging Nova Scotian named Andrew Prossin, a friend
of Hatfield's. The thirty-five-year-old Prossin is as hooked on polar
expeditions as he is on sailing. He has rounded the Horn sixty

times and has spent the equivalent of a year of the past ten sailing between Cape Horn and Antarctica. As Hatfield was expected to round the Horn at about the same time *Peregrine Mariner* was returning to Ushuaia from a ten-day Antarctic trip, the two men had planned to rendezvous at the Horn and for Prossin to film Hatfield's rounding.

Prossin had been in regular phone contact with Hatfield for the better part of two days. On Wednesday afternoon, *Peregrine Mariner* was anchored off the Antarctic Peninsula. When the weather worsened, Prossin called Hatfield that evening to see if they would still be able to meet. Hatfield said he hoped they would be able to, and told Prossin about the problem with his keel. Prossin could hear the banging down the phone and it concerned him. "I thought, it's only a matter of time before it bangs too hard and something cracks," he said.

Prossin loves the beauty of Antarctica and enjoys sharing it with his visitors. His experience in that part of the world made him Hatfield's unofficial Cape Horn adviser. Prossin knows that the Drake Passage in early March can be a lion or a lamb. It is the end of the short Antarctic summer, the equivalent of late August in the Northern Hemisphere. But the Southern Ocean doesn't obey the seasons. Some days are sunny and some days less windy, but it is always blowing and a large swell is always running. On warm days, the temperature will be a couple of degree above freezing, with snow catching in the crevices on deck. "What can I say?" Prossin says with a shrug. "It's the Furious Fifties. It just doesn't compare to anywhere else, so it's almost pointless to try."

Andrew Prossin planned
to rendezvous with *Spirit
of Canada* as it rounded
Cape Horn.
(Andrew Prossin)

Ships like *Peregrine Mariner* are engineered to withstand the conditions they face in those waters. As much as any ship is, they are unsinkable. But when a bigger than average storm blows through the Drake Passage, even *Peregrine Mariner*'s skipper must be careful. Prossin tells a story, which is a reminder of what can happen. During a late summer storm in 2002, with the wind blowing seventy to seventy-five knots and waves as tall as a six-story building, a nasty wave struck the bridge deck of a passenger ship. It was the highest deck on the ship, about fifty feet above the water level. The impact blew out windows on the bridge, where the steering is located. Many instruments were shorted out, and the boat limped back to Ushuaia controlled by an officer who stayed on the bridge and phoned instructions to the engine room where the course was altered manually.

Prossin's ship and others were on standby in case they needed to assist the stricken vessel. When they got on board, they found that a number of passengers had been injured. They had been

Peregrine Mariner's radio antenna is seventy feet high, and the waves
in this photograph are about the same height. *(Gordon Crowe)*

thrown across their cabins from the motion. The steel on bridge
deck was battered, as if a wrecking ball had been swung repeatedly
at the bridge.

Prossin had been plotting *Spirit of Canada*'s position from the
moment he learned Hatfield's keel was broken. The two men
talked frequently, and during each conversation Hatfield reported
his latitude and longitude. By early Thursday evening, about
twenty-four hours after the first call, *Peregrine Mariner* was plough-
ing through heavy seas in the Drake Passage. The wind was blowing
at fifty knots and the waves were building. As it passed through the

eye of the storm, wind and waves dropped a bit and a patchy sun came out. The boat was about to be belted by the back edge of the hurricane. Hatfield was farther to the west and was already facing those conditions.

On Thursday and early Friday, Prossin called Hatfield several times, asking about the conditions, about how the keel was holding up, and they discussed whether Hatfield should aim for Stanley in the Falkland Islands or put into Ushuaia. By midday Friday, the wind was so fierce, *Peregrine Mariner* was making little headway. Whenever the bow went into a trough, the top of the wave was parallel to the bridge deck, a distance of seventy feet. That afternoon a garbage container made from an oil drum lashed to a railing was crushed like a pop can.

A little after three p.m. Friday, after Hatfield had cut away his rig and spoken to Kelly Gilkison, he called Prossin. Hatfield believed *Peregrine Mariner* was much closer than it was and wanted the reassurance that the boat was standing by. He assured Prossin that he was still in control of his boat and was not prepared to abandon ship, even though he'd lost his mast. His engine was running and he was heading towards Ushuaia, about 100 miles to the north up the Beagle Channel. Hatfield knew that if he allowed himself to be rescued, his race would be over, and he was too stubborn, or foolish, to accept that, not after what he had been through. He told Prossin that he would struggle on, but agreed to drag his life raft into the cockpit, in case it was needed.

Prossin was afraid for his friend. He could see for himself how dreadful the waves were — unimaginably hard to navigate for a person in a small boat. It was a miracle Hatfield was alive, but how long could he hang on in these conditions? Still, until Hatfield issued a "mayday," the universal distress call, there was nothing Prossin could do but wait.

This oil drum, used as a garbage can
on a mid-level deck aboard *Peregrine
Mariner*, was crushed by waves
breaking over the stern.
(Gordon Crowe)

He consulted with the ship's captain, Leonid Sazonov, and
Adrian Trus, a friend of Prossin's who worked for Peregrine as a
tour guide. Trus, who lived in Toronto and was a member of
Ashbridge's Bay Yacht Club, also knew Hatfield, having sailed with
him and helped build *Spirit of Canada*.

The question was whether the ship should make all haste to
Hatfield's position or wait for the seas to moderate. Sazonov offered
a sobering piece of advice. He said he could make good speed, but
that if he turned the boat to go north, the ship would be taking
sixty-foot waves on its beam. He told Prossin that the force "would
break windows, break equipment and hurt people."

Prossin again called Hatfield and learned that *Spirit of Canada*
was now moving slowly north towards the Beagle Channel. Hatfield
said he was managing, but didn't tell Prossin the boat's fore hatch
had been ripped away and that a quarter of the boat was flooded.
"If I had known that hatch was gone we would have gone to him
immediately," Prossin said.

He met again with the captain, and they decided that if Hatfield issued a mayday, or abandoned ship, *Peregrine Mariner* would move at full speed toward him. In the meantime, the ship would continue to proceed cautiously.

Prossin told Hatfield the news. "We'll get to you as quick as we can," he said.

For the rest of Friday night and into the early hours of Saturday the storm continued unabated as Hatfield inched his way north to the mouth of the Beagle Channel. There, he would find some protection from the wind. The rollover had broken the lashing that kept his keel vertical, and it was flopping side to side, making the boat difficult to steer through the steep waves. Each lurch made Hatfield's stomach churn. What was going on under the hull? Was the damage getting worse? Was the hull cracking? Was the boat about to sink?

Hatfield says those hours standing in the cockpit and steering as the small diesel engine pulled the boat to safety, were the most tiring part of his ordeal. The waves were striking broadside, trying to flip the boat over. "It was unnerving," he says. "But what could I do? You just sit in the cockpit and steer."

Hatfield had been running on empty for so long now, he had entered another realm. He was in the mental place where marathon runners float in the last portions of their races, outside of themselves, watching themselves run. The young French sailor Raphaël Dinelli described a similar experience when he capsized and was dismasted in the 1996 Vendée Globe, the race that killed Gerry Roufs.

Dinelli described the creeping lethargy that settled over him as he stood on the upturned hull of his boat for almost twenty-four hours in near-freezing conditions. At first, he felt a deep sense of injustice that he should die like this. Then he noticed that he was no longer in his own body, he was outside himself and moving down some steps. He knew that, at the bottom, lay death. He observed this dispassionately as he felt himself, he says, "pass the first threshold of descent." He was continuing down, now quite prepared to die, when a race rival, Pete Goss, rescued him. Goss had sailed 160 miles upwind in the teeth of a hurricane to get to Dinelli. At some points in this mad dash, Goss had believed his own death was imminent. French President Jacques Chirac later awarded Goss the Légion d'honneur for his feat.

Friday night, Hatfield alternately steered and pumped out the forward compartment while he plodded north towards the shelter of the Beagle Channel. By midnight his radio phone was dead. He had no means of contacting the outside world, but race officials were polling his boat hourly. They were reassured to find that *Spirit of Canada* was moving slowly in the right direction.

By three a.m. the wind and waves had abated enough for *Peregrine Mariner* to make all speed towards Hatfield at fifteen knots. Shortly after dawn, as Hatfield sat slumped in the cockpit, nearly catatonic from exhaustion, he heard a whir and click. It was his autopilot trying to engage. He believes the engine's regulator, which feeds current to the alternator, had finally dried out and was able to send a charge. Hatfield steered the boat to the middle of the channel, about a mile wide at that point, and turned the autopilot on. He figured he could manage a short nap. He doesn't remember another thing until the persistent ring of a depth alarm penetrated his consciousness. He had been asleep for three hours and the channel had narrowed around him. If he'd slept through the alarm, his boat would have been wrecked on Navarino Island.

"It's quite unbelievable," he says. "Land was 100 yards away. It was just good luck. That's the way I am. I don't have a lot of bad luck but I have lots of good luck."

In the Beagle Channel, the conditions were nearly perfect. The seas were slight, the sun shining from a cloudless sky and an air temperature of 15 degrees Celsius (60 degrees Fahrenheit). It was a beautiful day. On board *Peregrine Mariner* all eyes were peeled for the first glimpse of Hatfield. Adrian Trus missed the moment because he was packing a rigid inflatable boat with supplies. It had been decided that Trus would be put on board *Spirit of Canada* to guide the boat into Ushuaia. *Peregrine Mariner* was heading there to unload its passengers in time for connecting flights. It was running late.

Trus is a good-natured, barrel-chested man in his early forties. He knew Hatfield well, having spent many a summer night banging around the race buoys near Toronto with him. As he passed the bar on the main deck of *Peregrine Mariner*, he snagged a six-pack of Guinness, figuring his friend might well need a drink. The other supplies he was packing included diesel fuel, two VHF radios, a spare engine battery and another battery for Hatfield's Iridium phone, a flashlight, sleeping bag, boots, dry clothes, food, water, and other provisions.

Peregrine Mariner caught up to Hatfield at midday and dropped anchor about a mile away. The inflatable was lowered and Trus,

When Andrew Prossin caught up with Derek Hatfield twenty-four
hours after *Spirit of Canada* rolled over, the sea was dead calm.
(Andrew Prossin)

Prossin, and Aaron Lawton, another Torontonian and tour guide,
climbed on board. Within a few minutes they were astern *Spirit of
Canada* and could see Hatfield standing in the cockpit.

"Are you ready for this?" Trus said.

That's when it hit Prossin that what they were about to see was
a man well past his limits. The hair on his neck stood up.

Hatfield's shoulders were slumped and he just stared at the
inflatable as it drew closer. Then he raised his arms, with the palms
of his hands turned up, as if to say: What the hell. Can you believe
this? There was something about his eyes too, Prossin says. They
had the look of someone who, like Dinelli, had walked down the
stairs and almost reached the bottom. But somehow Hatfield had
managed to climb back up again and having done so felt the simple
wonder of being alive.

"When you think about it, it's unbelievable," Prossin says. "This is a guy whose number was up and somebody threw him back. If you're in a boat that rolls and you're not tethered, basically that's it."

As Adrian Trus loaded the supplies on board, a Chilean gunboat arrived. The border between Chile and Argentina in this area is still disputed, and both nations patrol the waterways. The reunion was cut short. *Peregrine* had an Argentine pilot on board to help navigate the channel, but Hatfield had strayed to the Chilean side. The gunboat demanded that *Peregrine* return to the Argentine side or hire a Chilean pilot. *Peregrine* beat a hasty retreat.

Trus took control of *Spirit of Canada* and headed her towards Ushuaia, still forty miles or about eight hours away. Hatfield was silent, wandering aimlessly around the boat and looking at things. Trus gave him dry clothes, put the autopilot on, and went below to clean up.

The cabin was like a storm sewer after a heavy rain. The floor was six inches deep with fuel and salt water, mixed with packages of dried food that had split open and rehydrated. Cutlery, tools, and broken equipment were underfoot everywhere. Trus pumped it out as best he could and went back on deck. It was a beautiful day, not a cloud in sight. Just two old pals motoring along. Hatfield had stopped roaming and now sat silently. Trus sneaked glances at him, wondering whether his friend had lost his mind. He had never seen Hatfield so uncommunicative, so distant, so lost inside his own thoughts. After a while, Trus offered Hatfield a beer. And then another. That seemed to revive him. They got the charts out and plotted their course and time to Ushuaia. Hatfield started talking about what had happened, little pieces of the story, punctuated by silences. "He knew he was lucky to be alive," Trus says. "He knew it was an act of God that he was alive. What else can you say?"

After the second beer, Hatfield called his parents to tell them he was fine. Then he began talking about repairing the boat, buying a new mast, and getting back in the race. Just after midnight Saturday, *Spirit of Canada* tied up at the dock in Ushuaia, alongside *Peregrine Mariner*. By then Hatfield was a different man. The thousand-yard stare was gone. Trus's company, the cold beer, his parents' voices, the rescue by his friend. They had reknit the threads of his life.

Patianne Verburgh embraced Hatfield at the dock. "It was like visiting someone in hospital after a car accident," she says. "You see they only have a broken arm and you think, that wasn't so bad. Then you see the car and you wonder: Oh my God, how did they survive?"

Gordon Crowe, a Toronto sailor and management consultant, was also there at the dock. Crowe and his wife, Margaret, a psychiatrist, were passengers on *Peregrine Mariner*. He clasped Hatfield in a big hug and as an afterthought reached into his wallet and pulled out a fistful of cash. It was about a thousand dollars in American bills, which he stuffed into Hatfield's pocket.

"I didn't need it," Crowe says later. "I was going home."

17

To Brazil

**"Courage is rarely reckless or foolish. . . .
Courage usually involves a realistic estimate
of the odds that must be faced."**

– MARGARET TRUMAN

~~~~~~~~~~~~~~~~~~~~~~~~~~

As DEREK HATFIELD stepped ashore in Ushuaia, the rest of the
fleet was moving north to Salvador, Brazil, in a three-thousand-
mile sprint up the coast of South America in steadily improving
conditions.

Bernard Stamm and Bruce Schwab made first for the Falkland
Islands, which left Thierry Dubois in the lead. He chose to pass to
the south of the Falklands and then turn north. This gave him
several hundred more miles of sea room. Brad Van Liew chose the
same route, even though passing through the Strait of Le Maire to
the west of the Falklands and passing to the north of the islands was
a shorter and more direct route to Salvador. A large storm was
approaching and Van Liew thought it more prudent to sail east
to get out of the worst of it, but catch enough of the system to

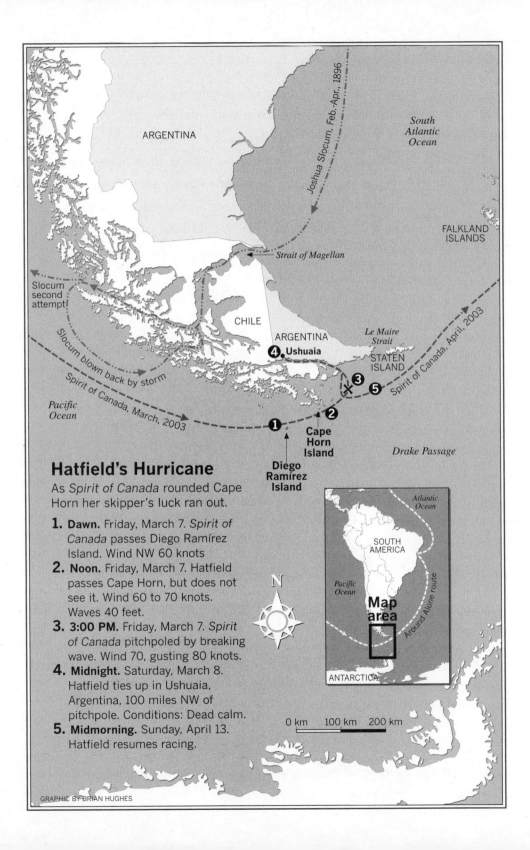

ARGENTINA

Joshua Slocum, Feb.-Apr., 1896

South Atlantic Ocean

Strait of Magellan

FALKLAND ISLANDS

Slocum second attempt

Slocum blown back by storm

CHILE

ARGENTINA

Spirit of Canada, April, 2003

Le Maire Strait

4 **Ushuaia**

STATEN ISLAND

3

5

Spirit of Canada, March, 2003

Pacific Ocean

1

2

Cape Horn Island

Drake Passage

Diego Ramírez Island

Hatfield's Hurricane

As *Spirit of Canada* rounded Cape Horn her skipper's luck ran out.

1. Dawn. Friday, March 7. *Spirit of Canada* passes Diego Ramírez Island. Wind NW 60 knots

2. Noon. Friday, March 7. Hatfield passes Cape Horn, but does not see it. Wind 60 to 70 knots. Waves 40 feet.

3. 3:00 PM. Friday, March 7. *Spirit of Canada* pitchpoled by breaking wave. Wind 70, gusting 80 knots.

4. Midnight. Saturday, March 8. Hatfield ties up in Ushuaia, Argentina, 100 miles NW of pitchpole. Conditions: Dead calm.

5. Midmorning. Sunday, April 13. Hatfield resumes racing.

N

Atlantic Ocean

SOUTH AMERICA

Pacific Ocean

Map area

Around Alone route

ANTARCTICA

0 km   100 km   200 km

GRAPHIC BY BRIAN HUGHES

give him a lift. "The shorter route was simply not possible," he says.

Before making his decision, Bianchetti carefully considered the two options. Choosing the outside route meant he could expect consistent winds, though they would be weaker than near shore. The inside passage between the Argentine coast and Staten Island was shorter and windier. *Tiscali*, *Pindar*, and *Hexagon*, chose to go through the strait, gambling that they would have plenty of time before the bad weather hit. Tim Kent and Kojiro Shiraishi also chose to sail up through the strait.

The day after his Cape Horn rounding, Bernard Stamm was sailing his wounded boat at eight knots towards the Falklands. The wind had diminished, but he had still managed to cover 234 miles in the twenty-four hours since his keel cracked. His shore crew noted dryly, "For a boat using only 20 per cent of her potential this is rather encouraging."

Stamm had approached the Horn feeling calm and confident. He had a good lead over *Solidaires* and, he says, "Everything was going well." He was preparing to celebrate and toast to the wind gods and Neptune, when at a speed of thirty knots, the boat was laid on her beam. For a moment *Bobst Group* was airborne, then she slammed into the trough of the wave. Stamm heard what he called "that dreaded noise," a forewarning of serious problems.

He went on deck and took down all his sail. *Bobst Group* righted herself but was still swept along by the winds, even though the boat was barepoled. Stamm inspected the keel well, and found the same problem with his keel as Hatfield had. He bound it with rope which he then winched tight to hold the keel firm.

By the evening of February 25, Stamm was tied up in Stanley

Harbour. There, two stainless steel plates were attached to pieces of wood on either side of the keel housing and bolted through to provide stiffness and support. Just eighteen hours after he arrived, at midday on Day Seventeen of the leg, he was back at sea. He had incurred a forty-eight-hour penalty for stopping and was 220 miles behind Dubois so he was determined to get going as soon as he could. Even his shore crew urged him to slow down. "We told Bernard that he needs to be careful and take it easy on the boat," Benoît Lequin said later. "But he is not the kind of person to listen. He is all about speed. Only speed. Sailing faster than anybody else."

Stamm set off in chase of Dubois, who was paying the price for choosing to sail south of the Falklands. The weather map showed a confusing pattern of pressure systems on his path to Salvador, "full of potholes," as Dubois put it. This was normal for the transition between the Southern Ocean and the South Atlantic High, but it meant that Dubois's lead was not a sure thing. He joked at one point that, based on the wind direction, "the best route to Salvador is to cut across land."

Graham Dalton finished his repairs on Tierra del Fuego the day after Stamm had finished his. Then, three days later, on March 1, misfortune struck Dalton again.

The day was not out of the ordinary, just another cold, blustery early fall day. Dalton was about six hundred miles north of the Horn and about two hundred miles offshore. He was down below at his navigation station considering his tactical options. A front was coming through from the west and the wind was blowing thirty-five knots and the sea was building. Without warning, *Hexagon* lurched. The ninety-five-foot mast buckled and crashed onto the deck, breaking into three pieces and ending up leaning over the starboard side. Dalton was stunned by this latest disaster. Then the boat rolled in a swell and the mast broke into a fourth piece.

From the deck, Dalton could see that pieces were thumping against the hull. His first thought was to save the biggest piece and use it to make a jury rig to get to the nearest Argentine port. He winched it on deck, tied it down, and went below to call race headquarters. While he was on the phone, a wave broke over the boat with such force that it snapped the ropes holding the mast and the broken piece started thrashing. Dalton climbed back on deck, but the conditions were so dangerous he immediately retreated, closing all hatches and each of *Hexagon*'s watertight compartments. Now, if the boat was holed, only one section would flood, and this would stop the boat from sinking. But, as a precaution, he got all of his safety equipment out so it would be ready to deploy. He sat for hours listening to the mast bang against his hull.

Brad Van Liew was the nearest sailor, about 170 miles to the south and east, ten to fifteen hours away in these conditions. He was told by race headquarters to make for Dalton's position, just in case. At first, he found the sailing fast and relatively easy, but as the front that had hit Dalton caught up to Van Liew, the wind shifted, carrying fifty-knot gusts that rocked *Tommy Hilfiger*. Van Liew says he "had the hammer down" because he didn't know what was going on. All he knew was that Dalton had not cut away his rig, a decision Van Liew believed to be unwise. "You only have to punch one four-inch hole in the boat and you can't keep up with the water coming in," he says.

Seven hours of hard sailing closed the gap by half. By then, Dalton had cut away the mast and the danger that *Hexagon* would sink was over. Van Liew was called off. Dalton proceeded under engine power to a rendezvous with a fishing boat sent from

Mar del Plata, Argentina by his shore crew. At the expected time, he spotted a boat and made radio contact. But it was not the boat that was supposed to meet him; it was a Uruguayan fishing boat. The captain offered Dalton fuel and dropped a line on a buoy off his stern. It floated down to *Hexagon* and Dalton attached it. Because the rope was long, he put *Hexagon*'s motor in reverse to increase his distance from the fishing boat. The line went taut, snapped, and before Dalton could react, snaked itself around his propeller. The Uruguayan boat hauled *Hexagon* alongside. Dalton refuelled *Hexagon*, and a diver unsuccessfully tried to remove the rope. After nightfall, the fishing boat departed. Dalton was left with full fuel tanks but a useless engine. He did try to remove the fouled line himself and drifted all that night through a squid fishing fleet.

The next day, March 6, the Argentine coastguard put *Hexagon* on tow and headed for Puerto Madryn. Dalton decided to stay on board *Hexagon*, and several hours into the trip he heard a noise coming from the box protecting the keel. He took a look and was alarmed to see that the pin securing the pivoting keel to the ram had come loose. He reattached it and wondered at the role fate plays in life. Had he not stayed on *Hexagon* and had the pin fallen out, who knows what damage might have been done. Dalton tried to remain positive. "I am still not beaten," he said.

The rest of the fleet struggled up the South Atlantic in a hard, tedious slog, which seemed even slower after the pace they'd set in the Southern Ocean. It was getting hotter, the days were longer, sunnier, and sweatier. On March 5, a week after his Falkland Islands repair, Stamm had whittled Dubois's lead to sixty-five miles. On March 9, the fourth week at sea, Stamm passed his rival. The next day he sailed into Salvador, four hours ahead of Dubois. He was first to cross the finish line, but because of his Falklands stopover, he came second on adjusted time. It was another spectacular performance by a skipper who had amazed everyone with his courage, his daring, and his sailing skills.

Dubois was angry and frustrated at being beaten for the fourth time. It was particularly galling this time because Stamm had beaten him after spending eighteen hours in the Falklands making repairs. Dubois has a reputation as a fiercely competitive man, whose dark moods can make him unpredictable and difficult to read. At the end of each of the first three legs, he had refused to celebrate his own safe arrival. This is a ritual of the race. Each skipper is given a bottle of champagne, which he or she dutifully sprays on the assembled crowd after a few sips.

"I do not celebrate coming in second," he had said each time.

This time he had won the leg, and after the cork was popped in the sizzling Brazilian heat, "the champagne was passed around like a hot croissant," Web correspondent Brian Hancock says, "no one wanting to hand it over." Dubois's wife, Muriel, declined a drink when the bottle was passed to her. So everyone was surprised when he grabbed the bottle, and with a huge smile, doused the crowd.

"In Salvador Dubois finally let up on himself," Hancock says. "He seemed resigned to having Stamm beat him and content to settle for second place."

The route to Salvador took the fleet through Brazil's Pampo oil fields, a 115-mile long, 40-mile wide swath of ocean crammed with rigs and supply vessels, north of Rio de Janeiro. On the day Stamm and Dubois arrived, Emma Richards passed through the field and nervously counted forty-two separate radar blips, indicating rigs and other boats in her path. She didn't sleep for thirty hours. Still,

Emma Richards arrives in Salvador, Brazil. The ball
at *Pindar*'s stern is a satellite receiver. *(Billy Black)*

she kept her good humour, joking that she had reefed and unreefed
so many times, "my biceps are now officially bigger than Popeye's."
Van Liew likened crossing the oilfield to travelling through the set
of the film *Waterworld*. He was struck by the stink and mess as flares
of burning waste gas shot into the sky.

This exhausting piece of sailing had been preceded by days of
squalls and thunderstorms. Richards had reported that the evening
sky was lit up with forks of lightning. On occasion, the lightning
was so close she watched it lick the water less than a quarter mile
away. She had been frightened and had put on her thick rubber-
soled sea boots. They at least provided more moral support if not
complete protection from lightning.

At first, Richards had tried to sail around the more ominous
storm cells. But, as Tim Kent had remarked on the voyage from

Brixham to Cape Town, it was hard to tell which ones would strike and which wouldn't. She soon gave up trying to dodge them and kept going in a straight line.

The weather was the opposite of what the sailors had faced in the Southern Ocean and, Van Liew thought, nearly as unbearable. The heat and humidity were as oppressive as the bitter cold had been. The squalls were intense with major shifts in every direction. Lightning strikes replaced icebergs as the thing to be feared most.

On March 14, after a passage of almost five weeks, Emma Richards arrived in Salvador to claim fourth place. She was a day behind Simone Bianchetti, but a week ahead of Bruce Schwab, who had spent two days in the Falklands fixing his boom.

18

Friends

**"Friendship is the hardest thing in the world
to explain. It's not something you learn in school.
But if you haven't learned the meaning of friendship,
you really haven't learned anything."**

– MUHAMMAD ALI

⁓⁓⁓⁓⁓⁓
⁓⁓⁓⁓⁓⁓

*A*S DEREK HATFIELD motored slowly north towards the safety of the Beagle Channel, Patianne Verburgh was on a plane bound for Santiago, Chile. For all she knew the boat might have rolled over again, or Hatfield may have been forced to abandon the boat and deploy his life raft. She pushed away these thoughts and held firmly to the belief that he would make it safely ashore. The big question was: How could they find the money to fix the boat and get back in the race?

After changing planes, midday Saturday, March 8, found her in the Buenos Aires airport waiting for a connection to Ushuaia. She ran into Richard Bearda, Graham Dalton's shore manager who was waiting for a connecting flight to Puerto Madryn. Bearda suggested that if Hatfield was serious about continuing, the Buenos Aires firm of King Harken SA might be able to supply a new mast. King Harken earned a reputation for fast, efficient, high quality work when it helped Brad Van Liew after he dismasted in the 1998 race.

While Hatfield had thirty days or more, in 1998 Van Liew had been under pressure for a quick turnaround. Had he not finished the race within the prescribed time, he would have been disqualified. He figured he had about ten days to get back to shore, order a mast, have it built in Brazil, delivered to Uruguay. He had to find a way to pay for it, because his sponsor Balance Bar was only prepared to match him dollar for dollar.

"There were no Andrew Pindars in our life then," Van Liew says.

It took two days to motor back to port. His wife and shore manager, Meaghan, had raised the cash.

A week after the dismasting, the new mast was on a flatbed truck crossing the Rio de la Plata and headed for the border. In Montevideo, about two and a half hours away, a crew was standing by when Van Liew received a call that Uruguayan customs was holding the truck up for no apparent reason.

Uruguay's President Didier Opertti had been the guest of honour at a recent Around Alone cocktail reception at the Yacht Club Uruguayo. When he heard of the hold up, the club's commodore called President Opertti's office and the mast was soon on its way.

The rig came through downtown Montevideo with a police escort and with thirteen King Harken guys hanging off the back. They rigged the boat, went for a forty-five-minute test sail, and off Van Liew went. "King was remarkable, a truly amazing bunch of guys," he says. "The rig was beautifully made and fit the demands perfectly."

Word had quickly spread through the fleet of Hatfield's monumental disaster. "We have a good man down and he needs help," Paris said. The men's friendship went back to the 1995 Bermuda One-Two, an annual single-handed, double-handed race between Newport and Bermuda that is 635 miles each way. The following year Paris had been unable to mount a campaign for the Europe 1 Star, the race Hatfield had finished seventh. While *Spirit of Canada* was under construction in New Brunswick, Paris had visited Hatfield. They had shared the nervous days before the race started. Derek and Patianne, and Alan, his wife, Becky, and son, Tucker, had been billeted in the same house in Newport.

Hatfield was popular in the race community. He was easy-going, low-key, and he didn't complain about the handicap of a low-budget campaign. He got on with it, handling his difficulties with stoic indifference. He was respected as a fierce competitor, scoring points for aggressively racing a small boat as if it were ten feet longer. He took a positive view when things went wrong and was quick to compliment others when things went right for them. These intangibles inspired others to help him.

His rescue and resurrection at the bottom of the world was led by four-time Around Alone and Vendée Globe veteran Josh Hall. Without Hall's intervention, and the subsequent support of Emma Richards's patron, Andrew Pindar, he might not have been able to continue. Hatfield's quest would have withered and died in Ushuaia, leaving him with a broken boat and a shattered dream. As Paris said, "Time and finances were not on his side."

When Hatfield moored in Ushuaia that evening, he was physically and emotionally spent. He was penniless in the remotest part of a country and didn't speak the language. His boat was badly damaged. He was thousands of miles from anywhere that could build provide a new mast, even if he had had the money to pay for one.

Josh Hall had been in a similar spot and understood the implications. In the spring of 2003, this exceptionally accomplished man was forty-three and had been a racing sailor for eighteen years. He had logged 180,000 ocean-racing miles, the equivalent of six circumnavigations of the earth. Hall was at the top of his game, among the elite, and a key part of Emma Richards's campaign.

Hall had formed close ties with the British firm Gartmore Investment Management. Despite a series of setbacks he had managed to persuade Gartmore to buy him bigger and better boats. In 1990, he placed third in his first Around Alone in an Open 50. In his second try four years later, Hall hit something in mid-Atlantic. The boat sank and he was rescued. Gartmore didn't give up on him. Instead they commissioned an Open 60, which Hall entered in the 1998 Around Alone. He was forced to retire in that race when he lost the top of his mast after leaving New Zealand. Gartmore rescued him again. In the 2000 Vendée Globe, he came ninth.

Hall had leased *Gartmore Investments* to Emma Richards for the 2002 Around Alone, and Richards had renamed her *Pindar* after her sponsor. Hall was hired as her shore manager. Hall's job was to arrange provisions, supervise repairs, and see to the details that keep an Open 60 in top shape as it races around the world. Because he knew all about the psychological, physical, and practical demands of offshore racing, he was as much Richards's mentor as hired hand.

Hall had met Hatfield during the 1995 Bermuda One-Two, and they had renewed their acquaintance during this race, with Hall offering Hatfield advice on tactics, weather, and boat handling. By the third leg, he was helping Hatfield ship equipment from port to port in *Pindar*'s containers.

As Adrian Trus and Hatfield were motoring up the Beagle Channel, Hall was on the phone to Andrew Pindar, chairman of the British printing and Internet publishing company. Pindar has a

Emma Richards's patron, Andrew
Pindar, invested about $1.85
million in her Around Alone
campaign. *(Pindar)*

fondness for sailing and believes the skills required to sail around
the world alone are similar to those needed to run his business.
Pindar is chairman of a private firm founded in 1836 and later
acquired by his great-grandfather. The company had 2003 sales of
£95 million ($215 million U.S.) with about one-quarter of the
business coming from North America.

Pindar dipped into sailing sponsorship in 1985 when his
company provided the prize money for a cross-Channel race. His
sponsorship remained modest until he was introduced to Richards
soon after she left university. Pindar liked what he saw and took a
gamble, putting Richards on his staff in 1999. He provided the
means by which she could pursue sailing, and, in return, if she continued to win races, Richards would lend the company a unique
marketing presence.

Pindar's instincts were good and both parties have benefited
from the relationship. Richards is a rising star in a resurgent sport.
She is usually mentioned in conjunction with her boat, or her

patron, keeping the Pindar name front and centre. In advance of the 2002–03 race, Richards signed a new three-year agreement. Virtually all the firm's marketing efforts are spent on her, and Pindar's investment in her Around Alone campaign topped £750,000 ($2.8 million U.S.).

Andrew Pindar joined the Around Alone fleet at each stopover, where he sponsored events and hosted receptions. It was a canny way to combine business with pleasure, raising awareness of his company, exploring new business opportunities, and relaxing a little.

Pindar has seen the intangible benefits of its sponsorship. During the race, more than one hundred thousand unique visitors logged on to the portion of Pindar's Web site that housed Richards's diary and other race information. Almost 80 per cent of the visitors were from North America, where Pindar is actively expanding AlphaGraphics, its chain of printing and copying stores. Most then clicked over to the corporate portion of Pindar's Web site to learn more about the firm.

Richards gives motivational presentations to Pindar's clients, suppliers, and staff. She also talks to schools and sailing groups, averaging one appearance a week. For Pindar, her experiences personify the skills required to succeed in business: setting and achieving goals, persevering in the face of adversity, and being flexible and creative when solving problems. Pindar says her delivery is impressive.

Andrew Pindar likes sailors and what they do. He enjoys spending time with them and respects their achievements. Pindar met Hatfield at a function he sponsored in Newport before the start of the race. He liked Hatfield right away. "I found him quiet, determined, resolute and very professional, a man of great depth and determination," he says. As the race went on, he found Hatfield's determination to carry on despite repeated setbacks compelling. He helped out, here and there, when he could. He tried to find

Hatfield sponsorship, even approaching the McCain family of New Brunswick. He knew the McCains because they own a potato processing plant in Scarborough, Yorkshire. Pindar had bought his home there from a McCain family member. The McCains weren't interested.

Andrew Pindar was drawn to help Hatfield because he knows that sometimes you need a break. If you get it, it can be the difference between a great thing or nothing at all. Pindar got that break in 1996 when Office Depot in the United States gave his firm a big contract. It was an act of faith by a huge company that didn't have any particular reason to choose his firm, and it was the turning point in Pindar's fortunes. Now here was a chance for him to give someone a chance.

Hall tracked Pindar down in Indian Harbour, Florida, where he was relaxing after a ski trip in Montana. Hall told Pindar he was prepared to throw in his time and energy to help Hatfield out, but the bigger problem was money. Hall estimated that a new mast, electronics, living expenses, and miscellaneous repairs would cost between $70,000 to $115,000 (U.S.).

Pindar gave the go-ahead with generous and loose terms. Pindar would cover Hatfield's costs up to £50,000 ($110,000). Hatfield would repay the loan as his Canadian fundraising efforts raised money. Or he would work it off in public speaking and personal service engagements after the race. They would figure it out later.

"Derek was in the unfortunate position of losing his mast and I was in the fortunate position of being able to pay for a new one," Pindar says. "Helping him was just the right thing to do."

On the other side of the Atlantic Ocean, another guardian angel was at work. On Friday, March 7, as Al Power sat watching a lacrosse game at the Air Canada Centre in Toronto, his wireless Blackberry pinged with an incoming message. It was an annoying interruption to the action between the Toronto Rock and the Vancouver Ravens, but as president of multinational car parts firm Decoma International, Power was used to being on call. The e-mail was from the Around Alone Web site with a news alert of Hatfield's disaster. Power had been following Hatfield's quest for a few months and had signed up for e-mail updates on the race.

A recreational sailor, Power had heard Hatfield's story over a drink at a Christmas party in December 2002. He was intrigued. When he learned how hard up the campaign was, Power made a five-thousand dollar donation when Hatfield arrived in Tauranga in February. In return for the donation, he asked that Hatfield speak at his annual employee banquet. Power thought nothing more of it until, a week or so later, he got a telephone call from a boat in the middle of the Southern Ocean thanking him for the aid. He was impressed by how grateful Hatfield was for the help. "It was a great Canadian success story, but in typical Canadian fashion no one had come forward," Power says.

Power decided he'd offer more help by spending thirty thousand dollars to buy Hatfield a new set of sails for the final leg between Salvador and Newport. The sails would fly Decoma's colours and those of its controlling shareholder, Magna International.

After he read the e-mail, Power could hardly concentrate on the game. How bad was the damage to *Spirit of Canada*, he wondered? Was Hatfield hurt? Was the boat sinking? That night when he got home, Power tried Hatfield's satellite phone number, but it was dead. He sent Patianne Verburgh an e-mail commiserating and encouraging Hatfield to continue. He offered a loan. Decoma has a parts plant in Brazil and that subsidiary could help with difficult Latin American currency and financial transactions. "I said anything we could do to help, we would," Power said.

Verburgh was in transit and didn't get the message until Saturday. By then she had spoken to Josh Hall. It seemed to her to be prudent to take advantage of Hall's expertise and Andrew Pindar's help. She thanked Power and told him what she and Hatfield had decided. He offered to help out anyway.

Decoma and Magna set aside 1.5 per cent of pre-tax profits for social causes. It is part of the philosophy of the company's founder, Frank Stronach. (Decoma's profit before interest expenses and taxes in 2002 was $177 million. The available pool for good causes was $2.6 million.) Power was Decoma's chief executive and had some discretion in where the funds could be directed. He informed his board of directors he intended to send a cheque for $150,000 to the *Spirit of Canada* campaign.

"It may not be as good a social cause as cancer, but it still falls under the guidelines," Power says.

By the time Patianne Verburgh reached Ushuaia, she knew a hand of friendship extended across oceans and countries. Now it was up to Hatfield to reach out and grasp it. If he had the energy and determination to keep going, the money was there. Once he was ashore, she told him the good news. "I think he was blown away by it," Hall says.

The question that remained was whether Hatfield was so shattered he couldn't continue. The Derek Hatfield that Adrian Trus knew had been absent for the first half of the trip up the Beagle Channel. Hall also wondered whether Hatfield would find the toughness within himself to soldier on. A lot of skippers would have said enough is enough and quit but Hall had a hunch Derek wouldn't. "That's why I got involved. I wouldn't have done it for just anybody, and neither would Andrew Pindar," he says.

Ushuaia is a Patagonian Indian name that means the "bay that goes westward." That accident of geography is a good thing in one of the stormiest and windiest places in the world. The city's deep, natural harbour is surrounded and protected by a semicircle of rugged peaks on the west, north, and east.

Ushuaia is often described as a poor man's Banff. In the summer, hikers, trekkers, cruise-ship passengers, and Antarctic sailors use this most southerly city in the world as the staging point for their holidays. The city's population swells to forty thousand at the height of the tourist season and it offers visitors good restaurants and hotels. There are two hospitals and several medical clinics, at least six banks. There are even a few Internet cafés and everyone seems to have a cellphone. Buildings are mostly wood frame and the tallest building in town is five stories. The modern airport handles up to three flights a day to Buenos Aires. There is even a small yacht club.

Even though it rains one day in three all year round, the streets are dusty and dry as the constant wind wicks away the moisture. There are no trees, although shrubs grow in well-protected gullies.

The hottest months are January and February, when the average daytime temperature is just shy of 16 degrees Celsius (60 degrees Fahrenheit), but the temperature can vary by 20 degrees or more in a few minutes. In winter there's lots of snow, but the oceans on either side moderate the temperature. The coldest month is July, when the overnight low hovers around freezing and the daytime high is around 4 degrees Celsius (40 degrees Fahrenheit).

Ushuaia sits on the island of Tierra del Fuego, named by the Portuguese explorer Ferdinand Magellan who sailed around the island in 1520. He saw Indian campfires along the coast and called the place "Land of Fire." Tierra del Fuego is part of an archipelago that is slightly smaller than Ireland. About 70 per cent of the islands belong to Chile, and the border between Chile and Argentina runs across the middle of the largest island and then down the centre of the Beagle Channel.

Charles Darwin's ship, *Beagle*, stopped in Ushuaia in 1832 during its voyage around the world, hence the Channel's name. To the north of Ushuaia lies the Strait of Magellan, which separates Tierra del Fuego from the mainland. About 100 miles south of Ushuaia lies Cape Horn.

Derek Hatfield's first hours ashore in the early hours of Sunday, March 9 were a blur. He greeted well-wishers at the dock, cleared Argentinian customs and then walked over to the *Peregrine Mariner*. Captain Sazonov wanted to shake the hand of the crazy Canuck who had survived such a terrible storm. Andrew Prossin was coping with angry passengers who had missed their flights home because of the diversion to help *Spirit of Canada*. Normally the flight to Buenos Aires waited for late cruise ships, but this time it hadn't. Hatfield stumbled down the street to the Albatross Hotel and collapsed in the first bed he had seen in twenty-seven days.

Within a week Hatfield was in Buenos Aires ordering a new mast from King Harken. Other options had been explored and discarded as too impractical or too expensive. One former Around Alone sailor offered to send his mast to Ushuaia, but as Hall says, "It's not like mailing a parcel." It would have had to be disassembled, cut in sections, and shipped by plane. Hall was able to scrounge space on a RAF Hercules leaving England on its monthly flight to the Falkland Islands, but wasn't able to find a mast to put on the plane. When he called Hatfield to tell him the bad news on March 14, Hatfield surprised him. "You won't believe it," he told Hall. "I'm in this place called King Harken and they are asking me whether I want aluminum or carbon fibre."

As Hatfield was struggling to reorganize on shore, the rest of his fleet was arriving in Salvador, Brazil, at the end of the fourth leg. Van Liew turned in another magnificent performance, finishing on March 15, after a month and a few days at sea. He was just sixteen hours behind Emma Richards and eight hundred miles ahead of Tim Kent. The last few days of the leg had been punishing. Van Liew recorded a temperature of 46 degrees Celsius (115 degrees Fahrenheit) in the cabin, describing the conditions "as a brutal steam room gone mad." He'd pounded upwind through big seas, and it had been so wet on deck he'd stayed below as much as possible. He was drinking several gallons of water per day and still felt dehydrated. "I want air conditioning! I want a salad! I want anything cool, crisp and refreshing!" he joked. "Did I mention it was hot out here?"

Van Liew's fourth consecutive first place finish matched the record set in 1991 by Frenchman Yves Dupasquier. With one leg left to go, he had a chance to put himself into the record books of the sport.

Van Liew felt quite ambivalent about his second safe passage around the Horn, savouring the dangers even as he swore it was his last time. He saw the passage as a gauntlet, where survival was more important than racing, but no sooner did those words come tumbling out than he admitted an addiction to living on the sharp edge of life. He thought the modern notion of adventure banal and blamed "cheesy reality TV shows" for cheapening real adventure. For him, adventure is about tests that push people to their limits in a quest to feel "the flow of juices never felt before." The men he admired were the explorers Magellan and Columbus, and he felt honoured to be doing what they had done five hundred years earlier.

Tim Kent's journey was long and arduous too, but he embraced the hardships and felt invigorated by them. Kent had found self-confidence and a sense of belonging during his journey, and a sense of fulfillment he had not thought possible.

He had found the stretch between the Horn and Salvador tougher than the passage around the Horn. On March 19, as he entered his sixth week at sea, he was still four hundred miles shy of Salvador. For three days he had sailed through a frightening tempest of thunder and lightning, and blasts of wind that had come out of nowhere. At one point he'd seen nine squalls boiling around him. Later that day he'd passed into the southern trades. "Shortly after dawn this morning, I sailed through the last of the squalls," he wrote in his log. "It was like emerging from a dark movie theatre on a sunny day. I blinked and headed below for sunglasses; I had not seen a cloudless sky for three days."

At about midnight on March 23, just a day shy of six weeks at sea, *Everest Horizontal* crept into Salvador. Kent was thrilled to see

the fleet waiting to greet him with raucous cheers of encouragement and the obligatory bottle of Mumm's. "Just 4,000 miles from
Newport," he said. "I find that pretty amazing."

About twelve hours later, Kojiro Shiraishi sailed in. The heavy
squalls that had lashed the area earlier in the day drifted out to sea
as *Spirit of Yukoh* took third place in Class II, Shiraishi's best showing
of the race. He had sailed a trouble-free, conservative leg. His wing
rotation mast had helped him add speed in the Southern Ocean and
good equipment and experience had helped him sail safely.

Alan Paris arrived on April Fool's Day after forty-nine days at
sea. About thirteen hundred miles north of Cape Horn, a stay
supporting his mast had snapped, slowing him down. This piece
of rod rigging, which supported his mast on the starboard side,
was the same stay that had broken en route to New Zealand,
forcing him to stop over in Tasmania. Now, after consulting with
his shore crew, he rigged a block and tackle with his strongest
Spectra line, fastened one end to the spreader, the other to the deck,
and lashed it tight. He tied off another line so that the two made a
V between spreader and the deck. The fix was strong enough to get
him to Salvador.

During the middle weeks of March, Graham Dalton was also
trying to get back to sea. After Richard Bearda, his shore manager,
crossed paths with Patianne Verburgh in the Buenos Aires airport,
Bearda made his way to Puerto Madryn. *Hexagon* arrived there
early on Saturday, March 8 as Hatfield was motoring up the Beagle
Channel. Dalton tipped his hat to the Canadian. "I was where he
is now with a broken boom, which we were able to fix in situ,"

Dalton said. "To have to ship a mast to such a remote area will be very hard; I wish him the best of luck."

In the end it was Dalton who needed the luck. After a week of trying to raise funds, he still did not have the wherewithal to have his third mast of the race built. Josh Hall offered to help ship one to the Falklands on the same flight he had offered to Hatfield. But there had to be something to ship. There wasn't.

On March 14, as Hatfield shook hands on his King Harken deal, Dalton withdrew from the race. "You are successful in life not because of your successes, but because of your failures and how you deal with them," he said. "The disappointment I feel is complete. I would not wish it on any of the other skippers in this race."

King Harken was eager to help Hatfield. They promised to have the finished product on a truck within ten days. In return, Hatfield switched his order for other equipment to the company, maximizing the reward to King Harken and minimizing the number of suppliers he had to deal with. The rig's designer, Boston naval architect Ted Van Dusen, sent the mast's specifications to King Harken and stood by to answer technical questions.

Meanwhile, in Ushuaia, the Russian engineers aboard *Peregrine Mariner* were doing what engineers everywhere love to do – dismantling, repairing and fussing over broken equipment. They used the deck crane to move *Spirit of Canada*'s keel ram to *Peregrine Mariner*, where they lovingly rebuilt it. The repair took fifteen hours over four full days, and it was done at no cost to Hatfield. The good news was that nothing else had been damaged by the keel's swinging back and forth. Andrew Prossin provided Hatfield

After almost a month in Ushuaia, Argentina, Derek Hatfield was
almost ready to leave. Here he surveys his new mast and sails.
(Spirit of Canada Ocean Challenges)

with the use of his Ushuaia shipping agent, who organized plane
tickets and hotels for Hatfield's rescuers.

By March 28, the mast was on its way to Ushuaia, and three of
Hatfield's Toronto friends, Brian Champion, the principal sail
designer at Quantum Sails in Toronto, Stacy Northcotte also with
Quantum, and Bruce Boulanger, a friend and former sailmaker,
were on their way to help rig and tune the mast and reinstall vital
systems. A fourth friend, Oakville marine electrician Paul Thornton
arrived with a suitcase full of electronic components to rebuild the
burned out communications panels, reconfigure the computers,
and ensure all the equipment worked properly. Thornton had wired
the boat when it was being built, and now he replaced the main
electrical panel. He also hooked up new instruments and checked
the charging system.

When the mast arrived, the group spent a marathon seventy-two hours installing ropes, wiring, lights, and instruments, stepping the mast, tuning rod rigging, and mounting runners.

Meanwhile in Toronto, a fundraising event was held at the Ashbridge's Bay Yacht Club on March 29. Some 144 people paid $125 a plate for dinner, and throughout the evening there were live and silent auctions of holidays, boating equipment, and services for sailors. The food for the five-course meal was donated to the club, so most of the money raised through ticket sales went to Hatfield. The ABYC staff, led by food and beverage manager Robert Faulkner, donated their time. Andrew Prossin stepped up again, donating a ten-day Antarctic excursion for two. A Toronto Maple Leafs hockey jersey signed by Gary Roberts went for almost $1,000. By the end of the evening Hatfield had $45,000 in the bank. He called in to the event and said that he was overwhelmed by the support. "I could not have done it without you," he said. "Thank you, that's all I can say until I can say it to you all in person."

The dinner was one of the many acts of support for Hatfield. Pindar and Decoma's cash and guarantees were worth at least $260,000, and this generosity overshadowed the fact that the campaign so far had been paid for by small donations from many hundreds of people. For many of them, *Spirit of Canada*'s journey evoked a sense of national pride, the romance of long distance sailing, and gave them a vicarious enjoyment of an adventure that most people dream about, but never try. Their support also spoke to Hatfield's character as many of those who gave him money said that they felt his spirit of endurance embodied Canada's national character.

That's why an assembly-line worker at the General Motors plant in Oshawa, Ontario, wrote a cheque for $2,700. Rick Eyre of the Whitby Yacht Club figured he had earned that amount during the seventy-two hours Hatfield lived through his rollover. It's why sailors aboard the HMCS *Fredericton* preparing to leave Halifax for a tour of duty in the Persian Gulf, passed the hat and sent a cheque for $350. It's why most yacht clubs in the Golden Horseshoe made donations not once, but twice, to support Hatfield. "People just want to help Derek succeed," Prossin said. "Maybe by helping him, you can live a little bit too. Sure, what he's doing is expensive and, sure, it's risky, but it is inspiring. I guess the world's a better place because of people like Derek."

The organizer of many of these efforts was Ann Harley, who had met Hatfield in 1996 and became a friend. Harley, a retired accountant and member of Toronto's prestigious Royal Canadian Yacht Club was tireless and tenacious in fundraising for Hatfield. She begged, borrowed, cajoled, encouraged, challenged, and at times browbeat. She wrote press releases, called journalists, planned events, worked the boat show, and anything else she could to move things forward. Without Harley's friendship and guiding hand, the grassroots campaign would have melted away.

This backing was a constant source of surprise to Hatfield. He needed the money, but he was too embarrassed to keep asking for it. He hated being a spectacle, but the nature of the venture meant he was the focus of attention. He underestimated how much he inspired others, how much his adventure had seized their imaginations.

"It is truly amazing, truly unbelievable," Hatfield said. "I just hope I don't let everybody down."

LEG V

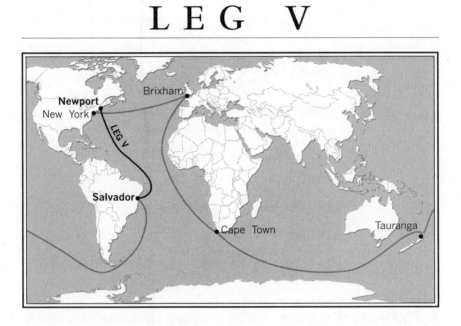

ROUTE: Salvador, Brazil, to Newport, Rhode Island

DEPARTURE: April 13, 2003

DISTANCE: 4,015 nautical miles

19

Going Home

"What would life be if we had no courage to attempt anything?"

– VINCENT VAN GOGH

ON THE MORNING of April 8, a month to the day that Derek Hatfield capsized at Cape Horn, he slipped his lines at the dock in Ushuaia and set sail again.

Hatfield waved goodbye to Patianne Verburgh and set out down the Beagle Channel. It was a twelve-hour trip at five knots to the Drake Passage. From there it was another six hours to the spot where he had been dismasted. Race rules obliged him to return to the point where he had turned on his engine, and a transponder on the boat would relay his latitude and longitude to race headquarters for verification. Hatfield had intended to leave two days earlier, but severe weather, with wind gusts to sixty miles an hour, delayed his departure. Storms were more frequent now as winter approached the south.

Hatfield was optimistic he could travel the three thousand sea miles to Salvador, Brazil, in about two weeks, for an average of two hundred miles a day, even though his best average so far had been between Cape Town and Tauranga, when he had averaged 180 miles a day. On the Brixham – Cape Town leg (excluding the five days in Spain) he had averaged 161 miles a day.

"I'm anxious to get away from here, it's a dangerous place," he said as he set out. "It's a little spooky to pass over the same spot again, but I guess it's only water."

As he motored down the Beagle Channel, the wind increased. The forecast had called for moderate conditions, but by the time he reached the end of the channel it was dark and blowing fifty knots. He shortened the mainsail to its third set of reefs, but a batten car on the mast broke and the top batten, which keeps the sail stiff, started to whip, threatening to tear the sail. Hatfield was in trouble again and facing fearful wind and waves. To continue would have required him to beat upwind, in the dark, near uncharted rocks and islands with no hope of rescue should anything go wrong. And it is the land sailors worry most about, not the sea.

Hatfield turned around and ran downwind. About four hours later he managed to get into the shelter of an island in a shallow bay. It was pitch black, the bay was littered with rocks, and the only way he could tell how far he was from land was by checking his radar. His tiny anchor wasn't enough to hold the boat so he motored back and forth all night, his heart in his throat as the depth sounder and radar beeped warnings. All the while the wind howled and rain clattered off the coach top.

"It was a nightmare," Hatfield said later. "It blew all night and kept blowing all the next day. I couldn't leave the bay to get back to the open ocean, I couldn't stay there, and I couldn't stop."

At dawn, disconsolate and exhausted, Hatfield did the only prudent thing. He turned around and headed back up the Beagle Channel. About twelve hours later he arrived at the Ushuaia Yacht Club, fell into bed, and slept for twenty hours. The wind blew for two more days.

"It was probably scarier than the rollover itself," Hatfield said. "This boat draws 12 feet and I was fooling around in water 30 feet deep with rocks. It was nerve-wracking. Very nerve-wracking. This is a difficult, nasty, violent place."

Four days later, on Sunday, April 13, the starting gun sounded in the sweltering equatorial heat of Salvador. The fleet had spent a month in Brazil's third-largest city, one that offers a heady blend of South American and West African cultures, reflecting its colonial past of slavery and plantation farming.

Salvador sits on a peninsula on the northeast coast of Brazil where a natural port and favoured location made it the Portuguese colony's capital for two hundred years. The settlement was founded in 1549 and made its fortune from the slave trade, sugar cane, tobacco, and cacao. In 1808, during the Napoleonic Wars, the Portuguese royal family lived in temporary exile in Salvador.

Today, the city is home to 2.5 million people and is divided between an upper city on the hills surrounding the harbour and a lower city around the waterfront. The marina where the Around Alone fleet stayed is a short distance from an elevator that connects the lower town with the upper central square. This area dominates the immediate downtown and is alive with music, street food, bars and restaurants. The city has a blend of colonial architecture set in a labyrinth of hills and narrow streets. Because of its slave roots, it is a centre of Afro-South American art, culture, and music. West African ingredients influence local cooking. Up and down the coast are spectacular beaches.

In the evening, the skippers enjoyed the city's nightlife, heading into the old town of Pelourinho. Their drink of choice was a *caipirinha*, literally translated as a "little peasant girl," a concoction made of a local rum called *cachaça*, mashed lime quarters, and sugar. One of the attractions of the old town are the street dancers who perform a dance called *capoeira*. First developed by slaves as a martial art, it has evolved as a dance with acrobatic movements, kicks, and sweeps.

Salvador is so close to the equator that the heat is constant and the humidity can be debilitating. The average daily temperature is 24 degrees Celsius (76 degrees Fahrenheit), rising to 31 degrees Celsius (88 degrees Fahrenheit) in January and February, the height of summer. In April, while the Around Alone fleet was there, it had cooled off to the high twenties (mid-eighties Fahrenheit). With 80 per cent humidity it felt far hotter.

Shore crew would work on the boats just after sun-up when it was still cool enough to work. By about nine in the morning the sun has soaked up all available moisture and turned it into humidity. The heat becomes oppressive, and by eleven a.m. it is unbearable. In the late afternoon it cools off slightly.

In Salvador, *Bobst Group* was hauled and the mast and keel removed, and the keel was totally rebuilt. Alan Paris repaired his broken shroud. Harken sent Tim Kent a new forestay and furling unit to replace the one he had cut away en route to the Horn. Kent also replaced solar panels that had been torn away by the force of the waves. *Pindar*'s crew spent three days going over the mast and rigging. Two new wind instruments at the top of her mast were installed, one as a backup, and the hydraulic rams that drove her autopilots were replaced. The latest computer maps were installed on *Pindar*'s computers. In a sign of the times, the latest anti-virus software was installed on each of her three laptops. The Around Alone skippers were almost paranoid about giving out their on-board e-mail addresses. They usually sent and received messages through intermediaries to keep their systems bug-free.

It was a long stop and some took the chance to go home. Brad Van Liew went back to Charleston for a few days, where Tate Van Liew celebrated her first birthday. Bernard Stamm flew to France to join his wife for the birth of their second child. Thierry Dubois's wife and daughters joined him in Salvador, as did Alan Paris's wife and son.

The fleet took their leave of Salvador in light air, on a warm, steamy day. The overcast sky kept the sun from searing their skin. Soon the familiar pattern emerged, with Bernard Stamm and Brad Van Liew leading their classes. The surprise was Simone Bianchetti. *Tiscali* displaced Thierry Dubois as the sailor chasing Stamm. Bianchetti had gained strength on each leg since his October dismasting in the Bay of Biscay.

The first five hundred miles was on an east-northeast heading along the bulge of Brazil. It was slow going, with light air and fickle changes of wind direction. There were two ways of navigating this route. One was to stay inshore and catch the thermals rising off the land; the other was to sail far from shore and hope the breeze filled in and stayed. Stamm and Bianchetti chose the nearshore route, while Dubois went farther out. By the third day at sea it was clear that the nearshore tactic was better. Stamm had a twenty-three-mile lead on Bianchetti. Dubois was 170 miles back.

Once past the bulge, the boats turned north, picking up the

southern trade winds to the equator and passing through the Doldrums again. The Doldrums are narrower on this side of the Atlantic, but still slowed the fleet down. From there the boats picked up the northern trades and sailed a straight course to Newport.

While the fleet sweated it out in their first days out from Salvador, Hatfield donned gloves and layers of fleece and once more sailed towards the place where he had nearly lost his life. He had learned a lesson from his attempt the previous week and enlisted the help of a cruising sailor in Ushuaia to help him escape. New Zealander Greg Landreth and his wife, Keri Pashuk, charter their fifty-four-foot steel-hulled ketch *Northanger* in those waters, taking passengers on Antarctic and Patagonian tours. They agreed to accompany Hatfield to the mouth of the Beagle Channel and act as a "floating dock" for *Spirit of Canada* in case the Horn was in an ugly mood. It was a staged departure that took two and a half days because of strong headwinds, but it was the proper way to do it.

Stage one saw the boats sail down the Beagle Channel where on the night of April 12, Hatfield moored off *Northanger* in a small bay, using the larger boat as a floating dock. Early the next morning in moderate winds he said his goodbyes and cast off from *Northanger*'s side in the lee of an island. He sailed forty-eight miles to a point approximately five miles beyond where he had been dismasted, then turned and set a course for the Falklands.

Like Dubois and Van Liew before him, he chose the outside route and two days later had travelled more than four hundred and fifty miles. He was well east of the Falklands, heading north and making good time. The weather was getting better though it was still very cold. Hatfield still felt unsettled, but every mile from the

Horn lifted his spirits. It was great to be back at sea, and the new rig and sails were performing well.

So far, the race had been remarkably free of medical emergencies, but two days out from Salvador Alan Paris hit a whale. *BTC Velocity* was sailing along at about seven knots, and Paris was down below at his navigation station when there was a bang and the boat came to a dead stop. When he stood up to see what had happened, there was a second bang and the boat was rocked again. Paris was off balance and thrown back onto the navigation station.

He went on deck and found the water around the boat awash with blood. There were two whales, one under the boat and one off the port side. He released the mainsail to ease the boat's forward progress and to let the whale swim away. It did so slowly. He tightened the sail and moved off with the uninjured whale following him. Paris worried it would ram him in revenge, but after a few minutes, Paris changed course and both whales disappeared.

Paris couldn't find any damage to his boat, but the pain in his side where he had smashed it against the navigation station was bad. The next morning when he touched his ribs, there was such a sharp pain he almost passed out. Paris called the Clipper Ventures emergency medical referral system. He was put in touch with an emergency room doctor. The consultation revealed one fractured rib, maybe two, but there was no danger of the broken rib puncturing a lung. If this had happened, the doctor said, the symptoms would have already shown themselves.

A week later on Easter weekend, the ninth day of the leg, Paris was already feeling better. The wind was light, the temperature pleasant, and it rained for an hour Easter Sunday, perfect for a cockpit shower. After seven days at sea, he desperately needed the shower. As he bathed, he realized that the stabbing pain in his rib cage had been replaced by a dull ache. He was encouraged that his rib was healing.

Medical emergencies in solo races present a unique challenge because the sailors must diagnose problems when their judgment is most likely to be clouded by fever or pain. The treatment may even involve self-surgery. In the 1998 Around Alone, Victor Yazykov's right elbow became severely infected. With the help of illustrated instructions received via e-mail, the Russian administered pain-killers, lanced and drained the wound, and stitched it up.

The renowned Argentine single-hander Vito Dumas came close to amputating his arm while sailing the mid-Atlantic in 1942. Dumas recounted the incident in *Alone Through the Roaring Forties*, his story of the circumnavigation. It began innocently enough when Dumas cut his hand. It was a fairly minor wound but it failed to heal in the wet, cold, salty conditions. The wound became infected and then septic. Two weeks after the accident, his arm was so swollen that Dumas could not close his fist. He used his good arm to strap the infected limb to a bunk. With the other hand and his teeth, he filled a syringe with penicillin and injected himself. A few days later, Dumas was feverish and drifting in and out of consciousness. He didn't care whether the boat was on course, or sank. He could not sleep because every jolt caused excruciating pain. He injected his last vial of penicillin and decided, in a lucid moment, he would cut the arm off if it did not improve. He believed the alternative was death. "With an axe, or my seaman's knife, at the elbow, at the shoulder, I knew not where or how, [but] somehow I would have to amputate," he wrote.

He lay in his bunk that night with a terrible fever, dreaming, hallucinating, and occasionally waking because of the pain in his arm. Some hours later he came fully awake and realized his bunk was damp. The abscess had burst and pus was flowing from a three-inch gash. Using his rigging knife, Dumas dug out the core of the abscess, and cleaned, disinfected, and bound the wound. Within twenty-four hours the swelling had subsided and he was able to take the helm again. He would never know whether he actually could have cut off his own arm.

Dr. Ian Cohen, a sports medicine specialist at the University of Toronto, acted as Hatfield's medical adviser. Cohen worked with several high performance athletes during the early 1990s and was team doctor for the Toronto Argonauts of the Canadian Football League. In 2001, he was the official doctor for the crew of *Defiant*, the Canadian boat which won the Canada's Cup race on the Great Lakes.

Throughout the Around Alone Hatfield spoke to Cohen regularly to allow the doctor to gauge his physical as well as his mental state. The arrangement was that should something major happen, Hatfield would pick up the phone and call, day or night. Luckily, he had no need. Hatfield had on board a medical CD-ROM and a textbook. Before the skippers left Newport there had been a medical check to ensure they had prescription drugs, including antibiotics, as well as needles, surgical tools, disinfectants, anesthetics, bandages and splints. Tucked into the medical kit was a five-page list of potential problems, divided into such categories as toothaches, heart and liver problems, broken bones, and lacerations.

Kojiro Shiraishi had cracked a tooth in the third leg, and just days after Paris's encounter with the whale, Tim Kent felt an ominous ache in one of his molars. It was one of his most-feared medical emergencies. As a pre-fluoride kid growing up in the 1950s, he associated trips to the dentist with drilling, filling, and pain. He called a dentist onshore who prescribed a combination of antibiotics and painkillers. A day later, the tooth was banging away in his jaw. He got a second opinion from an English emergency-room doctor available to the fleet, who suggested Kent switch from painkillers to plain old aspirin. It worked. With a few days the combination of drugs had settled the pain.

After three days at sea, Hatfield had travelled six hundred miles and was north of the Falklands. Conditions were good, but he still worried. Normally a boat undergoes a few weeks of sea trials to tension a new mast correctly. There had been no time to do that in Ushuaia so he was constantly adjusting the stays as the mast settled in. The weather files told him he would have a few more days of light air and then a storm during the Easter weekend.

For once the forecast was dead-on. He had escaped the Southern Ocean, but Southern Ocean weather was not ready to release him yet. That Easter weekend turned out to be almost as dangerous as his experience at the Horn. A fast-moving low-pressure system descended on Good Friday and blew through Saturday and half of Sunday. It was a full-blown howler, almost too much to take. First the Horn, then the blast that forced him back to Ushuaia and now this monster. "I thought, Gimme a break," he said later. "Isn't it three strikes and you're out?"

The wind picked up quickly and forty knots soon became fifty and then sixty. For a full twenty-five hours the wind blew hard and gusted even higher. The boat was knocked down at least ten times. Hatfield lost track after a while. Had it continued to blow in the same direction for another few hours he believes it might have been all over, but then the wind shifted. The waves were still big, about twenty-five to thirty-five feet, but they weren't the killer height they had been near the Horn. He could handle the wind, and as long as the waves didn't climb any higher, he could bear off on a broad reach and run with the storm. "You get a little anxious about losing the rig," he said later. "I thought, If I lose it here, I'm toast for sure."

The rig held and the boat suffered only minor damage, the most frustrating of which was a tear in the new mainsail. It ripped about two feet along the luff – the edge where it attaches to the boom. Hatfield also fell in the cockpit during the height of the storm, a blow that knocked the wind out of him for a few minutes and left him stiff and sore for days.

Meanwhile, the rest of the fleet was racing north in favourable winds. By now, Thierry Dubois had realized his tactical decision to go offshore was wrong. He had hoped to emerge from the Doldrums with a better angle for the northern trade winds. By the time he saw that this was not going to happen, it was too late. He pushed hard, but lagged the leaders by several hundred miles.

By Day Ten, a week and a half into the leg, Brad Van Liew's lead over the small boat fleet was unassailable. He was about 350 miles east of Martinique, with Tim Kent 180 miles behind. In Class I Bianchetti was close to Stamm and still in second place. But he was pushing *Tiscali* too hard and a section of the mainsail track at the top of the mast ripped away. Luckily, the wind was light. Bianchetti's only option was to climb the mast and reattach the track. It took two days. "My body is shattered," he said when he'd finished. Eleven times he climbed the eighty-five-foot spar and clung there for four hours each time, tackling the repair.

After only two and a half weeks at sea, on May 1 at 7:20 a.m., Bernard Stamm crossed the line in Newport. He was a record first

Bernard Stamm arrived first in every leg, even though he lost
Leg IV on adjusted time. Here he salutes his arrival in Newport,
Rhode Island, on May 1, 2003. *(Bobst Group/Armor Lux)*

across the line in each of the five legs. It was Stamm's first major
title and he had won in commanding style.

The victory had been a long time coming. In November 2000,
Stamm had set off in the Vendée Globe in the newly launched *Bobst
Group*, but was forced to retire when his autopilot failed. Then in
February 2001, he had set a new monohull transatlantic record
sailing between Sandy Hook, New Jersey, and Lizard Point in
England. He also set a twenty-four-hour distance record on that
voyage, sailing 420 miles in one day at an astonishing average speed
of 17.49 knots.

There is more to Stamm than his sailing skills. Around Alone
Web site correspondent Brian Hancock recalls Stamm's arrival in
New Zealand at the end of Leg III. He had endured one of his worst

nights at sea, beating into a fifty-knot wind and steep seas that threatened to break his boat. Stamm had been asked beforehand to give away prizes at a local festival. While some might have begged off after two days without sleep, Stamm showed up "still in his foul-weather gear with his shaggy hair crusted with salt," Hancock said. "He stepped onto the stage and in front of 5,000 people with great aplomb waved to the crowd and handed out the prizes."

On May 3, the twentieth day of the leg, as the rest of the fleet closed in on Newport, the weather deteriorated. A northeaster was brewing. The seas were steep and the wind was coming more or less from the direction the fleet wanted to go, which meant they had to beat towards the finish. Bianchetti was thirty miles from Newport early that morning when he heard a loud bang, felt the boat lurch and knew the mast had snapped. He waited for the rig to crash to the deck, but nothing else happened.

Bianchetti grabbed a flashlight and went on deck. The top twenty feet of his mast had broken above the top spreaders. Bianchetti lashed the broken piece down, hoisted a small staysail up front and eased his mainsail until it was flapping. "I was going to make the finish even if I had to swim, towing the boat," he said later.

At 7 a.m. on May 3, he struggled across the line as spectators and support boats cheered him on. His second-place showing gave him third overall for the race, edging out Emma Richards. It was a remarkable performance for a man who many thought was finished when he dismasted in the second leg. Instead he had clawed his way back, gaining ground in each leg.

At 3 p.m. that day, Thierry Dubois finished third to take second overall. He had recovered from his earlier tactical error, but could not make up the lost ground. Bruce Schwab arrived fourth to place fifth overall.

Emma Richards arrived May 4, rounding out the Class I fleet. She had plenty to celebrate. She had become the youngest woman to sail around the world via Cape Horn alone. Stamm, Dubois, Bianchetti, and Schwab showered her with hugs, kisses, and champagne. That day Derek Hatfield crept into Salvador, Brazil, where the lone familiar face to greet him was Patianne Verburgh.

"Salvador at last!" he said. "What a relief."

The surprise in the final leg was "Tenacious Tim" Kent, who was giving Brad Van Liew a run for his money. With three thousand of the four thousand miles behind them, the two boats were separated by less than two hundred miles. "Tim's been rather persistent," Van Liew said.

On April 30, two and half weeks into the leg, Van Liew was six hundred miles from the finish and sixty miles north of Bermuda. He was bracing for the northeaster that the bigger boats had missed. Van Liew told a reporter that the previous week had been frustrating, aggravating, slow, and tedious, but still he felt enormously satisfied. He had won every leg so far and barring disaster, would win this one as well. It would be a crowning achievement. He had set a record for the fastest one-day passage in a fifty-foot boat, travelling 345 miles in twenty-four hours on the approach to Cape Town. On the first leg, he missed setting another record by a whisker. He was the fastest American racing sailor alive.

Van Liew also felt a little unsettled. He had worked towards this goal for five years and now it was almost over. If you added the time and energy involved in mounting his 1998 campaign, these ventures had absorbed the better part of a decade – almost a third of his life. What could fill this void? What could top this achievement?

An exuberant Brad Van Liew celebrates victory with a bottle of champagne soon after arriving in Newport. *(Billy Black)*

Van Liew's commitments to his sponsors would keep him busy for a few months, but he figured that was it for solo sailing. Like Autissier before him, he had had enough. "I'm done in the Southern Ocean," he said. After two safe roundings of the Horn, the odds of something happening had hugely increased. And now he was a father he wasn't going to fight the odds.

As Bianchetti struggled towards the finish, Van Liew was about two hundred miles behind, facing forty-knot winds from more or less dead ahead. He was pounding through steep, short, boat-breaking seas and exhausted by several knockdowns that reminded him of Stamm's rounding of New Zealand's Cape Reinga in January. At one point, as Van Liew spoke to his wife, Meaghan, on the phone, the boat was leaning so far over, he was bracing himself with one foot on the cabin wall. "I haven't slept in two days," he said. "I feel like I am going to be sick or start hallucinating. The only thing I can compare it to would be trying to sleep on a roller coaster."

Within twelve hours, the system was spinning off to the east and conditions had eased. Twelve hours after that, at 5:53 a.m. on May 4 as the sun was rising, Van Liew sailed to victory in Newport, in a light breeze. Whatever doubts he'd had about himself had been vanquished. There was no question now that Brad Van Liew was one of the best solo sailors in the world.

As Tim Kent approached Newport, he felt as if the risks he had taken had paid off. He had shucked off his career, set aside his commitment to family and friends, and had invested everything in the great unknown. Now he envisioned a future that included more ocean racing and a career writing and speaking about his experiences. He could not see returning to a job of selling academic textbooks. He would be in debt for the rest of his life, but he said, "[T]he trip has been worth every penny, every exhausting hour, every frightening moment." He was performing at the same level as his heroes. That emotional high carried Kent towards Newport, but then the storm wiped the smile from his face. It caught him as he crossed the Gulf Stream. With the current moving northeast and the wind blowing from the north, the cross-seas were treacherous. The seas he faced were worse than those faced by Van Liew, although they were separated by less than two hundred miles.

He had gone fifteen miles beyond the edge of the Gulf Stream, judging by the change in the water temperature, when a gust of wind hit him. Before he could react, there was a "a sickening tearing" and his big jib sail blew out. He unfurled the storm jib, and it was just as well he did as, within minutes, the wind built from the mid-twenties to the mid-forties. The storm intensified and was soon blowing at fifty-five knots. Kent sailed ten miles in the next eight hours.

The storm came on so suddenly all he was wearing was a pair of light nylon pants. As he struggled to get the boat under control, the life raft in the cockpit broke loose and began slamming around. The line on the windward side of the boat that controlled the damaged jib became tangled with the furling lines for the storm sail. It was such a mess that Kent couldn't tack and change direction. Because of the storm's violence, he didn't feel it was safe enough to go forward on deck to try and sort it out. Half an hour later his instruments told him the water temperature had begun to rise, indicating he was being pushed back into the Gulf Stream. The boat was at a crazy angle of heel, and gusts kept slamming it over even further. On deck all of the lines were coated with oil. He had apparently sailed through an oil slick. He couldn't keep his feet on the pitching deck.

Kent crawled forward on his hands and knees, with the deck dropping out from under him whenever the boat sailed off one of the relentless, huge waves. He worked his way to the tangled line, freed it, and then crawled back to the cockpit. He couldn't tack because he couldn't get enough momentum to force the bow through the wind. He tried as hard as he could, transferring the ballast to the other side of the boat and throwing down the helm. The boat came head to wind and stalled. The wind was shrieking and spindrift was blowing off the tops of waves. *Everest Horizontal* started to move backwards. As it gained momentum, he turned the helm and backed the boat through the tack.

By late evening the waves were still huge, but the storm was abating. At least *Everest Horizontal* was moving in the right direction. By noon the next day the sky was clear, the sailing fast, and

Kent was enjoying his last miles at sea. At 11:42 a.m. on May 5, after three weeks and two days, *Everest Horizontal* crossed the finish line to take second in Class II for the leg and the race.

Two days later on May 7, a flotilla of boats greeted Kojiro Shiraishi. Around Alone veteran Minoru Saito fired the gun as Shiraishi crossed the line, marking his second solo circumnavigation. His first had made him the world's youngest solo circumnavigator. Earlier that day, Derek Hatfield restarted from Salvador, Brazil, after an enforced two-day stopover. He was inching his way east along the bulge of Brazil.

On Mother's Day, Sunday, May 11, after four weeks and a day at sea, Alan Paris entered the history books as the first Bermudan racing sailor to circumnavigate the earth. Of all the skippers, including Hatfield, Paris had spent the most time at sea – 202 days since the race started on September 15, almost seven of the past eight months. As the bright yellow hull of *BTC Velocity* crossed the line, it looked as if she had been out for a daysail, as did her skipper, who was tanned and relaxed. Since his collision, Paris had sailed with less sail than he would otherwise have set, as he was not sure he would be able to adjust his sails in a hurry because of his injury. *BTC Velocity* came fourth in the leg and fifth overall in Class II.

Only Hatfield was left on the course. He turned the corner on the bulge of Brazil the day Paris arrived in Newport. He had made good time, managing six hundred miles in four days since leaving Salvador, but he felt strange about being the last one left and still so far from Newport. It made it harder to concentrate. With nothing left to race for, it was less important that every last ounce of speed be wrung from the boat. All Hatfield had to do to claim third was finish. An hour or two, or a day or a week, wouldn't make any difference. "It feels odd to be the last one standing," he said. "You know the attrition rate will be high, you just hope it isn't you."

20

The Unforgiving Sea

**"Destiny is not a matter of chance;
but a matter of choice. It is not a thing
to be waited for. It is a thing to be achieved."**

– WILLIAM JENNINGS BRYANT

JUST BEFORE 11 a.m. on May 31, 2003, Derek Hatfield drifted across the finish line in Newport under slate-grey skies in a wisp of a breeze. It was seven weeks to the day that he had left Ushuaia, and three weeks and two days since leaving Salvador. He had sailed a very respectable leg, finishing in the same time as Kojiro Shiraishi and six days faster than Paris. He had averaged 167 miles a day, or seven knots an hour, in the last leg. He laid claim to third place in the small boat class, based on accumulated points. He had completed the 27,000-mile official course in a time of 245 days, 13 hours, 44 minutes, and 45 seconds.

While the world's eyes were focused that week on the fiftieth anniversary of Sir Edmund Hillary's conquest of Mount Everest,

Hatfield was ending a quest of no less epic proportion. "What he's done is like falling off Mount Everest while climbing it, then still managing to make it to the top," his father told *Toronto Star* reporter Josh Rubin. "A lot of people try to do something like this. He actually did it."

Hatfield sailed into Narragansett Bay at about six-thirty in the morning and was greeted by a seven-boat flotilla of relatives and friends, many of whom had made their way by car and plane at short notice to meet him. Hatfield sailed the final three weeks without incident. As he crossed the equator the heat was intense, and he had spent most days hidden under an air mattress for relief from the sun. It was more than 38 degrees Celsius (100 degrees Fahrenheit) by day in the tiny cabin. Occasional squalls at night brought respite. He pushed as hard as he could, but felt a sense of loss as one by one his friends and adversaries dispersed. He had not seen the other sailors since February, although many sent e-mails of encouragement and spoke with him by phone. They would gather one last time for the prize-giving ceremony, but he would miss that too.

On May 16, as the sailors got ready for that big event, Hatfield was still two weeks away, entering the northern trade winds that would carry him on the last leg of his journey. The steady breeze brought relief from the heat. Hatfield was connected to the proceedings in a pre-arranged phone call. A standing ovation for his efforts echoed down the several thousands of miles that separated him from his comrades. Hatfield said later that he was very moved by the applause.

And then it was over. A rough crossing of the Gulf Stream with high winds and square waves, the current moving one way, the wind the other, then drifting slowly to the finish. He crossed the

A thin, but relaxed-looking Derek Hatfield celebrates his
finish in Newport on May 31, 2003. *(Gordon Crowe)*

line to the cheers, a spray of champagne, feeling elation, sadness,
relief, satisfaction, and loss. He found everything loud and chaotic
after being so long at sea.

Three days later, Hatfield looked tanned, fit, and rested, a contented
man, but the enormity of his achievement had not sunk in. He
had struggled as hard as a man can to complete the journey. He had
come as close to death as possible, yet survived. He had given up
everything most people hold dear or are afraid to lose – his life
savings, a job, financial security – and had set out on a selfish and

solitary journey, one he felt impelled to make. Had he found what he was looking for?

"I wish I'd done it sooner," he said.

After the prize-giving ceremony, the fleet scattered. *Solidaires* sailed for France. *Bobst Group Armor Lux* also crossed the Atlantic to France. Bruce Schwab announced his intention to enter *Ocean Planet* in the 2004 Vendée Globe.

Tiscali's broken mast was repaired in Newport and she sailed across the Atlantic to Italy. Within a few weeks, her skipper-poet was dead. In the early hours of June 28, while aboard a boat in Savona, Italy, Simone Bianchetti had a stroke. His wife, Inbar, called an ambulance. It arrived quickly, but it was too late. The story circulating among the Around Alone skippers was that he had been partying hard for a week. Italy's first racing circumnavigator was buried three days later in his hometown of Cervia. He was thirty-five.

Pindar was returned to Josh Hall. He has since chartered it to a French sailor who plans to enter the 2004 Vendée Globe. Emma Richards's savvy patron bought Graham Dalton's *Hexagon* with the aim of building a team around Emma for the 2005 Volvo Ocean Race. *Hexagon* cost about $3.6 million (U.S.) to build (£1.6 million), but Andrew Pindar got her for a knockdown price. "Let's just say we paid something commensurate with her condition," he said later.

Hexagon's keel was removed and the boat shipped by container from Argentina to Tilbury, Essex, on the east coast of England. She was refitted and in November, Richards entered the Transat Jacques

Vabre, a double-handed race from Le Havre to Salvador. Her co-skipper was New Zealander Mike Sanderson. He was also now her boyfriend. They had known each other for years, but had become romantically involved during the Around Alone race. This time Emma was unlucky. They withdrew on the third day when their electronic instruments were knocked out and thousands of litres of water drained into the hull after a hose broke. The boat limped into Brest.

Bernard Stamm also entered the race. During the same violent storm, he was up forward and a sudden lurch threw him against the boat's forestay. He broke a rib and suffered other injuries. Four days later he was in considerable pain and retired. He put in to the island of Madeira for treatment. More bad luck.

Tommy Hilfiger was repainted and renamed *Beefeater Bold Spirit*. Van Liew sailed up and down the east and west coasts of the United States in the summer of 2003, unwinding and hosting party cruises on behalf of Beefeater Gin. In November, he sold the boat to a young American who plans to enter the 2006 Five Oceans race, the renamed Around Alone.

In January 2004, Van Liew retired from solo racing after seven years of campaigning. He has launched a marketing company with his wife, offering sailors public-relations advice, race management and training, and non-profit fundraising. Among his clients is the hopeful to whom he sold *Tommy Hilfiger*.

Tim Kent's adventure continued after the race and almost ended in tragedy. In June, he entered the Bermuda One-Two, the single-handed–double-handed race between Newport and St. George's, Bermuda, a mere "weekender" after the Around Alone. On the single-handed leg, Kent came third. On the return voyage, when he was 100 miles from Bermuda, the bulb on his keel snapped in thirty-knot winds. He was sailing at about twelve knots in a steadily building breeze when he heard two sharp bangs. The boat didn't slow down as if it had hit something, but rounded up and fell on her side.

With the mast and sails in the water, Kent climbed around the stern. He saw that the lead keel bulb had snapped off. *Everest Horizontal* was crippled. He climbed back into the cabin where his crew, Rick McKenna, was unlashing the safety gear he had carried during the Around Alone. Kent had just grabbed the waterproof box of flares and a headlamp and was reaching for the EPIRB when *Everest* rolled right over. It trapped both of them under the boat. McKenna was in the cabin and swam out and to the stern. Kent released the tether on his safety harness and followed him out.

They climbed on the bottom of the boat. Kent says about four minutes elapsed between the sound of the keel breaking and the rollover. The men didn't have time to grab the "go bag," a watertight duffel with a VHF radio, a hand-held GPS, and provisions. Almost immediately, they spotted the lights of a cruise ship on the horizon and Kent set off several rocket flares. The ship was the *Nordic Empress* of the Royal Caribbean Line, which had left Bermuda some hours after the race began. Within ninety minutes both were on board the cruise ship.

"It is pretty depressing, but I feel lucky," Kent said a few days later. "We survived, that's what matters. If this had happened in the Southern Ocean, the results wouldn't have been quite so happy. I guess I'm kind of like Derek. Somebody has decided our work on earth isn't finished yet."

Within twenty-four hours, Alan Paris and Brad Van Liew offered to help salvage the boat. Paris made arrangements with local salvers in Bermuda, while Van Liew was to fly and join him. At the last minute, Van Liew called it off when his wife's brother was killed in an accident in Chicago.

Everest Horizontal was found floating upside down in the Gulf Stream a few weeks after she capsized. Divers cut away her rig, rolled the boat over, and she was towed to Bermuda. *(Tim Kent)*

Nine days after the rollover, Kent was waiting impatiently dockside in St. George's. A racing sailboat had spotted *Everest Horizontal* on July 2, barely visible in the ocean swells, and relayed the coordinates. The mast had broken in three places and much of the rigging was tangled or broken. The boat was empty, the wave action having flushed the inside clean. The crew tied a line around the keel, rolled the boat over, cut away all the rigging and loose parts, and towed her back to Bermuda.

The adventure did not end there. Hurricane Fabian swept over Bermuda in early September 2003. At the height of the storm, *Everest Horizontal*'s mooring lines parted and she was driven onto the rocks in St. George's Harbour. Her rudders were sheared off and the hull damaged. "At the lowest point of the Around Alone Race, I never imagined that we would find ourselves in this sad shape," Kent said. By spring 2004, she was still in Bermuda and Kent had been hired by Harken Yacht Equipment as a sales manager for international clients.

As Kent thought about these problems, he returned to the damage done to his keel bulb during the tow into Tauranga, when the boat had been dragged over a rock. Now Kent wondered whether this was the ultimate cause of the capsize. Had the impact bent or weakened the bolts holding the bulb to the keel blade? But if that was the case, surely the bulb would have snapped long before Kent made it to Newport. The only sure thing is that all eight, one-inch stainless-steel keel bolts snapped at once, almost killing the two sailors on board.

Like many of the others before him who had not completed the race, John Dennis found it hard to let go. He followed the fleet from port to port, but was kept at a distance by race officials. Dennis maintained a relationship with Bayer, and from their point of view he was still an asset. If nothing else, he proved that diabetics could lead an active life. Dennis flew to New Zealand when the fleet gathered there and spoke to groups of diabetics on behalf of his sponsor. Then he flew back to Cape Town and double-handed *Bayer Ascensia* to Brazil. He was in Salvador when the fleet gathered there. As he was now out of the race, Around Alone organizers requested he moor his boat in a nearby basin. Dennis wanted to join the fleet and sail home solo from Salvador, but that put the race committee in an awkward position. Should something happen, the nearest boat to Dennis would have to abandon the race to help him. In the end, he waited for two days after the fleet's departure and double-handed the boat to Newport.

Dennis was in Newport when Derek Hatfield arrived on May 31. They greeted each other cordially, but still rivals did not share a drink or a meal. Bayer had given *Bayer Ascensia* to Dennis, and he had put it up for sale. He hoped to get $155,000 (U.S.). Over breakfast at Belles Café in the Newport Shipyard, Dennis said he was making public appearances on behalf of the pharmaceutical company and outlined a dreamlike plan to raise $16 million (U.S.) to build a seventy-foot boat for the 2005 Volvo Ocean Race. The boat would carry an all-diabetic crew.

Christmas 2003 found Dennis looking for work in the real-estate industry. His agreement with Bayer was over, and aside from a few speaking engagements he was at loose ends. He had abandoned his Volvo Ocean Race plans and had sold *Bayer Ascensia* for $50,000 (U.S.) to meet pressing financial obligations.

Derek Hatfield spent the summer and fall of 2003 making personal appearances and fulfilling speaking obligations to Decoma and Pindar. He spent time in England during the Cowes (race) Week in August and helped Emma Richards prepare the new *Hexagon* for the Jacques Vabre race.

Hatfield put together a business plan to enter an Open 60 in the 2006 Five Oceans. He tried to acquire *Solidaires* but could not reach an agreement with Thierry Dubois. In the end he decided to build a new boat from scratch. In January 2004, at the Toronto Boat Show, he announced a campaign with major support from Decoma. He is building a new *Spirit of Canada*, an Open 60 that is the next generation *Hexagon*, designed by the same naval architect. Decoma is providing factory space, equipment, and technical help. It is interested in the high-tech materials used in racing sailboats and sees helping Hatfield as research of sorts. Decoma wants to explore whether carbon fibre and Kevlar have applications in car parts.

Hatfield says the campaign will cost about $3 million from start to finish and has once again thrown all of his personal resources into it.

"I want to win this time," Hatfield says.

The 2006 race will be quite different, if it is run at all. As the fleet left New Zealand for the Horn, Sir Robin Knox-Johnston announced that sports promotion company Fast Track Events had bought a substantial stake in his company and would run the 2006 race. Fast Track Events will look at how the race can be repositioned to rejuvenate interest from sponsors and the ocean-racing community. For starters, the race will be two months shorter and exclude Open 40s. All entries must be between fifty and sixty feet.

The renaming of the race Five Oceans shifts the emphasis from adventure and personal challenge to racing and competition. The Open 40s have been the riskiest for the skippers and the race committee members, who are responsible for the safe running of the event. At the same time, the smaller boats attract "gentleman adventurers" like Kent and Hatfield, the characters who add colour to the race. These skippers broaden interest in the sport, particularly in North America, where ocean racing attracts little attention.

Mike Garside believes the day is done for this class of competitor and that this is a natural evolution of the event. Global firms like IBM and Volvo want to sponsor events in which professional athletes compete and achieve the excellence they believe is the metaphor for their products. There isn't room in their marketing plans for well-meaning eccentrics in mid-life crisis. "The day of the adventurer is done," Garside says. "It is not the way ahead."

Brad Van Liew agrees that the race has become a proving ground for professional sailors. He has sailed both types of race and believes that cutting out the adventurers will take the soul out of the event. But he agrees with race organizers that Open 40s are too small, and thinks that building and equipping a fifty-footer is not out of reach of someone aiming for forty feet.

"Both aspects of this race are very important," he says. "If you take the gentleman adventurer out, then the race has lost its legacy and some of its lustre, because these skippers are what makes this event a story."

The race was not a financial success for Clipper Ventures. Knox-Johnston, Clipper's chairman, was unable to find a deep-pocketed title sponsor and ran the race at a loss. But even if the race wasn't a financial success, it was successful in other ways. In the previous five runnings, attrition had been 40 per cent; four out of every ten entries withdrawing for one reason or another. In this race, it was half that – only three of thirteen. Belgian Patrick de Radiguès quit after the first leg because his sponsor preferred he compete in the Route du Rhum, which left France in November 2002. John Dennis and Graham Dalton were the other casualties.

Compared to the carnage in the 1998 Around Alone and the 1996 Vendée Globe, the 2002 Around Alone was as good as it gets. The fleet was solid and well prepared. Novices like Tim Kent were fast learners. As well, the Southern Ocean weather, although still dangerous, was less severe than it had been in previous races. In 1998, Brad Van Liew had feared for his life, spending the better part of two weeks in atrocious weather of the sort only Derek Hatfield faced this time. The boats in 2002 were undeniably faster, with Bernard Stamm putting in astonishing average speeds, unheard of even a few years ago. When this speed was paired with the maturing of Internet and satellite communications, the boats were able to get a jump on bad weather, or position themselves to take maximum advantage of it.

The safety requirements put in place after the 1996 Vendée Globe proved effective. Even after *Spirit of Canada* took her beating at Cape Horn, her hull, deck, and superstructure looked almost as pristine as the day she was launched. When the boat popped upright after the rollover, the forward hatch was gone and the compartment filled with water, but the seaworthiness of the boat – and the integrity of the other three watertight compartments – was unaffected. *Everest Horizontal* floated upside down for almost two weeks in the Gulf Stream. The boats are as safe as they have ever been.

Confucius said that man's greatest glory lies in rising up every time he falls down. In the nine months of the Around Alone the sailors fell many times as they raced at the edge of their abilities, through Nature's darkest and ugliest moods, in her most remote and dangerous waters. On their passage through the Southern Ocean and around Cape Horn they saw chunks of ice the size of small cars. Mountainous waves dwarfed their small boats and winds blew so fiercely that the sailors could not turn to face them.

It was a place of danger and death, where few sane people go under any circumstances, let alone by themselves in a small boat. Yet these sailors were not mad, or unbalanced. They felt the risks were acceptable as they engaged in a solitary dance with the unforgiving sea, which punished them day after day with a relentless indifference. Often they passed dangerously close to the edge and caught a glimpse of the end of their life at a moment when the wind was too strong, or the waves too high, or they had been knocked down once too often. And still they found the strength to rise each time. From afar we watched and marvelled. They were afraid but they managed their fear and acted in spite of it, resolute and determined, uncomplaining and unrepentant in their solitary pursuit of a selfish goal.

Millions followed their journey from the safety of their homes or offices. Emma Richards alone received nearly 360,000 e-mail messages during the race. The fascination is partly because in the West we live in an age without challenge, a time of unparalleled safety and comfort, where physical danger is rare or even non-existent. We will never know as Derek Hatfield knows, what we are capable of enduring, how far we can bend before breaking, or what we will do to live for another minute.

Those of us who followed their adventures did so because we admire, even envy, their self-sufficiency and courage. We felt the world was a better place because of them. Their adventuring spirit inspired us and left us feeling that one day, perhaps, we just might set sail ourselves, cast off the burdens of our lives, and leave it all behind to sail on our own sea of dreams.

APPENDICES

2002/2003 STANDINGS

CLASS I – 60 FEET

SKIPPER	COUNTRY	LEG I	LEG II	LEG III	LEG IV	LEG V	POINTS[1]	ELAPSED TIME[2]
Bernard Stamm	SWI	1st	1st	1st	2nd	1st	49	115:17:27
Thierry Dubois	FRA	2nd	2nd	2nd	1st	3rd	45	118:12:51
Simone Bianchetti	ITA	5th	6th	4th	3rd	2nd	35	159:19:35
Emma Richards	GBR	4th	3rd	6th	4th	5th	33	131:19:46
Bruce Schwab	USA	6th	5th	5th	5th	4th	30	159:05:42
Graham Dalton	NZL	7th	4th	3rd	withdrew		–	–
Patrick de Radiguès	BLG	3rd	withdrew	–	–	–		–

CLASS II – 40 & 50 FEET

SKIPPER	COUNTRY	LEG I	LEG II	LEG III	LEG IV	LEG V	POINTS[1]	ELAPSED TIME[2]
Brad Van Liew	USA	1st	1st	1st	1st	1st	50	148:16:55
Tim Kent	USA	3rd	2nd	2nd	2nd	2nd	44	169:23:06
Derek Hatfield	CAN	2nd	3rd	3rd	5th	5th	37	245:13:45
Kojiro Shiraishi	JPN	5th	4th	4th	3rd	3rd	36	180:23:06
Alan Paris	BER	6th	6th	5th	4th	4th	30	202:10:10
John Dennis	CAN	4th	5th	withdrew	–	–		–

1.) 1st=10 pts, 2nd=9 pts, 3rd=8 pts, 4th=7 pts, 5th=6 pts, 6th=5 pts

2.) Days:Hours:Minutes, including penalties

Web Resources

Here are a few Web sites readers may want to explore.

RACE SITES:
2002 Around Alone: www.aroundalone.com/
2005 Challenge Business: Global Challenge
    www.challengebusiness.com
2005 Clipper Round the World Race: www.clipper-ventures.com
Toronto Star: www.thestar.com/hatfield
Transat Jacques Vabre: www.jacques-vabre.com
Vendée Globe: www.vendeeglobe.com
Volvo Ocean Race: www.volvooceanrace.org

2002 AROUND ALONE COMPETITORS:
Thierry Dubois: http://solidaires.free.fr/
Derek Hatfield: www.spiritofcanada.net
Emma Richards: www.pindar.com/aroundalone
Bruce Schwab: www.bruceschwab.com
Kojiro Shiraishi: www.jp.real.com/kojiro
Bernard Stamm: www.bernardstamm.com
Brad Van Liew: www.tommy.com/freedomamerica

Bibliography

Adams, David. *Chasing Liquid Mountains: Adventures of a Solo Yachtsman.* Sydney: Pan Macmillan, 1997.

Bullimore, Tony. *Saved: The extraordinary tale of survival and rescue in the Southern Ocean.* London: Warner Books, 1997.

Dinelli, Raphaël. *Rescue from Beyond the Roaring Forties: The story of Pete Goss's rescue of Raphaël Dinelli.* London: Adlard Coles Nautical, 1998.

Dugard, Martin. *Knockdown: The Harrowing True Account of a Yacht Race Turned Deadly.* New York: Pocket Books, 1999.

Dumas, Vito. *Alone Through the Roaring Forties.* Camden, Maine: International Marine/McGraw Hill, 2001.

Hughes, John. *The Sailing Spirit: Meeting the BOC Challenge.* Toronto: Seal Books, 1988.

Lundy, Derek. *Godforsaken Sea: Racing the World's Most Dangerous Waters.* Toronto: Seal Books, 1998.

——— *The Way of the Ship: A Square-Rigger Voyage in the Last Days of Sail.* Toronto: Alfred A. Knopf Canada, 2002.

Moitessier, Bernard. *The Long Way.* New York: Sheridan House, 1995.

Acknowledgements

If the Around Alone fleet had not set sail there would not have been a story to tell. My biggest thanks are to the sailors, whose courage and bravery is remarkable. They shared their journey with candour and humility, offering up the detail that adds texture to the story. They were generous with their time, gracious, and patient.

Derek Hatfield and I began talking nine months before he set sail. The discussions with him and other sailors continued throughout the race and beyond, adding up to almost 100 hours of taped conversation at land and sea, often in very trying circumstances. Derek did not raise his voice once, or lose his temper, or utter an oath. Brad Van Liew's irrepressible exuberance was, well, irrepressible. His spontaneous tutorials on tactics, strategy, and the things that make these boats fly were as entertaining as they were impressive.

Tim Kent demonstrated how far determination and a positive attitude can carry you. John Dennis showed age truly is a state of mind. John Hughes recreated his incredible journey, while Ann Harley helped make connections where none were obvious. Andrew Prossin explained the beauty and wonder of Antarctica. Josh Hall, Andrew Pindar, and Mike Garside all aided with pieces of the physical, emotional, and financial complexities of single-handed racing.

If the sailors had the story, the *Toronto Star* and its Web site, www.thestar.com, were quick to see it was worth telling. Offshore yacht racing is the ideal Internet sport. Toronto Star deputy managing editor Phil Bingley, in charge of the paper's new media assets, was quick to see that. He agreed to devote thestar.com's scant resources to covering the race for the better part of a year. Saturday *Star* editor Steve Tustin was equally enthusiastic. He made precious space available in his paper to provide regular feature treatment of the Around Alone. I am grateful for their support.

My wife, Leigh, was, as always, my first reader and most gentle critic. Friends and colleagues Bill Comeau, Wayne Lilley, Pat McKeough, Ian Somerville, and Paul Wilson read the raw material and made comments that improved the manuscript immeasurably. The enormously talented Brian Hughes created the visual feast of maps and illustrations. Gordon Crowe graciously allowed the use of his photos. Finally, all writers need a good editor. Mine was Dinah Forbes. Thank you all.